PRO/CON VOLUME 7

THE CONSTITUTION

Published 2003 by Grolier,
a division of Scholastic Library Publishing
90 Sherman Turnpike
Danbury, Connecticut 06816

© 2003 The Brown Reference Group plc

Library of Congress Cataloging-in-Publication Data

Pro/con
  p. cm
Includes bibliographical references and index.
Contents: v. 7. The Constitution – v. 8. U.S. Foreign Policy – v. 9. Criminal Law and
the Penal System – v.10. Health – v. 11. Family and Society – v. 12. Arts and Culture.
 ISBN 0-7172-5753-3 (set : alk. paper) – ISBN 0-7172-5754-1 (vol. 7 : alk. paper) –
ISBN 0-7172-5755-X (vol. 8 : alk. paper) – ISBN 0-7172-5756-8 (vol. 9 : alk. paper) –
ISBN 0-7172-5757-6 (vol. 10 : alk. paper) – ISBN 0-7172-5758-4 (vol. 11 : alk. paper)
ISBN 0-7172-5759-2 (vol. 12 : alk. paper)
 1. Social problems. I. Scholastic Publishing Ltd Grolier (Firm)

HN17.5 P756 2002
361.1–dc21

                                                                    2001053234

Printed and bound in Singapore

SET ISBN 0-7172-5753-3
VOLUME ISBN 0-7172-5754-1

For The Brown Reference Group plc
Project Editor: Aruna Vasudevan
Editors: Sally McFall, Karen Frazer, Chris Marshall, Phil Robins,
Andrew Campbell, Leon Gray, Lesley Henderson
Consultant Editor: Ronald C. Lee, Jr., Chairman of the Social Studies
Department, Keith Country Day School, Rockford, IL
Designer: Sarah Williams
Picture Researchers: Clare Newman, Susy Forbes
Set Index: Kay Ollerenshaw

Managing Editor: Tim Cooke
Design Manager: Lynne Ross
Production Manager: Alastair Gourlay

GENERAL PREFACE

"All that is necessary for evil to triumph is for good men to do nothing."
—Edmund Burke, 18th-century English political philosopher

Decisions

Life is full of choices and decisions. Some are more important than others. Some affect only your daily life—the route you take to school, for example, or what you prefer to eat for supper— while others are more abstract and concern questions of right and wrong rather than practicality. That does not mean that your choice of presidential candidate or your views on abortion are necessarily more important than your answers to purely personal questions. But it is likely that those wider questions are more complex and subtle and that you therefore will need to know more information about the subject before you can try to answer them. They are also likely to be questions where you might have to justify your views to other people. In order to do that you need to be able to make informed decisions, be able to analyze every fact at your disposal, and evaluate them in an unbiased manner.

What is *Pro/Con*?

Pro/Con is a collection of debates that presents conflicting views on some of the more complex and general issues facing Americans today. By bringing together extracts from a wide range of sources—mainstream newspapers and magazines, books, famous speeches, legal judgments, religious tracts, government surveys—the set reflects current informed attitudes toward dilemmas that range from the best way to feed the world's growing population to gay rights, from the connection between political freedom and capitalism to the fate of Napster.

The people whose arguments make up the set are for the most part acknowledged experts in their fields, making the vast difference in their points of view even more remarkable. The arguments are presented in the form of debates for and against various propositions, such as "Is Pornography Art?" or "Is U.S. Foreign Policy Too Interventionist?" This question format reflects the way in which ideas often occur in daily life: in the classroom, on TV shows, in business meetings, or even in state or federal politics.

The contents

The subjects of the six volumes of *Pro/Con 2—The Constitution, U.S. Foreign Policy, Criminal Law and the Penal System, Health, Family and Society*, and *Arts and Culture—* are issues on which it is preferable that people's opinions are based on information rather than personal bias.

Special boxes throughout *Pro/Con* comment on the debates as you are reading them, pointing out facts, explaining terms, or analyzing arguments to help you think about what is being said.

Introductions and summaries also provide background information that might help you reach your own conclusions. There are also comments and tips about how to structure an argument that you can apply on an everyday basis to any debate or conversation, learning how to present your point of view as effectively and persuasively as possible.

3

VOLUME PREFACE
The Constitution

The U.S. Constitution is one of the most celebrated political documents of all time. Drafted between May and September 1787 in Philadelphia by a total of 55 representatives from 12 of the 13 states, it is also one of the oldest written constitutions in the world. While little of the document was entirely original—the Framers drew on their knowledge of British government and colonial self-rule—its genius lay in its solutions to such problems as balancing strong government against too much individual or institutional power, and preventing large states from dominating smaller ones.

The Framers dealt with the first issue by separating government into three separate branches—the executive (presidency), legislative (Congress), and judiciary (Supreme Court and lower courts). The second issue, negotiating power between the states, was resolved by having a Senate made up of two senators from each state and a House of Representatives based on population: The larger a state's population, the greater the number of representatives it would have. In 1791, four years after the Constitution was written, a solution was found to the issue of safeguarding individual liberties from government interference. The first 10 amendments to the Constitution, known as the Bill of Rights, specified a list of individual freedoms, including freedom of speech, assembly, and worship.

Is the Constitution still valid?
The United States in the late 18th century was very different from what it is at the start of the 21st. For example, a number of the Framers were slave owners. Critics of the Constitution use such information to argue that the document is outmoded, reflecting a society of 200 years ago. Defenders point out that the Constitution is a living document and can be altered either through Supreme Court interpretations or formal amendments, of which there have been 27 since 1787.

Most controversies surrounding the Constitution have to do with its interpretation. The Framers wrote that the government has an obligation to provide for the "general welfare" of its citizens, for example, but does that justify a welfare system, or is it contrary to the Constitution's aims? The Second Amendment guarantees citizens the right to bear arms, but some historians believe that this right was only intended for the raising of a militia in time of emergency.

While many people agree with the civil rights leader Dr. Martin Luther King, Jr., that the Constitution contains "magnificent words," others question whether it is still achieving the aims of its authors in a far more complex and uncertain age than theirs. Interpreting the Constitution is one crucial way of ensuring its continuing relevance, but does this give too much power to certain legal or political bodies, such as the Supreme Court or the president? And in the wake of the terrorist attacks of September 11, 2001, does the requirement for tighter security outweigh the protection of civil liberties? These issues and others are explored in *The Constitution*.

HOW TO USE THIS BOOK

Each volume of *Pro/Con* is divided into sections, each of which has an introduction that examines its theme. Within each section are a series of debates that present arguments for and against a proposition, such as whether or not the death penalty should be abolished. An introduction to each debate puts it into its wider context, and a summary and key map (see below) highlight the main points of the debate clearly and concisely. Each debate has marginal boxes that focus on particular points, give tips on how to present an argument, or help question the writer's case. The summary page to the debates contains supplementary material to help you do further research.

Boxes and other materials provide additional background information. There are also special spreads on how to improve your debating and writing skills. At the end of each book is a glossary and an index. The glossary provides explanations of key words in the volume. The index covers all twelve books, so it will help you trace topics throughout this set and the previous one.

marginal boxes
Margin boxes highlight key points of the argument, give extra information, or help you question the author's meaning.

summary boxes
Summary boxes are useful reminders of both sides of the argument.

further information
Further Reading lists for each debate direct you to related books, articles, and websites so you can do your own research.

other articles in the *Pro/Con* series
This box lists related debates throughout the *Pro/Con* series.

background information
Frequent text boxes provide background information on important concepts and key individuals or events.

key map
Key maps provide a graphic representation of the central points of the debate.

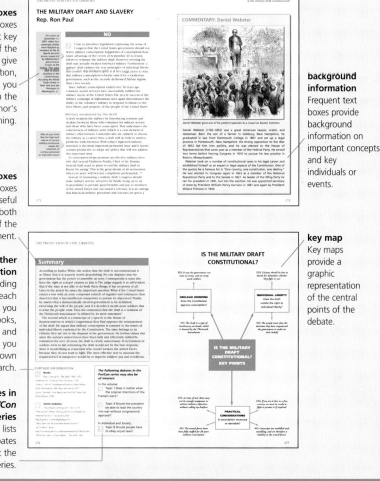

CONTENTS

PART 1
THE CONSTITUTION, GOVERNMENT, AND THE RULE OF LAW

INTRODUCTION

In the early summer of 1787 deputies representing 12 of the 13 states—Rhode Island was the exception—assembled at the State House in Philadelphia to revise the Articles of Confederation under which the United States government was created. Soon, however, the 55 deputies decided not to amend the existing articles but to draft a new frame of government. The Constitution they created remains the basis of U.S. government today.

Since that summer 27 amendments have been added to the Constitution. The first 10—the Bill of Rights—were adopted as early as 1791 as a condition placed by some states on ratification of the Constitution. Further amendments have been added as circumstances have changed. For example, the Thirteenth Amendment (1865) abolished slavery, the Nineteenth Amendment (1920) gave women the right to vote, and the Twenty-Second Amendment (1951) limited presidents to two terms of office. The most recent amendment was ratified in 1992 and deals with congressional pay increases.

The Constitution set out the structure of government and the responsibilities of its various branches, and it outlined the basic rights of citizens. It separated the government into three parts—the executive, or presidency; the legislative, or Congress; and the judiciary, or Supreme Court—so that each could guard against abuses of power by the others. While the legislative branch creates laws, the executive is responsible for implementing them, and the judiciary reviews their constitutionality.

At around 4,500 words, including the signatures of the 39 deputies who signed it, the original document was one of the shortest written constitutions in the world. It has been widely hailed since for its clarity, and in the 19th century British Prime Minister William Gladstone called it "so far as I can see, the most wonderful work ever struck off at a given time by the brain and purpose of man."

Despite the Constitution's clarity, however, its precise meaning has long been a source of controversy. Some debates stem from people's varied interpretations of the wording of the document; others reflect the different circumstances of daily life today from those of more than 200 years ago.

Defining the rule of law
One of the main principles on which the Constitution is based is the rule of law, which means that people's relationships with each other and with

the state are governed by a set of rules rather than by an individual—such as a king or queen—or a group of individuals. Not only are American citizens subject to the law, but so are its government and leaders.

The rule of law is intended to limit the abuse of power by an individual or a government, and thus it serves to protect the rights and liberties of the individual citizen.

world. They assert that the Framers set up a system that may sometimes have problems, but that for the most part works. Kathleen M. Sullivan and Wendy McElroy examine whether the Framers' original intentions still matter in the first topic in this book.

Sometimes the system breaks down, however, and abuses of power occur. For example, in the 2000 presidential elections the Supreme Court halted a

---

"Men do not make laws. They do but discover them. Laws must be justified by something more than the will of the majority. They must rest on the eternal foundation of righteousness. That state is most fortunate in its form of government which has the aptest instruments for the discovery of the law."

—CALVIN COOLIDGE (1872–1933), 30TH PRESIDENT, IN 1914

Like other parts of the Constitution, however, the rule of law has come into question at times. It depends on a legal system that should not be subject to outside pressures and influence, yet it can and sometimes does come under such influence. The theory is not always the same as the practice.

Such contradictions lead some people to believe that the Constitution needs updating. They claim that the Framers established a set of rules that were by their very nature a compromise, and that the system needs to be developed in order to suit changing circumstances.

Supporters, however, counter that the Constitution has served people well, and that principles such as the rule of law mean that the United States has one of the fairest democratic systems in the

recount of ballots in Florida, effectively handing the presidency to George W. Bush. Professors from 137 law schools set up a website to protest against what they perceived as a violation of the rule of law. This has led to questions about whether the courts have too much power. Justices Scalia and O'Connor debate this issue in Topic 2.

The last two topics in this section look at what powers the Constitution allows to the presidency. Two classic statements, by Abraham Lincoln and Justice Hugo L. Black, are used to examine if the president has residual emergency powers in Topic 3. Similarly, in Topic 4 Caspar W. Weinberger and Louis Fisher look at whether the president needs congressional approval to lead the country into war.

THE MAKING OF THE CONSTITUTION, 1774 TO 1791

"The issue today is the same as it has been throughout all history, whether man shall be allowed to govern himself or be ruled by a small elite."

—THOMAS JEFFERSON,

CONSTITUTIONAL CONVENTION, JUNE 6, 1787

In 1774 representatives from all of Britain's North American colonies met to discuss the future relationship with their mother country. The Revolution became the struggle of these colonies to assert their independence and break with colonial rule. By 1789 these colonies had become independent states governed by a single constitution; two years later the Bill of Rights was ratified.

1774 Representatives from each of the 13 colonies meet at the Continental Congress to discuss how best to resist British rule.

1775 The Revolutionary War begins between the American colonies and Britain. **April 19:** The first military engagement takes place at Lexington and Concord, Massachusetts.

1776 June 11–28: Thomas Jefferson drafts the Declaration of Independence. Jefferson provides a list of grievances against the king to justify the breaking of ties between the colonies and Britain. It is revised by Benjamin Franklin and John Adams. **July 4:** The colonists formally issue the Declaration.

1777 The Articles of Confederation are drafted. They establish a "firm league of friendship" between the 13 states. Created during the throes of the Revolutionary War, the articles reflect the states' fear of a strong central government. Under the articles every state retains its "sovereignty, freedom, and independence." A committee of delegates composed of representatives from each state is formed instead of executive and judicial branches of government. These individuals comprise the Congress, a national legislature called for by the Articles. Congress is responsible for conducting foreign affairs, declaring war or peace, maintaining an army and navy, among other lesser functions. However, the Articles deny Congress the power to collect taxes, regulate interstate trade, and enforce laws. The Articles are adopted by Congress on November 15.

1781 The last battle of the Revolutionary War takes place; the Articles become operative on March 1, when the last of the 13 states signs the document.

1783 September 3: The Treaty of Paris is signed by Britain and the United States officially ending the Revolutionary War as the United States is recognized as a sovereign nation. Britain gives up a large tract of land west of the Appalachian Mountains that doubles the new nation's size. Thomas Jefferson heads a committee, formed to govern the new territory.

1784 Jefferson proposes the division of the new land into ten new territories that should be admitted into the union on an equal footing. He further suggests that slavery should be banned in these territories. Debate about the territories continues.

1785 The Land Ordinance is passed by Congress. It provides for a survey dividing the new territories into townships, which are in turn divided into lots of 640 acres each, with one lot set aside for public education.

1786 Thomas Jefferson's Ordinance of Religious Freedom is adopted by the Virginia legislature. It becomes the model for the First Amendment to the Constitution. Representatives from five states meet at Annapolis, Maryland, to discuss interstate trade. Alexander Hamilton and James Madison call another convention in Philadelphia since so few delegates attend.

1786–1787 Captain Daniel Shays, a veteran of the war and a farmer from Pelham, leads a rebellion of 1,500 men. They attack a federal arsenal in Springfield, Massachusetts. The Supreme Judicial Court sentences 14 of the rebel leaders, including Shays, to death for treason. They are later pardoned by the newly elected Governor John Hancock. Shays' Rebellion is considered one of the leading factors in the formation of the Constitution since the Constitutional Convention met to create a stronger central government that will "establish justice and insure domestic tranquillity."

1787 May 25: Fifty-five representatives from all the states, except Rhode Island, meet at Philadelphia to revise the Articles of Confederation. George Washington is voted president. They debate for five weeks before agreeing to make a new Constitution. James Madison drafts a plan for a new national government, the "Virginia Plan," which is rejected by smaller states that draw up the "New Jersey Plan" instead. Both are rejected. **July 13:** The Northwest Ordinance provides for the eventual incorporation of three to five new states in the Northwest Territories. **July 16:** The Great Compromise (Connecticut Compromise) is presented by Roger Sherman; it advocates proportional representation in the House of Representatives and equal representation in the Senate. It is adopted by a margin of one vote. **September 17:** The Constitutional Convention comes to a close as the representatives sign the Constitution.

1788 The Constitution goes into effect after receiving the approval of the requisite nine states. New Hampshire becomes the ninth and last state required to approve it.

1789 George Washington is elected first president of the United States. John Adams is vice president. War and Treasury Departments are established by Congress. Henry Knox will be the secretary of war; Alexander Hamilton will be the secretary of the treasury. The Federal Judiciary Act is passed by Congress; it creates a six-man Supreme Court with a chief justice and five associate justices. It also provides for an attorney general and for a judicial system of 13 district courts and three circuit courts. Washington nominates Thomas Jefferson as secretary of state. **September 25:** The First Congress of the United States proposes 12 amendments to the Constitution to protect the rights of individual citizens. The first two proposed amendments, which are concerned with the number of constituents for each representative and the compensation of congressmen, are not ratified.

1791 December 15: The Bill of Rights, composed of Articles 3 to 12 of 12 suggested changes to the Constitution, is ratified and becomes the first 10 amendments of the Constitution. See pages 24–25.

Topic 1

DOES IT MATTER WHAT THE ORIGINAL INTENTIONS OF THE FRAMERS WERE?

YES

"ARE THE FEDERALIST PAPERS STILL RELEVANT?"
THE CENTURY FOUNDATION
KATHLEEN M. SULLIVAN

NO

FROM "CONSTITUTIONAL INTENTIONS"
HTTP://WWW.ZETETICS.COM/MAC/ARTICLES/CONST.HTML
FIRST APPEARED IN *IDEAS ON LIBERTY*, JUNE 2000
WENDY McELROY

INTRODUCTION

At the height of the American Revolutionary War in 1777 Congress adopted and put into practice the Articles of Confederation. The move was primarily to finance the war effort, and it enabled Congress to tax the individual states in relation to their ability to pay. The states ratified the Articles of Confederation at the successful conclusion of the war in 1781, and they formed the first constitution of the new United States.

There were problems with the Articles from the beginning. They made no provision for a chief executive (a president) to speak for the nation or for a national court system (such as the Supreme Court) to enforce uniform laws. Congress could not levy taxes on individuals but only on the states, which were responsible for collecting the taxes according to their own provisions. If any of the states refused to pay, Congress had no powers of enforcement. Neither was Congress allowed to regulate foreign or domestic trade or to intervene in disputes among states. Finally, as though to set the seal on the unchallengeable rights of those proudly sovereign states, Congress was given no power to enforce any of its limited powers. In short, the Articles of Confederation represented a treaty between sovereign states, not the creation of a new nation.

The weaknesses in the Articles soon became obvious. Since Congress could not enforce tax collection, many states fell chronically into arrears, leaving Congress crippled with war debt and starved of funds to meet its expenses. Land disputes erupted between states in the Western territories, with some claiming a continuous strip all the way to the Pacific Ocean. For states such as Maryland that had no western frontier, this seemed grossly unfair. They wanted the Western lands handed over to a national government so that all could share in the eventual wealth. The states also exercised their right to impose tariffs on other states, which blocked economic progress and worked against any feeling of national unity. The lack of unity was clearly perceived abroad, and European powers such as Britain and France felt little reason to respect the new republic.

> *"If we do not come to some agreement among ourselves, some foreign sword will probably do the work for us."*
> —ELBRIDGE GERRY, MASSACHUSETTS POLITICIAN AND FRAMER OF THE CONSTITUTION

It was against such a backdrop that the Constitutional Convention was held in Philadelphia between May and September 1787. Most delegates agreed that the new United States was heading for disaster unless the Articles of Confederation were drastically revised. There was general agreement that they had to set out a framework that would enable the United States to conduct its affairs in a mature manner, at peace with itself and able to deal with foreign powers as an equal. This meant there had to be effective ways of raising taxes, enforcing laws, and defending the national interest.

The result of the deliberations at Philadelphia was the Constitution of the United States, which has proved to be one of the most durable blueprints for government in the world and an inspiration to many other nations. Its essential features are the division of powers between the federal and state governments and the further division of federal powers between the executive, the legislative, and the judicial, thus creating the famous system of checks and balances.

Since then political debates and arguments about what the Constitution means in this or that instance have continued unabated. Often these debates revolve around what the intentions of those who framed the Constitution (the Framers) actually were. The passage of time and the existence of circumstances that could not have been foreseen in the 18th century complicate such debates.

Many disputes have arisen out of the division of authority between the federal government and the states, most explosively in the 19th century over the issue of slavery. More recently there has been fierce debate about issues such as abortion and the funding of welfare, and whether they are federal or state matters.

In the first of the articles that follow, Kathleen M. Sullivan argues that the concerns guiding the Framers of the 1787 Constitution still apply, notably the need to control the problem of "faction," when rival groups adopt hostile political stances. If more powers were taken from the federal government and handed over to the states, there would be a risk of minority interests gaining the ascendancy.

Wendy McElroy disagrees, however. She suggests that the Constitution was the result of a series of compromises designed to be acceptable to a range of views—federalist and antifederalist (see page 19 for more information on the three main plans for a constitution).

ARE THE FEDERALIST PAPERS STILL RELEVANT?
Kathleen M. Sullivan

Republican Newt Gingrich was speaker of the House from 1995 to1998. His conservative "Contract with America" was a manifesto to roll back the powers of the federal government.

YES

Speaker Gingrich may have disappeared recently from prominent public view, but the constitutional revolution he helped launch keeps percolating. The Republican sweep of the 1994 elections has thrown into question the most basic aspects of our governmental structure. While the Framers of the Constitution sought to replace a weak federal government with a strong one, the constitutional revisionists want to throw federal power back to the states. While the Framers of the Constitution saw a strong federal government as the key to a strong national market, the constitutional revisionists portray government as the market's enemy. While the Framers of the Constitution built a representative democracy, the constitutional revisionists favor a populist regime of plebiscites and polls.

For more on Madison and the Federalist Papers see Volume 1, Government, pages 76–79 and page 106.

What would James Madison say to all this? That it ignores the basic premises of our founding. He and the other authors of the Federalist Papers—the great series of essays explicating the Constitution in 1787 to the people who soon would ratify it—would have much critical to say about specific aspects of the Contract with America. But above all they would remind the revisionists that the key reason to have a strong federal government is to solve the problem of "faction." Much has changed in the two centuries since the founding. The problems that faction creates for government have not.

In Federalist No. 10, Madison wrote that the divisive forces of faction would inevitably plague government on the small scale of the states. "Extend the sphere" of government to national dimensions, however, and such destructive factionalism could be kept in check. What did Madison mean by "faction"? "The propensity of mankind to fall into mutual animosities," and thus more "to vex and oppress each other than to co-operate for their common good." This propensity, he wrote, is "sown in the nature of man." Some factions arise from passion—the opinion that one is right and others wrong on matters of politics or of faith. (Think of current divisions over abortion or gay marriage.) Others arise from

Related to gay marriage is the issue of homosexuals serving in the military, see pages 100–113.

economic interest—"the most common and durable source of factions has been the various and unequal distribution of property." (Consider current struggles over the minimum wage and cuts in Medicare.)

> Do you agree that unequal distribution of wealth is the major cause of animosity among people?

When small is not beautiful

Why did Madison and the Framers believe that a strong federal government could solve the problem of faction? It was mostly a matter of scale. The smaller the government, the more homogeneous. Thus, state and local governments are vulnerable to the tyranny of local majorities. "Extend the sphere," however, "and you take in a greater variety of parties and interests," making it less likely that any majority faction can "outnumber and oppress the rest."

On the Framers' theory, decentralization of power is exactly the wrong prescription for a time when passions run high and interests are in sharp competition. Can anyone doubt that this is such a time? Black churches burn across the south while voters in California prepare to dismantle affirmative action. Vigilantes patrol the San Diego airport terminal to intercept illegal immigrants. The anti-government Freemen made federal agents stake them out for nearly three months. If anything, it is easier to foment factionalism today than in Madison's time: in the eighteenth century, there was no talk radio or world-wide-web. Yet today's constitutional revisionists would dismantle the federal government—the only institution anyone has come up with in our political history for keeping explosive divisions of faction under control.

> Do you agree that state-level and other local politics are more open to extremism than the federal government?

Current critics of the federal government suggest that it no longer fits Madison's ideal. Instead of national representatives detached from public sentiment, we have electronic polling and continuous C-Span coverage. Instead of a national capital too far away for local factions to dominate, advances in communication and transportation have made access by "special interests" to the nation's capital quite cheap. And instead of a limited federal government that would offer factions little in the way of spoils, federal income taxes now fuel federal agencies and programs on a scale unimagined by the Framers. Thus, say the critics, there is no reason today to suppose that the problem of faction is better solved by the federal government than by the states.

Not so fast. While it is true that much has changed since Madison's time, our history has, if anything, proved Madison right about the crucial role of the federal government in constraining faction. Consider, first, the Reconstruction Amendments to the Constitution, which abolished slavery

In 1932 Franklin D. Roosevelt was elected president on the promise of a New Deal—to employ the powers of federal government to halt the Great Depression.

and gave African Americans rights of equal citizenship, setting the stage for the civil rights victories of the 1950's and 1960's. In matters of race, only the federal government could control oppressive localism and prove, as Madison put it, "superior to local prejudices and to schemes of injustice."

Consider, second, the New Deal. Again, federal programs proved the answer to problems that proved intractable at the level of the states—this time, because capital and labor can freely move across state lines. There is a dark side to interstate mobility, as the great depression made quite clear. No state wants to be the first to adopt social security or abolish child labor unless others will do the same—lest their businesses and workers flee to rival states. By imposing social legislation uniformly across all states, federal programs begun under the New Deal stopped this race to the bottom, and its accompanying social harms.

Do you feel more closely involved with your state government or with the national government?

While forgetting these lessons of history, today's critics of the federal government also romanticize the states as the branch of government closest to the people. Most states today are too big to permit participatory democracy. And when they do, they practice government largely by passion and interest, not reason and deliberation, just as Madison predicted. Groundswells of passion led California voters, for example, to enact Proposition 187 (now enjoined), which would deny public services to illegal aliens and their children. And the referendum and initiative—once devised by progressives to express the people's will—are now more often vehicles for expression of narrow corporate interests.

Because the states are so big and their bureaucracies so elaborate, most citizens participate directly in government only at the local level, if at all. But at the local level, the problem of faction is most acute. Madison warned of the tyranny of local majorities, but today, in an atmosphere of voter cynicism and apathy unknown to the Framers, even minority factions can hold local sway. (Fundamentalist Christian groups, for example, have taken over local school boards right under the noses of more ecumenical local majorities.)

A hidden agenda

Theodore Roosevelt (1858–1919) was the 26th president. A Republican, he was in office from 1901 to 1909 and was a legendary foe of big business conglomerates.

So doubtful are contemporary claims for the states as vehicles for democracy that it is fair to suspect other motives behind today's calls for devolution. Decentralization can be an attractive cover for deregulation. As Theodore Roosevelt once said, "The effective fight against adequate control and supervision of individual, and especially corporate, wealth engaged in interstate business is chiefly done under cover;

and especially under the cover of an appeal to states' rights." Transferring power to the states might well reduce the role of government altogether. State governments are weaker than Congress. Many states have part-time legislatures. Few pay their legislators very much. Half the states have imposed term limits on state representatives, as they cannot now constitutionally do to members of Congress. And, as Madison noted, private interest groups may easily exert disproportionate influence at the state level. Just because factional capture has gotten easier at the federal level does not mean it has gotten any harder in the states.

Today's constitutional revisionists contemplate disempowering the federal government and empowering the very local forces that Madison and the Framers most feared. The Anti-Federalists lost the constitutional battle at the end of the eighteenth century. Nothing has changed in two centuries to make them right at the end of the twentieth.

Antifederalists were those political opponents of Madison and Hamilton who argued against the creation of a powerful federal government.

CONSTITUTIONAL INTENTIONS
Wendy McElroy

NO

X A frequent question arises in disputes about interpreting the United States Constitution: "What was the intention of the Framers, of the Founding Fathers?" This question contains an invalid assumption. It assumes that those who drafted the Constitution at the 1787 Convention were of one mind and of one intent. Professor of Law Eugene W. Hickok, Jr. wrote in his Introduction to the anthology 'The Bill of Rights: Original Meaning and Current Understanding,' "...during the summer of 1787 and during the formative years of the early Republic, there was considerable disagreement over the idea of appending a bill of rights to the new Constitution, as there was controversy over the Constitution itself." Hickok continues, "While it is something of an overstatement to describe the Constitution of 1787 as nothing but the product of political compromise, it is safe to say that the federal character of that Constitution ... was hammered out through compromise."

> The author is referring to the many different points of view represented at the Constitutional Convention.

A series of compromises
Perhaps the most infamous compromise embedded in the Constitution of 1787 was the 3/5ths rule which was included to soothe Southern fears of Northern domination. This 'rule' provided that a slave would count as 3/5ths of a person for the enumeration of population for the purposes of representation and taxation. This would dramatically increase the political presence of Southern whites within Union. Arguably, the most important compromise of the Constitutional Convention occurred on the question of equitable representation between the large and small states. The resolution: the new Congress should consist of two houses. In one, the representation should be proportional to a state's population; in the other, each state would have an equal vote.

> This was one of the key compromises. While the House would reflect the weight of sheer numbers, the Senate would protect the interests of the less populous states by giving all states the same number of votes.

The struggle for ratification
The text of the Constitution itself provided for continued compromise by including an Amendment process. But—in a political Catch 22—before amendments could be secured, the Constitution had to be ratified as is by nine of the 13 states who were bound together by the Articles of Confederation.

COMMENTARY: The Constitutional Convention

In September 1786 delegates from five of the states met at Annapolis, Maryland, to discuss the troubling situation facing the new republic—the seeming inability of the Articles of Confederation to provide for effective government. It was agreed at Annapolis to hold a subsequent convention as soon as possible to amend the Articles. The venue selected was Philadelphia, and the date was set for the following spring. The 55 delegates who arrived in Philadelphia in May 1787 represented all the states with the exception of Rhode Island. "Rogue Island," as the smallest of the 13 states was also sometimes referred to, feared that the Convention was a plot on the part of the largest states to take control of the nation.

With Washington presiding, the delegates settled to their task during a long, sweltering summer. Almost at once, however, there was a dramatic turn of events when the Virginia delegates presented the so-called Virginia Plan.

The Virginia Plan

Rather than tinkering with the Articles, this proposal, written by James Madison, dismissed them out of hand. It called for a powerful new federal government with two houses of Congress, a House of Representatives, and a Senate. In both cases the number of representatives allotted to each state was to be proportional to its population. The House would select both the president and the judiciary. The Virginia Plan was debated for two weeks and then was countered by the New Jersey Plan, put forward by William Paterson.

The New Jersey Plan

The smaller states were opposed to the Virginia Plan because it would place so much political power in the hands of the populous states such as Virginia and New York. The New Jersey Plan sought to protect the smaller states by proposing a single congress having equal state representation. In essence this was not a radical departure from the Articles of Confederation.

The Connecticut Compromise

The Convention was deadlocked between the two plans when Roger Sherman of Connecticut put forward a compromise. The Sherman proposal included the two houses of Congress envisaged by Virginia, but in a crucial concession to the smaller states Sherman argued that the Senate should be made up of two senators from each state. So while the larger states would get their proportional representation in the House, the smaller states would get their safeguard in the Senate. Sherman's subtle proposal, which became known as the Great Compromise, was accepted by the Convention and formed the cornerstone of the United States Constitution.

On September 17, 1787, 39 of the 42 delegates still in attendance put their names to the new constitution. By 1790 every state had ratified it.

At the outset, it was far from clear that a sufficient number would ratify and allow the Constitution to become the "law of the land."

The absence of a bill of rights was only one of the issues that sparked the ensuing controversy known as the Ratification Debates—that is, the state by state conventions held to ratify or reject the Constitution. Should the thirteen colonies become one nation under the Constitution or remain as affiliated but relatively sovereign states? After all, the states had different and sometimes conflicting interests. For example, commercial states were often at political odds with more agricultural ones on such issues as tariffs. During the American Revolution, some states had paid a steep price for their autonomy which they were not eager to surrender. Indeed, there is reason to suspect that a majority of 'Americans' in 1787 did not approve of the Constitution. For example, Rhode Island had not bothered to send delegates to the Constitutional Convention. Even the staunch federalist Alexander Hamilton estimated that the majority within his state of New York opposed the measure.

Manufacturers, for example, wanted protection from competing imports, while farmers wanted to buy equipment at the lowest possible price.

But Congress needed to pay the costs of the American Revolution, which included a huge foreign debt and the redemption of paper certificates it had issued as money to soldiers during the war. This required collecting revenues on a federal scale. On September 17, 1787, the Constitution was signed, without a bill of rights. On September 28, Congress ordered the states to call ratifying conventions.

As the ratification debates progressed, some aspects of the proposed Constitution encountered little opposition. For example, the idea of a three-way split of power within government—into the executive, the legislative, and the judicial powers—was relatively uncontroversial. Other aspects exploded. The anti-ratification side of the debate was called Anti-Federalist, and its ranks included Patrick Henry, John Adams, Elbridge Gerry, and George Mason. The pro-Constitution side was called Federalist, and it included James Madison, Alexander Hamilton, John Jay, and George Washington.

Patrick Henry refused to attend the Constitutional Convention because he said he "smelt a rat."

A hidden agenda

Thus, the question 'what was the intention of the Framers of the Constitution' is misleading in another manner as well. Not only did the Framers at the Constitutional Convention have differing intentions that produced a compromise document, but there were also founding fathers who absolutely opposed ratification. Yet, because the Federalists ultimately prevailed, the voices of Anti-Federalists such as the great orator Patrick Henry and George Mason—author of the Virginia Declaration of Rights from which Jefferson drew heavily in writing the Declaration of Independence—are usually ignored. Without their participation, however, it is unclear whether the Constitution would have subsequently adopted a Bill of Rights....

The Antifederalists were particularly concerned that a strong federal government might degenerate into a tyranny and trample on individual rights.

Conclusion

The Constitution of the United States should not be so idealized as to obscure its history. The document was born in an atmosphere of political compromise and political maneuvering. Its text, especially the Bill of Rights, was formed as much—and, perhaps, more—by its critics as by its advocates.

When asking the question, 'what was the intention of the Framers of the Constitution?,' it should not be forgotten that its main architect, James Madison, did not originally believe a Bill of Rights was necessary to secure liberty. Yet, on June 8, 1789, Madison asked the House of Representatives to consider the amendments offered by the state ratifying conventions. Even then the course was not an easy one. Consider the Tenth Amendment—which Justice Joseph Story, in "Commentaries on the Constitution of the United States", called "a mere affirmation" of a "necessary rule of interpreting the constitution." This Amendment states, "The powers not delegated to the United States by the Constitution, nor prohibited by it to the States, are reserved to the States respectively, or to the people." Much debate revolved around whether to use the word 'expressly.' Thus, the suggested amendments, which were attached as a compromise, were the objects of further compromise before becoming law.

Justice Joseph Story (1779-1845) was one of America's most distinguished jurists, serving on the Supreme Court from 1811 until his death.

Rather than ask 'what was the intention of the Framers' of the Constitution, it is valuable to inquire 'what compromise (if any) is reflected in a particular passage or amendment?' And to understand a compromise, it is necessary to listen carefully to the arguments from both sides.

Summary

Kathleen M. Sullivan believes passionately that the Framers' decision to strengthen federal powers in the 1787 constitution is as relevant today as it was then. She cites the Federalist Framer James Madison, who maintained that strong central government was vital to overcome the problem of "faction"—divisive forces that he believed would undermine government at a state level but which would be held in check by national governance. Although she acknowledges that much has changed since Madison's day, Sullivan uses the examples of unifying measures taken by the federal government—notably the abolition of slavery and the measures of the New Deal—that could not have been implemented by the individual states. Divisive and extremist groups could exert an influence at state level disproportionate to their real support if the balance of power were to shift from the federal government toward the states.

Wendy McElroy disagrees. For her, to talk of the Framers' intentions is not to understand history, since delegates to the Constitutional Convention had widely differing views, and some were actually strongly opposed to ratification. The outcome of the convention was compromise: One house of Congress would have equal representation for each state, while the other would reflect their different populations. And to meet the concerns of the Southern states, every slave was to count as three-fifths of a person for the purposes of representation and taxation. McElroy doubts whether a majority of citizens even approved of the new constitution at the time. So how can we cite the intentions of the Framers, she asks, when they were so diverse?

FURTHER INFORMATION:

Books:

Bowen, Catherine Drinker, *Miracle at Philadelphia: The Story of the Constitutional Convention, May to September 1787*. New York: Little Brown, 1986.

Collier, Christopher, and James Lincoln Collier, *Decision in Philadelphia: The Constitutional Convention of 1787*. New York: Ballantyne Books, 1987.

Ketch, Ralph, (ed.), *The Anti-Federalist Papers and the Constitutional Convention Debates*. New York: Penguin Books, 1986.

Morgan, Edmund Sears and Daniel J. Boorstin (ed.), *The Republic 1763–1789*. Chicago: University of Chicago Press, 1993.

Webster, Mary, *The Federalist Papers: In Modern Language: Indexed for Today's Political Issues*. Bellevue, Washington, D.C.: Merrill Press, 1999.

Useful websites:

www.usconstitution.net/consttime2.html
Day by day account of the proceedings of the Constitutional Convention and the ratification process.

home.earthlink.net/~gfeldmeth/lec.conconv.html
Discusses the issues facing delegates to the Constitutional Convention and the steps they took to address them.

> **The following debates in the Pro/Con series may also be of interest:**
>
> In *Government*:
>
> Topic 6 Should more power be given to state governments?

DOES IT MATTER WHAT THE ORIGINAL INTENTIONS OF THE FRAMERS WERE?

YES: Reforms such as the abolition of slavery and Roosevelt's New Deal could not have been enacted without strong federal government

YES: Individual states often have conflicting economic interests; a national perspective is vital

SOCIAL PROGRESS
Are major social reforms best implemented by federal government?

ECONOMIC PROGRESS
Does a strong economy require a "big picture" government?

NO: Some states have a record of passing more progressive laws than the federal government

NO: Many federal programs— for example, welfare—are cumbersome and expensive; control at state level is likely to be more cost-effective

DOES IT MATTER WHAT THE ORIGINAL INTENTIONS OF THE FRAMERS WERE?

KEY POINTS

YES: For example women would not have been granted the right to choose abortion had it not been for a 1973 ruling of the Supreme Court

FREEDOM OF THE INDIVIDUAL
Is personal freedom best protected by a strong federal government?

NO: Democracy would be better served if states were able to make their own decisions without being dictated to by a federal body

THE BILL OF RIGHTS

"A bill of rights is what the people are entitled to against every government on earth."

—THOMAS JEFFERSON TO JAMES MADISON, 1787

Since its beginnings the Constitution has been subject to controversy, not least over the interpretation of some of its phrases. On September 25, 1789, the first Congress of the United States proposed 12 articles outlining suggested amendments to the Constitution that would protect the rights of individual citizens. The last 10 of these articles, which constitute the Bill of Rights, were ratified by the states and formally adopted on December 15, 1791, forming the first 10 amendments to the Constitution.

The Preamble to the Bill of Rights

The Conventions of a number of the States having, at the time of their adopting the Constitution, expressed a desire, in order to prevent misconstruction or abuse of its powers, that further declaratory and restrictive clauses should be added, and as extending the ground of public confidence in the Government will best ensure the beneficent ends of its institution.

RESOLVED by the Senate and House of Representatives of the United States of America, in Congress assembled, two thirds of both Houses concurring, that the following Articles be proposed to the Legislatures of the several States, as amendments to the Constitution of the United States; all or any of which articles, when ratified by three-fourths of the said Legislatures, to be valid to all intents and purposes, as part of the said Constitution; namely:

ARTICLES in addition to, and Amendment of the Constitution of the United States of America, proposed by Congress, and ratified by the Legislatures of the several States, pursuant to the fifth Article of the original Constitution.

Amendment I

Congress shall make no law respecting an establishment of religion, or prohibiting the free exercise thereof; or abridging the freedom of speech, or of the press; or the right of the people peaceably to assemble, and to petition the Government for a redress of grievances.

Amendment II

A well regulated militia, being necessary to the security of a free state, the right of the people to keep and bear arms, shall not be infringed.

Amendment III
No Soldier shall, in time of peace be quartered in any house, without the consent of the owner, nor in time of war, but in a manner to be prescribed by law.

Amendment IV
The right of the people to be secure in their persons, houses, papers, and effects, against unreasonable searches and seizures, shall not be violated, and no warrants shall issue, but upon probable cause, supported by oath or affirmation, and particularly describing the place to be searched, and the persons or things to be seized.

Amendment V
No person shall be held to answer for a capital, or otherwise infamous crime, unless on a presentment or indictment of a grand jury, except in cases arising in the land or naval forces, or in the militia, when in actual service in time of war or public danger; nor shall any person be subject for the same offense to be twice put in jeopardy of life or limb; nor shall be compelled in any criminal case to be a witness against himself, nor be deprived of life, liberty, or property, without due process of law; nor shall private property be taken for public use, without just compensation.

Amendment VI
In all criminal prosecutions, the accused shall enjoy the right to a speedy and public trial, by an impartial jury of the state and district wherein the crime shall have been committed, which district shall have been previously ascertained by law, and to be informed of the nature and cause of the accusation; to be confronted with the witnesses against him; to have compulsory process for obtaining witnesses in his favor, and to have the Assistance of Counsel for his defense.

Amendment VII
In suits at common law, where the value in controversy shall exceed twenty dollars, the right of trial by jury shall be preserved, and no fact tried by a jury, shall be otherwise reexamined in any Court of the United States, than according to the rules of the common law.

Amendment VIII
Excessive bail shall not be required, nor excessive fines imposed, nor cruel and unusual punishments inflicted.

Amendment IX
The enumeration in the Constitution, of certain rights, shall not be construed to deny or disparage others retained by the people.

Amendment X
The powers not delegated to the United States by the Constitution, nor prohibited by it to the States, are reserved to the states respectively, or to the people.

Topic 2
IS THE SUPREME COURT TOO POWERFUL?

YES

FROM *PLANNED PARENTHOOD OF SOUTHEASTERN PA V. CASEY*
505 U.S. 833 (1992)
JUSTICE ANTONIN SCALIA

NO

FROM *PLANNED PARENTHOOD OF SOUTHEASTERN PA V. CASEY*
505 U.S. 833 (1992)
JUSTICE SANDRA DAY O' CONNOR

INTRODUCTION

On December 12, 2000, the Supreme Court ruled in the case of *Bush v. Gore* that manual recounts of the ballots cast in the 2000 presidential election in Florida could not proceed. The court's view was that the inconsistent standards used to evaluate ambiguously marked ballots in different counties violated the equal protection clause of the Fourteenth Amendment. In ending a lengthy and inconclusive attempt to accurately recount the ballots in Florida, whose 25 electoral votes decided the election, the court ruling in effect declared Texas Governor George W. Bush the winner. The Supreme Court's role in determining the outcome of the election, unusual though it was, highlighted the degree of power that this small institution of nine unelected members wields. Is the Supreme Court too powerful?

An important function of the Supreme Court's power is judicial review—the right of the federal courts to declare laws of Congress and acts of the executive branch void and unenforceable if they are judged to be in conflict with the Constitution. Judicial review is an important element of the constitutional system of checks and balances designed to prevent abuses of power by the other branches of government.

Critics argue that the power of judicial review can be potentially dangerous. According to *National Review* senior editor Ramesh Ponnuru: "We have come to hold an inflated view of judicial authority. We think it natural that judges should have the last word on constitutional matters. We habitually treat the Constitution as though it were whatever the Supreme Court says it is. We assume that the Court has the job of determining the limits of everyone else's powers, which means, of course, that it has more power than everyone else. Such power, effectively unchecked, is bound to be abused."

Debate over whether the Supreme Court is too powerful is as old as the Constitution itself. In 1788 Alexander Hamilton, writing in defense of the proposed Constitution, explained that the court's authority to decide whether a law is contrary to the Constitution was not designed to expand the power of the courts but to confine that of the legislature.

> *"Whoever attentively considers the different departments of power must perceive, that, in a government in which they are separated from each other, the judiciary ... will always be the least dangerous to the political rights of the Constitution."*
> —ALEXANDER HAMILTON, FRAMER OF THE CONSTITUTION

Critics of the proposed Constitution (dubbed Antifederalists) feared that the judiciary would encroach on popular government. Certainly there have been instances in history when decisions by the Supreme Court, the pinnacle of the federal judiciary, seemed to contradict popular opinion. In the Dred Scott case of 1857, for example, the court ruled that black people were not citizens and could not become so. The public outcry in the North against this decision was enormous, and it ultimately took a civil war to overrule what the Supreme Court had mistakenly assumed it could

treat as a purely legal issue. Further historical evidence that the Supreme Court may be too powerful can be found in *Lochner v. New York* (1905). In this case, on the grounds that such statutes "were meddlesome interferences with the rights of the individual," the court struck down a New York state law that had set maximum working hours for bakers.

Yet there appears also to be evidence to support Hamilton's contention that the judiciary is the weakest branch of government. In times of crisis the Supreme Court has proved either unable or unwilling to prevent the other branches from exceeding their authority. During World War I, for example, the court failed to overrule restrictions on speech. Several decades later, despite concerns that the president's usurpation of powers from Congress was chiefly to blame for America's involvement in Vietnam, it was repeatedly reluctant to enforce the War Powers Resolution of 1973 and thus stem the steady flow of war powers to the presidency.

The fundamental weakness of the judiciary that Hamilton spoke of was revealed even when the Supreme Court issued one of its boldest and most historic rulings in *Brown v. Board of Education* in 1954. The Court ruled that legally segregated public schools violated the Fourteenth Amendment. Yet the ruling was ineffective until the other branches of the federal government took steps to enforce it.

In the following pieces, excerpted from the 1992 abortion case *Planned Parenthood of Southeastern PA v. Casey*, two Supreme Court justices—Antonin Scalia and Sandra Day O'Connor—debate whether or not the Supreme Court is too powerful.

PLANNED PARENTHOOD OF SOUTHEASTERN PA V. CASEY
Justice Antonin Scalia

YES

The [Supreme] Court's description of the place of Roe in the social history of the United States is unrecognizable. Not only did Roe not, as the Court suggests, resolve the deeply divisive issue of abortion; it did more than anything else to nourish it, by elevating it to the national level, where it is infinitely more difficult to resolve. National politics were not plagued by abortion protests, national abortion lobbying, or abortion marches on Congress before *Roe v. Wade* was decided. Profound disagreement existed among our citizens over the issue—as it does over other issues, such as the death penalty—but that disagreement was being worked out at the state level. As with many other issues, the division of sentiment within each State was not as closely balanced as it was among the population of the Nation as a whole, meaning not only that more people would be satisfied with the results of state-by-state resolution, but also that those results would be more stable. Pre-Roe, moreover, political compromise was possible.

No longer room for compromise

Roe's mandate for abortion on demand destroyed the compromises of the past, rendered compromise impossible for the future, and required the entire issue to be resolved uniformly, at the national level. At the same time, Roe created a vast new class of abortion consumers and abortion proponents by eliminating the moral opprobrium that had attached to the act. ("If the Constitution guarantees abortion, how can it be bad?"—not an accurate line of thought, but a natural one.) Many favor all of those developments, and it is not for me to say that they are wrong. But to portray Roe as the statesmanlike "settlement" of a divisive issue, a jurisprudential Peace of Westphalia that is worth preserving, is nothing less than Orwellian.

Roe fanned into life an issue that has inflamed our national politics in general, and has obscured with its smoke the selection of Justices to this Court, in particular, ever since. And by keeping us in the abortion-umpiring business, it is the perpetuation of that disruption, rather than of any Pax Roeana that the Court's new majority decrees....

The Imperial Judiciary lives. It is instructive to compare this Nietzschean vision of us unelected, life-tenured judges—leading a *Volk* who will be "tested by following," and whose very "belief in themselves" is mystically bound up in their "understanding" of a Court that "speak[s] before all others for their constitutional ideals"—with the somewhat more modest role envisioned for these lawyers by the Founders.

"The judiciary ... has ... no direction either of the strength or of the wealth of the society, and can take no active resolution whatever. It may truly be said to have neither Force nor Will, but merely judgment....." The Federalist No. 78...

Or, again, to compare this ecstasy of a Supreme Court in which there is, especially on controversial matters, no shadow of change or hint of alteration ("There is a limit to the amount of error that can plausibly be imputed to prior Courts"...), with the more democratic views of a more humble man:

"[T]he candid citizen must confess that, if the policy of the Government upon vital questions affecting the whole people is to be irrevocably fixed by decisions of the Supreme Court, ... the people will have ceased to be their own rulers, having to that extent practically resigned their Government into the hands of that eminent tribunal." A. Lincoln, First Inaugural Address (Mar. 4, 1861)...

Friedrich Nietzsche (1844–1900) was a German philosopher whose ideas included that of the "superman" who would live above conventional morality. To learn more about Nietzsche, go to www.connect.net/ron/nietzsch.html.

The Federalist was a series of political essays written in the 1780s by Alexander Hamilton (1755–1804), John Jay (1745–1829), and James Madison (1751–1836). To read them, go to http://odur.let.rug.nl/~usa/D/1776-1800/federalist/fedxx.htm.

A frightening notion

I cannot agree with, indeed I am appalled by, the Court's suggestion that the decision whether to stand by an erroneous constitutional decision must be strongly influenced—against overruling, no less—by the substantial and continuing public opposition the decision has generated. The Court's judgment that any other course would "subvert the Court's legitimacy" must be another consequence of reading the error-filled history book that described the deeply divided country brought together by Roe....

But whether it would "subvert the Court's legitimacy" or not, the notion that we would decide a case differently from the way we otherwise would have in order to show that we can stand firm against public disapproval is frightening. It is a bad enough idea, even in the head of someone like me, who believes that the text of the Constitution, and our traditions, say what they say and there is no fiddling with them. But when it is in the mind of a Court that believes the Constitution has an evolving meaning...; that the Ninth

The Ninth Amendment reads: "The enumeration in the Constitution of certain rights shall not be construed to deny or disparage others retained by the people."

The chief justice of the Supreme Court in 1992 was William Hubbs Rehnquist (1924–), who was appointed in 1986 by President Ronald Reagan.

Amendment's reference to "other" rights is not a disclaimer, but a charter for action …; and that the function of this Court is to "speak before all others for [the people's] constitutional ideals" unrestrained by meaningful text or tradition—then the notion that the Court must adhere to a decision for as long as the decision faces "great opposition" and the Court is "under fire" acquires a character of almost czarist arrogance. We are offended by these marchers who descend upon us, every year on the anniversary of Roe, to protest our saying that the Constitution requires what our society has never thought the Constitution requires. These people who refuse to be "tested by following" must be taught a lesson. We have no Cossacks, but at least we can stubbornly refuse to abandon an erroneous opinion that we might otherwise change—to show how little they intimidate us.

Of course, as the Chief Justice points out, we have been subjected to what the Court calls "'political pressure'" by both sides of this issue…. Maybe today's decision not to overrule Roe will be seen as buckling to pressure from that direction. Instead of engaging in the hopeless task of predicting public perception—a job not for lawyers but for political campaign managers—the Justices should do what is legally right by asking two questions: (1) Was Roe correctly decided? (2) Has Roe succeeded in producing a settled body of law? If the answer to both questions is no, Roe should undoubtedly be overruled.

Tradition vs. intuition

In truth, I am as distressed as the Court is … about the "political pressure" directed to the Court: the marches, the mail, the protests aimed at inducing us to change our opinions. How upsetting it is, that so many of our citizens (good people, not lawless ones, on both sides of this abortion issue, and on various sides of other issues as well) think that we Justices should properly take into account their views, as though we were engaged not in ascertaining an objective law, but in determining some kind of social consensus. The Court would profit, I think, from giving less attention to the fact of this distressing phenomenon, and more attention to the cause of it. That cause permeates today's opinion: a new mode of constitutional adjudication that relies not upon text and traditional practice to determine the law, but upon what the Court calls "reasoned judgment" … which turns out to be nothing but philosophical predilection and moral intuition….

What makes all this relevant to the bothersome application of "political pressure" against the Court are the twin facts that the American people love democracy and the American people are not fools. As long as this Court thought (and the people thought) that we Justices were doing essentially lawyers' work up here—reading text and discerning our society's traditional understanding of that text—the public pretty much left us alone. Texts and traditions are facts to study, not convictions to demonstrate about. But if in reality, our process of constitutional adjudication consists primarily of making value judgments; if we can ignore a long and clear tradition clarifying an ambiguous text, as we did, for example, five days ago in declaring unconstitutional invocations and benedictions at public high school graduation ceremonies, *Lee v. Weisman*, 505 U.S. 577 (1992); if, as I say, our pronouncement of constitutional law rests primarily on value judgments, then a free and intelligent people's attitude towards us can be expected to be (ought to be) quite different. The people know that their value judgments are quite as good as those taught in any law school—maybe better.

In 1992 the Supreme Court ruled that the offering of prayers at public school graduation ceremonies violated the establishment clause of the First Amendment. For a summary of the case and ruling go to http://supct. law.cornell.edu/ supct/html/ 90-1014.ZS.html.

A vote on values?

If, indeed, the "liberties" protected by the Constitution are, as the Court says, undefined and unbounded, then the people should demonstrate, to protest that we do not implement their values instead of ours. Not only that, but the confirmation hearings for new Justices should deteriorate into question-and-answer sessions in which Senators go through a list of their constituents' most favored and most disfavored alleged constitutional rights, and seek the nominee's commitment to support or oppose them. Value judgments, after all, should be voted on, not dictated; and if our Constitution has somehow accidentally committed them to the Supreme Court, at least we can have a sort of plebiscite each time a new nominee to that body is put forward....

PLANNED PARENTHOOD OF SOUTHEASTERN PA V. CASEY
Justice Sandra Day O'Connor

NO

X Our analysis would not be complete, however, without explaining why overruling Roe's central holding would … seriously weaken the Court's capacity to exercise the judicial power and to function as the Supreme Court of a Nation dedicated to the rule of law. To understand why this would be so, it is necessary to understand the source of this Court's authority, the conditions necessary for its preservation, and its relationship to the country's understanding of itself as a constitutional Republic.

The root of American governmental power is revealed most clearly in the instance of the power conferred by the Constitution upon the Judiciary of the United States, and specifically upon this Court. As Americans of each succeeding generation are rightly told, the Court cannot buy support for its decisions by spending money, and, except to a minor degree, it cannot independently coerce obedience to its decrees. The Court's power lies, rather, in its legitimacy, a product of substance and perception that shows itself in the people's acceptance of the Judiciary as fit to determine what the Nation's law means, and to declare what it demands.

> The authority of the judiciary is assigned under Article III of the Constitution.

Principle-based decisions

The underlying substance of this legitimacy is of course the warrant for the Court's decisions in the Constitution and the lesser sources of legal principle on which the Court draws. That substance is expressed in the Court's opinions, and our contemporary understanding is such that a decision without principled justification would be no judicial act at all. But even when justification is furnished by apposite legal principle, something more is required. Because not every conscientious claim of principled justification will be accepted as such, the justification claimed must be beyond dispute. The Court must take care to speak and act in ways that allow people to accept its decisions on the terms the Court claims for them, as grounded truly in principle, not as compromises with social and political pressures having, as such, no bearing on the principled choices that the Court is obliged to make. Thus, the Court's legitimacy depends on making legally principled decisions under circumstances in which their principled character is sufficiently plausible to be accepted by the Nation.

The need for principled action to be perceived as such is implicated to some degree whenever this, or any other appellate court, overrules a prior case. This is not to say, of course, that this Court cannot give a perfectly satisfactory explanation in most cases. People understand that some of the Constitution's language is hard to fathom, and that the Court's Justices are sometimes able to perceive significant facts or to understand principles of law that eluded their predecessors and that justify departures from existing decisions. However upsetting it may be to those most directly affected when one judicially derived rule replaces another, the country can accept some correction of error without necessarily questioning the legitimacy of the Court.

"Appellate court" means "court of appeal," in which the decision of another court is reviewed and, if deemed erroneous, can be reversed.

Exceptions to the rule

In two circumstances, however, the Court would almost certainly fail to receive the benefit of the doubt in overruling prior cases. There is, first, a point beyond which frequent overruling would overtax the country's belief in the Court's good faith. Despite the variety of reasons that may inform and justify a decision to overrule, we cannot forget that such a decision is usually perceived (and perceived correctly) as, at the least, a statement that a prior decision was wrong. There is a limit to the amount of error that can plausibly be imputed to prior Courts. If that limit should be exceeded, disturbance of prior rulings would be taken as evidence that justifiable reexamination of principle had given way to drives for particular results in the short term. The legitimacy of the Court would fade with the frequency of its vacillation.

That first circumstance can be described as hypothetical; the second is to the point here and now. Where, in the performance of its judicial duties, the Court decides a case in such a way as to resolve the sort of intensely divisive controversy reflected in Roe and those rare, comparable cases, its decision has a dimension that the resolution of the normal case does not carry. It is the dimension present whenever the Court's interpretation of the Constitution calls the contending sides of a national controversy to end their national division by accepting a common mandate rooted in the Constitution.

The Court is not asked to do this very often, having thus addressed the Nation only twice in our lifetime, in the decisions of Brown and Roe. But when the Court does act in

Brown v. Board of Education of Topeka, Kansas (1954) was a landmark Supreme Court decision which ruled that segregation in public schools was unconstitutional. For more go to http://brownvboard.org/index.htm.

In legal terms a "precedent" is a judgment or decision of a court that is cited as an example or analogy to justify deciding a similar case or point of law in the same manner.

this way, its decision requires an equally rare precedential force to counter the inevitable efforts to overturn it and to thwart its implementation. Some of those efforts may be mere unprincipled emotional reactions; others may proceed from principles worthy of profound respect. But whatever the premises of opposition may be, only the most convincing justification under accepted standards of precedent could suffice to demonstrate that a later decision overruling the first was anything but a surrender to political pressure and an unjustified repudiation of the principle on which the Court staked its authority in the first instance. So to overrule under fire in the absence of the most compelling reason to reexamine a watershed decision would subvert the Court's legitimacy beyond any serious question….

The promise of constancy

The country's loss of confidence in the Judiciary would be underscored by an equally certain and equally reasonable condemnation for another failing in overruling unnecessarily and under pressure. Some cost will be paid by anyone who approves or implements a constitutional decision where it is unpopular, or who refuses to work to undermine the decision or to force its reversal. The price may be criticism or ostracism, or it may be violence. An extra price will be paid by those who themselves disapprove of the decision's results when viewed outside of constitutional terms, but who nevertheless struggle to accept it, because they respect the rule of law. To all those who will be so tested by following, the Court implicitly undertakes to remain steadfast, lest in the end a price be paid for nothing. The promise of constancy, once given, binds its maker for as long as the power to stand by the decision survives and the understanding of the issue has not changed so fundamentally as to render the commitment obsolete. From the obligation of this promise, this Court cannot and should not assume any exemption when duty requires it to decide a case in conformance with the Constitution. A willing breach of it would be nothing less than a breach of faith, and no Court that broke its faith with the people could sensibly expect credit for principle in the decision by which it did that.

Do you agree that the Supreme Court needs to stick by its decisions whatever the circumstances?

It is true that diminished legitimacy may be restored, but only slowly. Unlike the political branches, a Court thus weakened could not seek to regain its position with a new mandate from the voters, and even if the Court could somehow go to the polls, the loss of its principled character could not be retrieved by the casting of so many votes. Like the character of an individual, the legitimacy of the Court must be earned over time. So, indeed, must be the character of a Nation of people who aspire to live according to the rule of law. Their belief in themselves as such a people is not readily separable from their understanding of the Court invested with the authority to decide their constitutional cases and speak before all others for their constitutional ideals. If the Court's legitimacy should be undermined, then, so would the country be in its very ability to see itself through its constitutional ideals. The Court's concern with legitimacy is not for the sake of the Court, but for the sake of the Nation to which it is responsible.

Legitimacy in the balance

The Court's duty in the present case is clear. In 1973, it confronted the already-divisive issue of governmental power to limit personal choice to undergo abortion, for which it provided a new resolution based on the due process guaranteed by the Fourteenth Amendment. Whether or not a new social consensus is developing on that issue, its divisiveness is no less today than in 1973, and pressure to overrule the decision, like pressure to retain it, has grown only more intense. A decision to overrule Roe's essential holding under the existing circumstances would address error, if error there was, at the cost of both profound and unnecessary damage to the Court's legitimacy, and to the Nation's commitment to the rule of law. It is therefore imperative to adhere to the essence of Roe's original decision, and we do so today....

According to West's Encyclopedia of American Law, "due process of law" is "A fundamental, constitutional guarantee that all legal proceedings will be fair and that one will be given notice of the proceedings and an opportunity to be heard before the government acts to take away one's life, liberty, or property." For more information and a history go to www.wld.com/conbus/weal/wdueproc.htm.

Summary

Justices Scalia and O'Connor offer two competing answers to the question of the Supreme Court being too powerful. The case of abortion law makes clear, Scalia argues, that the court has abandoned the role that the Framers of the Constitution intended for it—the role of impartial interpreter of the law based on legal text and tradition—in favor of making new law by deciding what is the contemporary meaning of the Constitution. According to Scalia, when it comes to judgments about morality (or as he puts it, "values") that are not clearly defined by the Constitution, the Supreme Court should show deference to elected legislators or to the people themselves. And the idea that the Supreme Court "must adhere to a decision for as long as the decision faces 'great opposition' and the Court is 'under fire'" smacks, in Scalia's view, of "almost czarist arrogance."

In sharp contrast to Scalia, O'Connor believes that the American people respect the Supreme Court's authority to "speak before all others for their constitutional ideals." And yet the power of this institution, O'Connor asserts, rests on the fragile basis of public trust, and the court cannot be suspected of having bowed to pressure. She thus opposes any court reversal on abortion on the grounds that it would undermine popular respect for the court's legitimacy. According to O'Connor, "The court's power lies ... in its legitimacy, a product of substance and perception that shows itself in the people's acceptance of the Judiciary as fit to determine what the Nation's law means, and to declare what it demands." O'Connor does not argue that the court should never overrule previous decisions, but that it should do so only with principled justification. And in the case of Roe, she argues, "to overrule under fire in the absence of the most compelling reason to reexamine a watershed decision would subvert the Court's legitimacy beyond any serious question."

FURTHER INFORMATION:

Books:

Dershowitz, Alan M., *Supreme Injustice: How the High Court Hijacked Election 2000*. New York: Oxford University Press, 2001.

Irons, Peter, *A People's History of the Supreme Court*. New York: Viking, 1999.

Rehnquist, William H., *The Supreme Court*. New York: Vintage Books, 2002.

Useful websites:

www.roevwade.org/index2.html
Site of prolife organization Women and Children First.
www.supremecourtus.gov
U.S. Supreme Court site.

The following debates in the Pro/Con series may also be of interest:

In this volume:
Topic 1 Does it matter what the original intentions of the Framers were?

In *Individual and Society*:
Topic 8 Should people have to obey unjust laws?

Topic 15 Is abortion a right?

IS THE SUPREME COURT TOO POWERFUL?

YES: All Supreme Court decisions are founded on legal principle

YES: The people see the Supreme Court as "speak[ing] before all others for their constitutional ideals"

DECISION-MAKING
Does the Supreme Court base its rulings on the Constitution?

ROLE
Is the Supreme Court's perception of its role a legitimate one?

NO: The Supreme Court no longer relies on text and tradition but on value judgment

NO: The Supreme Court's view of its role seems to go beyond what the Founders intended

**IS THE SUPREME COURT TOO POWERFUL?
KEY POINTS**

YES: Unless the justification was utterly compelling, people might think the court had bowed to pressure, which would destroy its credibility

YES: To overrule is to admit error, and to overrule too often might suggest that a motive other than principle was driving the decision-making process

MISTRUST
Could reversing a divisive ruling undermine the court's legitimacy?

NO: Perhaps, but the mere fact that pressure for change exists should not prevent the court from overruling a decision if it is wrong

NO: Refusing to overrule an unpopular decision is trying to teach a lesson to those who refuse to bow to the court's opinion—especially when that unpopular decision is wrong

Topic 3

DOES THE PRESIDENT HAVE RESIDUAL EMERGENCY POWERS?

YES

FROM "MESSAGE TO CONGRESS," JULY 4, 1861
WWW.FURMAN.EDU/~BENSON/DOCS/LINCOLN.HTM
ABRAHAM LINCOLN

NO

FROM *YOUNGSTOWN SHEET & TUBE CO. V. SAWYER* (1952)
BASIC READINGS IN U.S. DEMOCRACY ONLINE
HTTP://USINFO.STATE.GOV/USA/INFOUSA/FACTS/DEMOCRAC/59.HTM
U.S. DEPARTMENT OF STATE, INTERNATIONAL INFORMATION PROGRAMS

INTRODUCTION

Does the president have residual powers—powers not specifically defined in the Constitution—that enable him to take exceptional measures in exceptional circumstances? For example, in a national emergency does he have the right to involve the military in domestic law enforcement despite the threat this poses to the long-standing tradition of military subordination to civilian authorities?

It might seem that the answer is simply no. After all, one of the purposes of a constitution is to limit government power so it cannot act arbitrarily against citizens. Presidential powers must derive from the Constitution and not from any source beyond it. Still, there is much debate about the scope of the presidential powers that can be inferred from the Constitution.

The Constitution makes the president head of the executive branch of government but not the legislative branch (Congress) and the judicial branch (Supreme Court). The legislative branch is responsible for making laws, the executive for executing them, and the judicial for seeing that they are properly constructed. The theory behind this—known as the "separation of powers"—says that different parts of government should be kept separate in a system of checks and balances in which no one element becomes too powerful. The president's power to act alone is therefore limited: He cannot, for example, *independently* declare a national emergency and suspend the ordinary processes of government.

The president's specific powers—he is commander-in-chief of the armed forces, for example—are mostly defined in Article II, Sections 2 and 3 of the Constitution. Compared to those granted to Congress in Article I, the president seems to have relatively few powers. In line with the "separation of powers" he cannot make laws himself —though he can recommend legislation to Congress and even veto (that is, reject) legislation that has passed Congress (Article II, Section 3 and Article I, Section 7, Clause 3).

"The Executive Power shall be vested in a President of the United States of America."
—ARTICLE II, SECTION 1, CLAUSE 1, THE CONSTITUTION

Complete separation of powers has proved difficult to maintain in practice, and presidents have sometimes argued that it is necessary—especially in times of war—to act in ways that seem to stretch the constitutional limits on their power. In the 20th century, especially, presidents have increasingly claimed that special circumstances have justified their changing the law unilaterally. (They have often been able to bypass Congress by issuing special "executive orders" in times of crisis.) Some people argue that the Constitution is flexible enough to allow this, if only in emergencies. Others insist that constitutional limitations are fixed, and that all attempts to stretch them are fundamentally improper.

Such discussions began with the Framers. James Madison (1751-1836) —often described as the "Father of the Constitution"—held that the presidency is strictly limited to specific powers set out in the Constitution. But Alexander Hamilton (1755-1804) argued that the difference between the wording of Articles I and II implied the availability of wider presidential powers. Where Article I says "all legislative powers herein granted shall be vested in a Congress," Article II omits the words "herein granted" and states simply that "the Executive Power shall be vested in a President."

Hamilton concluded that although the powers of Congress are strictly limited to those mentioned in Article I, the "Executive Power" held by the president extends beyond the list of specific powers granted in Article II to include any other powers that are executive in nature—including special emergency powers.

Subsequent debate has tended to fall along similar lines. Some people have argued that the president can do anything that the Constitution or laws do not expressly forbid, and that it is the president's responsibility to take whatever measures are necessary for the public good.

Others have insisted that the president has no residual powers that he can exercise merely because it seems to him that they are in the public interest. They maintain that he can do nothing that the Constitution or laws do not expressly permit.

There follow two classic statements of these opposing arguments. In the first President Abraham Lincoln (1809-1865) justifies before Congress in 1861 the emergency measures he took to protect the Union from the actions of Confederate rebels at the beginning of the Civil War (1861-1865).

In the second Supreme Court Justice Hugo L. Black argues that President Harry S. Truman (1884-1972) overstepped the constitutional bounds of his power when in 1952 he ordered the government seizure of steel mills during the Korean War (1950-1953).

MESSAGE TO CONGRESS
Abraham Lincoln

YES

☑ Fellow Citizens of the Senate and House of Representatives:

Having been convened on an extraordinary occasion as authorized by the Constitution, your attention is not called to an ordinary subject of legislation. At the beginning of the present Presidential term, four months ago, the functions of the Federal Government were found to be generally suspended within the several States of South Carolina, Georgia, Alabama, Mississippi, Louisiana, and Florida, excepting only those of the Post-Office Department.

The Union under threat

Within these States all the forts, arsenals, dock-yards, custom-houses, and the like, including the movable and stationery property in and about them, had been seized, and were held in open hostility to this Government, excepting only Forts Pickens, Taylor, and Jefferson, on and near the Florida coast, and Fort Sumter, in Charleston Harbor, S.C. The forts thus seized had been put in improved condition; new ones had been built, and armed forces had been organized, and were organizing, all avowedly with the same hostile purpose.

The forts remaining in the possession of the Federal Government in and near these States were either besieged or menaced by warlike preparations, and especially Fort Sumter was nearly surrounded by well-protected hostile batteries, with guns equal in quality to the best of its own and outnumbering the latter as perhaps ten to one. A disproportionate share of the Federal muskets and rifles had somehow found their way into these States and had been seized to be used against the Government. Accumulations of the public revenue lying within them had been seized for the same object. The Navy was scattered in distant seas, leaving but a very small part of it within the immediate reach of the Government. Officers of the Federal Army and Navy had resigned in great numbers, and of those resigning a large proportion had taken up arms against the Government. Simultaneously, and in connection with all this, the purpose to sever the Federal Union was openly avowed. In accordance with this purpose an ordinance had been adopted in each of these States declaring the States, respectively, to be separated from the National Union. A formula for instituting a combined government of these States had been promulgated, and this illegal organization, in the character of Confederate States, was already invoking recognition, aid, and intervention from foreign powers.

The defense of the Union

Finding this condition of things and believing it to be an imperative duty upon the incoming Executive to prevent, if possible, the consummation of such an attempt to destroy the Federal Union, a choice of means to that end became indispensable. This choice was made and was declared in the inaugural address. The policy chosen looked to the exhaustion of all peaceful measures before a resort to any stronger ones. It sought only to hold the public places and property not already wrested from the Government and to collect the revenue, relying for the rest on time, discussion, and the ballot-box. It promised a continuance of the mails, at Government expense, to the very people who were resisting the Government, and it gave repeated pledges against any disturbance, to any of the people or any of their rights. Of all that which a President might constitutionally and justifiably do in such a case, everything was forborne without which it was believed possible to keep the Government on foot....

See www.yale.edu/ lawweb/avalon/ presiden/inaug/ lincoln1.htm for the text of Lincoln's first inaugural address —March 4, 1861. Were his initial actions as president consistent with the words he spoke there?

The threat to free government

[T]his issue embraces more than the fate of these United States. It presents to the whole family of man the question whether a constitutional republic or democracy—a Government of the people, by the same people—can or cannot maintain its territorial integrity against its own domestic foes. It presents the question whether discontented individuals, too few in numbers to control administration, according to organic law, in any case, can always, upon the pretenses made in this case, or on any other pretenses, or arbitrarily without any pretense, break up their Government and thus practically put an end to free government upon the earth. It forces us to ask: "Is there, in all republics, this inherent and fatal weakness?" "Must a government, of necessity, be too strong for the liberties of its own people, or too weak to maintain its own existence?"...

So viewing the issue, no choice was left but to call out the war power of the Government; and so to resist force employed for its destruction by force for its preservation....

Lincoln now widens the discussion from the particular events that have taken place in the United States to a more abstract discussion of democratic governments. How does this help his argument?

Here Lincoln uses rhetorical questions to make his point. How effective is this?

Specific government actions

Recurring to the action of the Government, it may be stated that at first a call was made for 75,000 militia, and rapidly following this a proclamation was issued for closing the ports of the insurrectionary districts by proceedings in the nature of blockade. So far all was believed to be strictly legal. At this point the insurrectionists announced their purpose to enter upon the practice of privateering....

Other calls were made for volunteers to serve for three years, unless sooner discharged, and also for large additions to the Regular Army and Navy. These measures, whether strictly legal or not, were ventured upon under what appeared to be a popular demand and a public necessity, trusting then, as now, that Congress would readily ratify them. It is believed that nothing has been done beyond the constitutional competency of Congress....

Rebellion calls for extreme measures

Soon after the first call for militia it was considered a duty to authorize the commanding general in proper cases according to his discretion, to suspend the privilege of the writ of habeas corpus, or in other words to arrest and detain, without resort to the ordinary processes and forms of law, such individuals as he might deem dangerous to the public safety. This authority has purposely been exercised but very sparingly. Nevertheless the legality and propriety of what has been done under it are questioned and the attention of the country has been called to the proposition that one who is sworn to "take care that the laws be faithfully executed" should not himself violate them. Of course some consideration was given to the questions of power and propriety before this matter was acted upon. The whole of the laws which were required to be faithfully executed were being resisted and failing of execution in nearly one-third of the States. Must they be allowed to finally fail of execution, even had it been perfectly clear that by the use of the means necessary to their execution some single law, made in such extreme tenderness of the citizen's liberty that practically it relieves more of the guilty than of the innocent, should to a very limited extent be violated? To state the question more directly, are all the laws but one to go unexecuted and the Government itself go to pieces lest that one be violated? Even in such a case would not the official oath be broken if the Government should be overthrown, when it was believed that disregarding the single law would tend to preserve it?

"Privateering" means commissioning private merchant vessels and crews to fight in a war.

In fact, several states objected on constitutional grounds to Lincoln's unilateral call for troops. Four more states even joined the Confederates as a result.

"Habeas corpus" is "a writ inquiring into the lawfulness of the restraint of a person who is imprisoned or detained..." (Merriam-Webster's Dictionary). The Constitution guarantees a prisoner's right to obtain such a writ —except in certain circumstances (see page 43).

The president's responsibility to "take care that the laws be faithfully executed" is outlined in Article II, Section 3 of the Constitution.

But it was not believed that this question was presented. It was not believed that any law was violated. The provision of the Constitution that "the privilege of the writ of habeas corpus shall not be suspended unless when in cases of rebellion or invasion the public safety may require it," is equivalent to a provision—is a provision—that such privilege may be suspended when in cases of rebellion or invasion the public safety does require it. It was decided that we have a case of rebellion, and that the public safety does require the qualified suspension of the privilege of the writ which was authorized to be made. Now, it is insisted that Congress and not the Executive is vested with this power. But the Constitution itself is silent as to which, or who, is to exercise the power; and as the provision was plainly made for a dangerous emergency, it cannot be believed the Framers of the instrument intended that in every case the danger should run its course until Congress could be called together, the very assembling of which might be prevented, as was intended in this case, by the rebellion....

See Article I, Section 9, Clause 2 of the Constitution for the provision regarding habeas corpus.

In the first four months of Lincoln's presidency Congress did not convene. Lincoln assumed that when it did—to hear this speech—it would validate his actions retrospectively. Was this a reasonable assumption?

The responsibility of the executive

It was with the deepest regret that the Executive found the duty of employing the war-power, in defense of the government, forced upon him. He could but perform this duty, or surrender the existence of the government. No compromise, by public servants, could, in this case, be a cure; not that compromises are not often proper, but that no popular government can long survive a marked precedent, that those who carry an election, can only save the government from immediate destruction, by giving up the main point, upon which the people gave the election. The people themselves, and not their servants, can safely reverse their own deliberate decisions. As a private citizen, the Executive could not have consented that these institutions shall perish; much less could he, in betrayal of so vast, and so sacred a trust, as these free people had confided to him. He felt that he had no moral right to shrink; nor even to count the chances of his own life, in what might follow. In full view of his great responsibility, he has, so far, done what he has deemed his duty. You will now, according to your own judgment, perform yours. He sincerely hopes that your views, and your action, may so accord with his, as to assure all faithful citizens, who have been disturbed in their rights, of a certain, and speedy restoration to them, under the Constitution, and the laws.

Why does Lincoln talk so much about "responsibility"?

YOUNGSTOWN SHEET & TUBE CO. V. SAWYER (1952)
U.S. Department of State, International Information Programs

U.S. Department of State,
International Information Programs

| NO |

Harry S. Truman (1884–1972), 33rd president (1945–1953), took America to war with communist North Korea after it invaded South Korea in 1950.

...[T]he Steel Seizure case reminded the nation that even in a war, the president could not act beyond the bounds of his constitutional powers.

The background

In April 1952, President Truman ordered seizure of the nation's steel mills in order to forestall a strike which, he claimed, would have seriously harmed the nation during the Korean conflict. Although there was a law on the books, the Taft-Hartley Act, which gave the president the power to impose an eighty-day "cooling off" period when a strike was threatened, Truman refused to use that law, since he had opposed its passage in the first place. He also chose not to ask Congress for special legislation. Instead, he chose to take over control of the companies under his emergency war powers as commander-in-chief.

Also known as the Labor Management Relations Act, the Taft-Hartley Act of 1947 comprised a range of measures limiting union power, especially the power to strike. Congress had insisted on the act despite opposition from Truman.

The steel companies did not deny that the government could take over their property in emergencies. Rather, they claimed that the wrong branch of the government had proceeded against them; in essence, they sued the president on behalf of Congress on the basis that the presidential action had violated the constitutional doctrine of separation of powers. Six members of the Court agreed, and Justice Hugo Black's majority opinion made a strong case for requiring the president, even in wartime, to abide by established rules.

The significance of the case

From a constitutional standpoint, Youngstown remains one of the "great" modern cases, in that it helped to redress the balance of power among the three branches of government, a balance that had been severely distorted by the enormous growth of the executive branch and its powers first during the Depression, then during the war and the subsequent postwar search for global security....

Throughout the 20th century and beyond—beginning with the Great Depression (the severe economic slump of the 1930s)—presidents have increasingly argued that particular circumstances have necessitated greater presidential powers. Does the current "war on terrorism" justify such claims?

YOUNGSTOWN SHEET & TUBE CO. V. SAWYER
Justice Black delivered the opinion of the Court:

Charles Sawyer was Truman's secretary of commerce from 1948 to 1953.

Overview
"We are asked to decide whether the President ... was acting within his constitutional power when he issued an order directing the Secretary of Commerce to take possession of and operate most of the Nation's steel mills. The mill owners argued that the President's order amounts to lawmaking, a legislative function which the Constitution has expressly confided to the Congress and not to the President. The Government's position is that the order was made on findings of the President that his action was necessary to avert a national catastrophe which would inevitably result from a stoppage of steel production, and that in meeting this grave emergency the President was acting within the aggregate of his constitutional powers as the Nation's Chief Executive and the Commander in Chief of the Armed Forces of the United States....

This was an "executive order"—an order issued by the executive branch of government in special (usually emergency) circumstances.

To what extent are these arguments similar to those of President Lincoln in the previous article?

The President's actions are unauthorized
The President's power, if any, to issue the order must stem either from an act of Congress or from the Constitution itself. There is no statute that expressly authorizes the President to take possession of property as he did here. Nor is there any act of Congress to which our attention has been directed from which such a power can fairly be implied....

Moreover, the use of the seizures technique to solve labor disputes in order to prevent work stoppages was not only unauthorized by any congressional enactment; prior to this controversy, Congress had refused to adopt that method of settling labor disputes. When the Taft-Hartley Act was under consideration in 1947, Congress rejected an amendment which would have authorized such governmental seizures in cases of emergency. Instead, the plan sought to bring about settlements by use of the customary devices of mediation, conciliation, investigations by boards of inquiry, and public reports. In some instances temporary injunctions were authorized to provide cooling-off periods. All this failing, unions were left free to strike....

Under the Taft-Hartley Act the government was empowered to obtain an 80-day injunction preventing any strike that it considered a danger to national health or safety.

Limited military and executive powers
It is clear that if the president had authority to issue the order he did, it must be found in some provision of the Constitution. And it is not claimed that express constitutional language grants this power to the President. The contention

is that presidential power should be implied from the aggregate of his powers under the Constitution. Particular reliance is placed on provisions in Article II which say that 'The executive Power shall be vested in a President'; that 'he shall take Care that the Laws be faithfully executed'; and that he 'shall be Commander in Chief of the Army and Navy of the United States.'

The order cannot properly be sustained as an exercise of the President's military power as Commander in Chief of the Armed Forces. The Government attempts to do so by citing a number of cases upholding broad powers in military commanders engaged in day-to-day fighting in a theater of war. Such cases need not concern us here. Even though 'theater of war' be an expanding concept, we cannot with faithfulness to our constitutional system hold that the Commander in Chief of the Armed Forces has the ultimate power as such to take possession of private property in order to keep labor disputes from stopping production. This is a job for the Nation's lawmakers, not for its military authorities.

See Article II, Section 3 and Article I, Section 7 of the Constitution for the clauses relating to presidential powers to recommend and veto (reject) legislation.

Nor can the seizure order be sustained because of the several constitutional provisions that grant executive power to the President. In the framework of our Constitution, the President's power to see that the laws are faithfully executed refutes the idea that he is to be a lawmaker. The Constitution limits his functions in the law-making process to the recommending of laws he thinks wise and the vetoing of laws he thinks bad. And the Constitution is neither silent nor equivocal about who shall make laws which the President is to execute....

The President is acting in the role of Congress

Here Justice Black makes a distinction between the president's emergency order and normal statutes (laws) enacted according to the Constitution in a manner approved by Congress.

The President's order does not direct that a congressional policy be executed in a manner prescribed by Congress—it directs that a presidential policy be executed in a manner prescribed by the President. The preamble of the order itself, like that of many statutes, sets out reasons why the President believes certain policies should be adopted, proclaims these policies as rules of conduct to be followed, and again, like a statute, authorizes a government official to promulgate additional rules and regulations consistent with the policy proclaimed and needed to carry that policy into execution. The power of Congress to adopt such public policies as those proclaimed by the order is beyond question. It can authorize the taking of private property for public use. It can make laws regulating the relationships between employers and employees, prescribing rules designed to settle labor disputes, and fixing wages and working conditions in certain fields of our economy. The Constitution does not subject this lawmaking power of Congress to presidential or military supervision or control.

Historical precedents

It is said that other Presidents without congressional authority have taken possession of private business enterprises in order to settle labor disputes. But even if this be true, Congress has not thereby lost its exclusive constitutional authority to make laws necessary and proper to carry out the powers vested by the Constitution 'in the Government of the United States, or any Department or Officer thereof.'

The founders of this Nation entrusted the lawmaking power to the Congress alone in both good and bad times. It would do no good to recall the historical events, the fears of power and the hopes for freedom that lay behind their choice. Such a review would but confirm our holding that this seizure order cannot stand.

To learn about the historical events that influenced the Framers, see Topic 1 Does it matter what the original intentions of the Framers were?

Summary

According to President Lincoln, the presidential office established by the Constitution allows and even requires the exercise of executive discretion in extraordinary situations. That, he argues, is necessary for the preservation of the Constitution itself and the rule of law. Lincoln's constitutional responsibility to suppress treasonous activity, ultimately derived in his view from the inaugural oath he took to "preserve, protect, and defend the Constitution," justified, for example, his suspension of habeas corpus. "Are all the laws but one to go unexecuted," he asked, "and the Government itself go to pieces lest that one be violated?"

In the case of *Youngstown Sheet and Tube Co. v. Sawyer* (1952) a majority on the Supreme Court rejected President Truman's argument that wartime emergency and his authority "as President of the United States and Commander in Chief of the Armed Forces" justified his seizure of the nation's steel mills. In his opinion for the court Justice Hugo Black emphatically rejects Truman's contention that the president has special emergency powers not specifically enumerated in the Constitution. According to Black, the president's power must stem from either an act of Congress or a specific provision in the Constitution itself. In seizing the mills, Justice Black argues, Truman went beyond his power to execute the law by exercising a lawmaking power that is reserved for the legislative branch alone.

FURTHER INFORMATION:

Books:

Anastaplo, George, *Abraham Lincoln: A Constitutional Biography*. Lanham, MD: Rowman & Littlefield, 1999.

Fausold, Martin, and Alan Shank (eds.), *The Constitution and the American Presidency*. Albany, NY: State University of New York Press, 1991.

Hardin, Charles M., *Presidential Power and Accountability: Towards a New Constitution*. Chicago, IL: University of Chicago Press, 1974.

Marcus, Maeva, *Truman and the Steel Seizure Case: The Limits of Presidential Power*. New York: Columbia University Press, 1977.

Neely Jr., Mark, *The Fate of Liberty: Abraham Lincoln and Civil Liberties*. New York: Oxford University Press, 1991.

Robinson, Donald L., *To the Best of My Ability: The Presidency and the Constitution*. New York: Norton, 1998.

Westin, Alan F., *The Anatomy of a Constitutional Law Case: Youngstown Sheet and Tube Co. v. Sawyer*. London: Macmillan, 1958.

Useful websites:

http://press-pubs.uchicago.edu/founders/
The University of Chicago Press's and Liberty Fund's Founders' Constitution site, with archive of historical documents relating to each clause of the Constitution. See especially documents relating to Article II.

http://memory.loc.gov/const/fed/fedpapers.html
Library of Congress archive of The Federalist Papers, early writings on the Constitution by Alexander Hamilton, John Jay, and James Madison. See numbers 47, 48, and 67–77.

The following debates in the Pro/Con series may also be of interest:

In this volume:

Topic 1 Does it matter what the original intentions of the Framers were?

DOES THE PRESIDENT HAVE RESIDUAL EMERGENCY POWERS?

YES: Although the Constitution lists specific executive powers, further residual presidential powers can also be inferred from it

YES: In certain exceptional circumstances—a national emergency or a war—the president may use residual powers to issue executive orders that bypass Congress

CONSTITUTION
Can the president claim powers other than those enumerated in the Constitution?

SEPARATION OF POWERS
Can the executive ever make laws?

NO: The president's powers are explicitly defined by the Constitution and clearly limited to those alone

NO: The Constitution states that the executive can recommend and veto laws, but it cannot make laws, which is the function of the legislative branch of government—Congress

DOES THE PRESIDENT HAVE RESIDUAL EMERGENCY POWERS? KEY POINTS

YES: To ensure that the vast majority of the laws of the land are executed, the president may, in exceptional circumstances, have to suspend some particular laws

YES: It is the president's duty to do all he possibly can in the service of his country—and that may mean anything that is not expressly forbidden by the Constitution

THE RESPONSIBILITY OF THE EXECUTIVE
Do presidents sometimes have a duty to stretch the constitutional limitations on executive power?

NO: As chief executive of the government, it is the president's duty to ensure that all the laws of the land are properly executed in line with the Constitution

NO: A responsible president is one who acts at all times strictly within the limits explicitly defined by the Constitution

Topic 4

SHOULD THE PRESIDENT BE ABLE TO LEAD THE COUNTRY INTO WAR WITHOUT CONGRESSIONAL APPROVAL?

YES

FROM "DANGEROUS CONSTRAINTS ON THE PRESIDENT'S WAR POWERS"
THE FETTERED PRESIDENCY: LEGAL CONSTRAINTS ON THE EXECUTIVE BRANCH
CASPAR W. WEINBERGER

NO

FROM "RESTORING CHECKS AND BALANCES"
PRESIDENTIAL WAR POWER
LOUIS FISHER

INTRODUCTION

A government makes no greater or graver decision than to commit its citizens to war. But who has the power to make such a decision in the United States? The Constitution states that "the Congress shall have power ... to declare war," and that "the President shall be commander-in-chief of the army and navy of the United States, and of the militia of the several states, when called into the actual service of the United States."

Consequently, many people argue that—according to the Constitution— the president may not engage in war on his own authority. Abraham Lincoln put the matter succinctly as a young congressman when he attacked President James K. Polk's use of his war powers to maneuver the United States into war with Mexico in 1845: "The provision of the Constitution giving the war-making power to Congress, was dictated, as I understand it, by the following reasons. Kings had always been involving and impoverishing their people in wars, pretending generally, if not always, that the good of the people was the object. This, our Constitution understood to be the most oppressive of all Kingly oppressions; and they resolved to so frame the Constitution that no one man should hold the power of bringing this oppression upon us."

Despite such rousing arguments, as commander-in-chief during the Civil War, Lincoln then broke all precedents in the use of presidential power by employing his war powers without a congressional declaration of war against the Confederacy.

The failure of the Constitution to specify the extent to which the president—as commander-in-chief— need take directions from Congress— the war power—has long been a subject of debate. As presidential scholar Richard J. Ellis wrote: "One of the most fascinating stories in the development of the presidency is how this 'joint possession' gradually became seen, even by Congress itself, as primarily a presidential dominion." Since World War II a new understanding of that power has emerged: that the president, not Congress, should be responsible for determining when the nation will go to war.

"When a crisis breaks, it is impossible to draw the Congress into the decision-making process in an effective way...."

—GERALD FORD (1913–),

38TH PRESIDENT

In 1950, for example, President Harry Truman did not seek congressional approval to engage American armed forces in defense of South Korea against an invasion by North Korea. The Gulf War of 1991 provides another example. President George Bush led the United States into war against Iraq despite the fact that Congress never issued a formal declaration of war. Admittedly, on the eve of the war Congress did authorize hostilities against Iraq; but when signing the legislation, President Bush insisted that he already possessed the authority, implying that he was not bound by the War Powers Resolution of 1973.

Enacted in the wake of the American failure in the Vietnam War (a war that Congress never declared), the War

Powers Resolution was intended to make it more difficult for presidents to lead the country into war and easier for Congress to reverse any such decision. To this end, unless Congress declares war or otherwise authorizes the use of American troops, the president is required to withdraw the troops from a hostile situation or hostilities within a maximum of 90 days.

The following articles raise important issues in the debate over the president's war powers. Caspar Weinberger, former secretary of defense under President Ronald Reagan, argues that the War Powers Resolution is unconstitutional and therefore should not be considered binding on the president. Though he concedes that the Constitution does give Congress a role in foreign policymaking, he contends that "the primary responsibility for international affairs and foreign policy lies with the president." In his view the War Powers Resolution is "incompatible with the ability of a strong president to carry on his [constitutional] duties as required." After all, effective foreign policy often requires "prompt, unambiguous, and decisive action," the sort of action that a slow and deliberative body such as Congress is not well suited to take. National security thus requires that the president have discretion in deciding when military power should be used.

Journalist Louis Fisher disagrees and denies that it is necessary to give the president power to decide when to go to war. Fisher claims that Congress must play a decisive role in determining when, as he puts it, "to expend the nation's blood and treasure." A decision as grave as that of whether or not to go to war, he concludes, requires "the thorough exploration and ventilation that only Congress can provide."

DANGEROUS CONSTRAINTS ON THE PRESIDENT'S WAR POWERS
Caspar W. Weinberger

YES

It is vital to recognize the ever-increasing involvement of Congress in all aspects of executive branch affairs. The consequences of this involvement are nowhere more significant than those raised by the War Powers Act.

No one will be very surprised to hear that I believe the War Powers Act is unconstitutional. Every president who has ever been subjected to it believed it to be unconstitutional, and I do not think that any president could support it and feel able to carry out his oath of office....

The War Powers Act, as we know, was inspired by the Vietnam experience and is based primarily on the conviction that executive authority should be limited and that there should be no way for a president to move decisively without congressional action....

An arbitrary date

The War Powers Act says that if Congress does not affirmatively authorize the presence of troops in certain situations, when hostilities are "imminent," then the president must take the troops out on the ninetieth day. From the point of view of the military, the ninetieth day may very well be an unsafe day for withdrawal, particularly if hostilities have occurred. Withdrawal may have to take place not as a result of a congressional vote but of a congressional nonvote. And there are, as everybody knows, a great many situations in which Congress may not be able to act within ninety days or, indeed, in the case of the budget, at all. During my tenure as secretary of health, education, and welfare we had more than two years of continuing resolutions rather than a budget because Congress could not agree on what should be done about abortion. Many things can block a resolution: Congress might adjourn, or the ninetieth day might be a holiday, for instance.

Yet one way or another, according to the War Powers Act, the troops would have to come out on the ninetieth day, no matter where they were, no matter what the situation was—and this by a nonaction of the Congress, a legislative veto,

In 1964 President Johnson received a congressional blank check to escalate the war in Vietnam. See commentary box, page 59.

Weinberger is arguing that troop movements must only be determined by military realities rather than general guidelines. Do you agree?

over which the president has no authority to act. Merely declaring the War Powers Act a bad law that can be cured by requiring a quick vote on whether to give money to the president to fund the military action is not much of a cure.

Definitions of war

Interestingly, in few situations has the executive branch sought a declaration of war. In our history, whereas more than 200 events have involved our troops abroad, we have had only six declarations of war. Increasingly, the country will face circumstances in which the line between hostilities, war, declarations of war, and events that require the participation of American forces is more and more blurred. We certainly will have many cases in which the president, as commander in chief, will have to deploy America's armed forces to defend our interests.

The assumption in the War Powers Act that the power to make war always belonged to the legislative branch and was simply being regained after being usurped by the president is plainly wrong, as the debates of the Founding Fathers show very clearly. With good reason Presidents Nixon, Ford, Carter, and Reagan have all believed that the War Powers Act is unconstitutional and incompatible with the ability of a strong president to carry on his duties as required.

None of these arguments deny Congress a role in foreign policy; clearly it has a role. It has the power to declare war. The Senate has the power to confirm appointments and advise and consent on treaties. Congress is also briefed regularly and holds its own hearings. Congress has the absolute and indisputable leverage on all of these matters because it has the power of the purse. No actions can be carried on without the necessary funding.

Not giving the executive branch of government—the presidency—an independent source of income was probably the Framers' greatest single restraint on presidential power.

With this in mind, one must recognize that the history of the country shows without any doubt that the primary responsibility for international affairs and foreign policy lies with the president. The founders placed this responsibility with the president because they had a far different view of presidential power than did the legislators who enacted the War Powers Act. Hamilton, of course, argued in *The Federalist* that the prime characteristic of the presidency is energy. By that, of course, he meant the capacity for prompt, unambiguous, and decisive action.

See Topic 1 Does it matter what the original intentions of the Framers were?

In the conduct of foreign affairs, among the greatest errors that can be made are indecision, delay, or frequent shifts in policy. These weaknesses quickly dispirit our allies. They send a signal of weakness that encourages our foes and invites aggression. A body whose principal strength is debate, working out compromises, or forming or determining consensus and that is under constant pressure for favorable political support will necessarily lack an ability—or even a willingness—to act decisively in a way that may be thought unpopular. This is not to say that public opinion should be flouted, but some situations require quick action, where debate and deliberation, which are the strengths of the Congress, cannot occur without potentially serious consequences to the nation's very ability to survive....

The long arm of the U.S. Navy

The "interests" the United States has in the Persian Gulf include the rich oil supplies of nations such as Saudi Arabia.

We have longstanding interests in the Persian Gulf, where our naval forces have been since the 1940s. I believe that it will be necessary for those forces to be there more or less permanently. We cannot defend the United States, we cannot defend freedom, we cannot preserve peace, by staying within our own borders. We must be a global presence—with our troops deployed as close as possible to areas where they might be involved. The Persian Gulf is clearly an area of immense importance to us and our allies, some of whom have no oil at all. All need the free flow of commerce in this area. The gulf effort has been a substantial success. We have had many convoys pass through the gulf uneventfully under American naval escort. Our allies have weighed in very heavily, too; in fact, there are more allied ships than U.S. ships now protecting commerce in the area.

This article was written before the collapse of the Soviet Union in 1991.

Moreover, we have successfully excluded the Soviets from a larger presence and role in the gulf, which they have sought for a long time and which would be against our interest. We have enhanced our credibility with the moderate states of the gulf and with our allies. Perhaps the greatest accomplishment is that we have moved this entire operation off the front page and it is now accepted as a routine and necessary continuing action.

Weinberger implies that congressional leaders leaked military secrets to the press. Should they be punished for this, or does the public right to know come before military security?

The policy was initiated by the president. It was important that it be done and be done quickly and decisively. It is also important to note that the executive branch has regularly given briefings to members of Congress, committees, and individuals in the leadership on this matter. We even went so far as telling them when a convoy was scheduled to start, within two or three days, a fact that duly found its way within hours, of course, to the front pages. It is important, however, that a president have the ability to take this kind of action. It is important that Congress be informed about it; it is important that the funding be provided by the people's representatives. It is also important, though, that no president face a situation like the one in the gulf in which those ships might have to be pulled out because of congressional inaction or one in which any American forces engaged in a vital action would have to be disengaged regardless of the military consequences.

Presidential responsibility

Although we should be concerned about the constitutionality of the War Powers Act, we should be equally concerned about the safety of our forces and about the necessity of deploying our forces in many parts of the world quickly and decisively. Of course, the president is responsible to the people and to Congress, and it is vital to consult with the Congress, as he does. But many in Congress seem to want something beyond consultation: they really want to run foreign policy. Yet Congress is not a body designed to deal with rapidly moving day-to-day events that are the hallmark of foreign policy and national security.

Weinberger repeatedly stresses the need for quick decision-making in foreign affairs. Do you think that is always the case?

It is an inherent and perfectly proper part of our system for lengthy debate to be held and consensus reached on all kinds of domestic policy. It is perfectly proper for the president to have to report to the Congress and to the American people. It is also proper, nevertheless, as the founders directed, that the president have the responsibility for the conduct of foreign affairs and that he not be fettered in a way that prevents him from fulfilling this duty....

The constitutional status of the War Powers Act must be determined, or Congress must become sufficiently aware of the problems so that it will not unconstitutionally and dangerously fetter the presidency. Our responsibilities and capabilities as a superpower are fundamental to the powers of the presidency but are now being challenged in an impractical, risky, and unconstitutional way. Unless this issue is resolved, our presidents will not be able to fulfill their intended role. Consequently the United States will not be able to take the actions that can keep our freedom and our peace.

Is being prepared and able to wage war the most effective way of keeping the peace?

RESTORING CHECKS AND BALANCES
Louis Fisher

NO

The drift of the war power from Congress to the President after World War II is unmistakable. The Framers' design, deliberately placing in Congress the decision to expend the nation's blood and treasure, has been radically transformed. Presidents now regularly claim that the commander-in-chief clause empowers them to send American troops anywhere in the world, including into hostilities, without first seeking legislative approval. Congress has made repeated efforts since the 1970s to restore legislative prerogatives, with only moderate success. Presidents continue to wield military power single-handedly, agreeing only to consult with legislators and notify them of completed actions. That is not the Framers' model.

Many justifications are advanced to defend this fundamental shift in constitutional power. Champions of executive power cite the need for secrecy and prompt action, qualities supposedly associated in some unique fashion with the Executive. The Framers knew about dangers and emergencies, and they understood the virtues of speed and secrecy. They lived at risk also but drafted a charter that vested in Congress the crucial responsibility for moving the nation from peace to war. Contemporary justifications for presidential dominance must be examined closely to discard, or at least qualify, explanations that initially may have superficial allure. Some have substance; most are shallow.

Fisher is employing one of the most effective methods of debate—setting out his opponents' arguments in order to demolish them.

Contemporary justifications

It is often argued that presidential power in the twentieth century must be defined more broadly than the model formulated by the Framers. They agreed that the President could "repel sudden attacks," but advocates of executive power want more elbow room than that. The climate after World War II, they say, is far more dangerous and much more in need of decisive presidential action. Promptness, we are told, is a quality of the Executive, not the Legislature.

Is there any evidence that the world has become more dangerous since World War II?

It is simplistic to claim that the conditions of the modern world make it necessary to vest in the President the crucial decision to go to war. If the current risk to national security is great, so is the risk of presidential miscalculation and aggrandizement—all the more reason for insisting that military decisions be thoroughly examined and approved by Congress. Contemporary presidential judgments need more, not less, scrutiny.

The Framers also lived at a dangerous time, possibly more hazardous than today. After granting the President power to repel sudden attacks, they relied for their safety primarily on Congress. In a succession of statutes, Congress authorized the President to respond to emergencies involving Indians, domestic rebellions, the Barbary conflicts, and other national security issues. Presidents acted on statutory, not inherent, authority. As noted in [David Friedman's study] "Waging War Against Checks and Balances":

> *Despite glib assertions of the novelty and gravity of the post-Korean war period, the threats confronting the United States during the first quarter century of government under the Constitution imperiled the very independence and survival of the nation. The United States Government fought wars against France and England, the two greatest powers of that period, to protect its existence, preserve the balance of power, and defend its commerce. Notably, both conflicts, the Franco-American War [the Quasi-War of 1798–1800] and the War of 1812, were authorized by statute.*

In the years following World War II, there has been more than enough time to seek authorization in advance from Congress before committing the nation to war. Even if one could argue that President Truman needed to take immediate "police action" to respond to North Korea's provocation, he had time after that to ask Congress to authorize extended hostilities. Presidents find time to seek advice from executive officials, often over a period of months, before acting. They even reach out to inform allies of planned attacks. Few uses of unilateral force by the President can be explained by genuine emergencies. Contrived emergencies, perhaps, but not real ones. In the period since World War II, only one situation justified presidential action in the absence of congressional authority: President Ford's evacuation of Americans and foreign nationals from Vietnam.

Does the specter of nuclear war—unknown to the Framers—require concentrating in the President the sole responsibility for launching missiles? That is a beguiling, but misleading, proposition. There is a difference between first use of nuclear weapons (any initiation of war requires prior

Two days after the North Koreans invaded South Korea on June 25, 1950, Truman ordered the Air Force and Navy to come to South Korea's aid.

When the South Vietnamese capital Saigon fell to North Vietnamese troops in April 1975, Marines hastily evacuated U.S. personnel along with refugees.

congressional authority) and retaliatory second strikes (a unilateral presidential power pursuant to the executive duty to repel sudden attacks). Policymakers generally assume that nuclear weapons would be used only after a conventional war escalates, over a period of weeks or months, to a nuclear confrontation. Time is available within the executive branch to debate and decide the use of nuclear weapons, permitting adequate opportunity for a congressional role....

This argument was developed during the Cold War. Is it still relevant if terrorism is the new threat?

Dangerous precedents

Defenders of presidential war power point to more than two hundred instances in which Presidents have used military force without an authorization from Congress. Those actions were minor adventures done in the name of protecting American lives or property, taken at a time when U.S. intervention in neighboring countries was considered routine and proper. Today, such invasions violate international law and regional treaties. Is the bombardment of Greytown, Nicaragua, in 1854 an acceptable "precedent" for the current use of American military power? Are we comfortable with citing America's occupation of Haiti from 1915 to 1934 or the repeated interventions in Nicaragua from 1909 to 1933? We should not speak nonchalantly about "more than 200 precedents," assuming that such numbers, by themselves, justify unilateral military action by the President. We need to examine the specific instances. Are they attractive precedents for the use of force today? None of the 200 incidents comes close to justifying military actions of the magnitude and risk of Korea in 1950, Panama in 1989, Iraq in 1990, or Bosnia and Haiti in 1994....

Does the existence of precedents —200 examples— make a difference in justifying presidential action?

As another justification for executive power, Presidents Truman, Bush, and Clinton have told the American public that mutual defense treaties (like NATO) and resolutions passed by the UN Security Council provide sufficient legal support for presidential military actions. There is no basis for these claims. Treaties entered into by the President and the Senate —whether for NATO or the UN Charter—cannot strip from the House of Representatives its constitutional duties over military commitments....

Congressional responsibilities

Members of Congress need to participate in the daily grind of overseeing administration policies, passing judgment on them, and behaving as a coequal, independent branch. When Presidents overstep constitutional barriers or threaten to do so, Congress must respond with solid statutory checks, not floor speeches and "sense of Congress" resolutions. Action by statute is needed to safeguard the legislative institution, maintain a vigorous system of checks and balances, and fulfill the role of Congress as the people's representatives. Members do more than represent districts and states; they represent popular control. Citizens entrust to Congress the safekeeping of their powers, especially over matters of war and peace. Legislators act as custodians of the people. If they neglect that function, citizens, scholars, and interest groups must apply constant pressure on Congress to discharge the constitutional duties assigned to it.

Congress may stand against the President or stand behind him, but it should not stand aside as it did year after year during the Vietnam War, looking the other way and occasionally complaining about executive usurpation. Members have to participate actively in questions of national policy, challenging presidents and contesting their actions. Military issues need the thorough exploration and ventilation that only Congress can provide.

Fisher concludes by reminding the reader why the War Powers Resolution of 1973 was passed—to prevent another disastrous war like Vietnam.

COMMENTARY: The Gulf of Tonkin incident

On the evening of August 4, 1964, President Lyndon Johnson went on TV to tell the American nation that he was extending the war in Vietnam by authorizing bombing raids against North Vietnam. The pretext for this action was an apparent attack on two U.S. warships by North Vietnamese PT boats that had taken place earlier that day in the Gulf of Tonkin off the North Vietnamese coast. The attack followed a similar one two days earlier on the U.S. destroyer *Maddox*, which had been on "routine patrol" in the same area. Newspapers took Johnson's account at face value, and so too did Congress, which on August 7 passed the Gulf of Tonkin Resolution with only two dissenting votes. It authorized Johnson "to take all necessary measures to repel any armed attack against the forces of the United States and to prevent further aggression."

It later emerged that what had actually happened was rather different. The *Maddox* was not on routine patrol but engaged in aggressive intelligence gathering. More misleading, the attack on August 4 was a figment of a U.S. sonar-operator's overexcited imagination. As Johnson shrugged later, "For all I know our Navy was shooting at whales out there." Armed with the Gulf of Tonkin Resolution, however, Johnson was able to commit the nation to a long conflict that eventually cost 50,000 American and millions of Vietnamese lives. The resolution was the closest thing there ever was to a declaration of war against North Vietnam.

Summary

Caspar Weinberger and Louis Fisher take strongly opposed positions on the question of whether the president should be able to lead the United States into war without congressional approval. Weinberger argues that in the interest of national security, the president should not be bound by the restraints that the War Powers Resolution attaches to the executive's war-making powers. As commander-in-chief, the president is responsible for defending American interests, and this requires that the president have the authority to deploy America's armed forces when he deems it necessary. To bolster his argument, Weinberger cites precedent: Throughout American history presidents have used military force abroad more than 200 times—and only on the rarest of occasions with congressional authorization. It is therefore historically inaccurate, he argues, to suggest that modern presidents have usurped a power that previously belonged to the legislative branch.

Fisher denies that history proves what Weinberger wants it to prove—namely, that there are well-established precedents for what presidents in recent decades have done or claimed the power to do. The more than 200 instances in which presidents have used military force without congressional authorization were, as he puts it, "minor adventures," none of which justify military actions of the "magnitude and risk" of Korea or Iraq, for example. In sharp contrast to Weinberger, Fisher argues for congressional discretion in determining when the nation will go to war, thus ensuring "popular control" over matters of war and peace. The chasm between Weinberger and Fisher can be summed up like this: Weinberger believes that war powers are essentially executive in nature, and thus he favors presidential preeminence in matters of war and peace; Fisher believes that war powers are essentially legislative in nature, and therefore he favors congressional preeminence. One thing seems certain: In dividing the war powers as they appear to have done, the Framers of the Constitution guaranteed an "invitation to struggle" between the executive and legislative branches of government for control over the decision to take the country into war.

FURTHER INFORMATION:

Books:
Westerfield, Donald L., *The Presidency, the Congress, and the Question of War*. Westport, CT: Praeger Publishers, 1996.

Useful websites:
www.yale.edu/lawweb/avalon/warpower.htm. Contains full text of War Powers Resolution 1973.
www.ford.utexas.edu/library/speeches/770411.htm President Ford speaks against the Resolution.

The following debates in the Pro/Con series may also be of interest:

In this volume:

Topic 1 Does it matter what the original intentions of the Framers were?

SHOULD THE PRESIDENT BE ABLE TO LEAD THE COUNTRY INTO WAR WITHOUT CONGRESSIONAL APPROVAL?

YES: Crises can blow up overnight, and the president is there to deal with crises

YES: A great power must never give the impression of weakness because that just increases the risk of war

NEED FOR SPEED
Are congressional procedures too slow to deal with fast-moving international affairs?

DECISIVENESS
By trying to hamstring the president, is Congress handing an advantage to our enemies?

NO: The president has the necessary power to "repel sudden attacks"; in other circumstances he should have to justify his policies to Congress

NO: If the president cannot persuade Congress of the rightness of his foreign policy, then perhaps the fault lies with the policy

SHOULD THE PRESIDENT BE ABLE TO LEAD THE COUNTRY INTO WAR WITHOUT CONGRESSIONAL APPROVAL?

KEY POINTS

YES: The Constitution expressly reserves to Congress the right to declare war

YES: Such congressional power would be our only safeguard if we were saddled with a reckless, warlike president

THE CONSTITUTION
Is it constitutional for Congress to tell the commander-in-chief how to deploy forces?

NO: The president is responsible for the forces' safety and cannot discharge that duty if he lets Congress dictate to him in such a way

NO: As commander-in-chief, the president is ultimately responsible for defending the nation's interests—which he cannot do without using executive authority

PART 2
EQUAL RIGHTS

The Constitution affords the American people certain rights that allow them to live in one of the most open democracies in the world.

Equal protection under the law

The Bill of Rights—the first 10 amendments to the Constitution—endorse specific individual rights, such as freedom of expression and the right to religious freedom. Those civil liberties are considered in Part 3 of this volume (see pages 126–127). This group of debates consider another right that lies at the heart of American life: the right to equality.

The Equal Protection clause of the Fourteenth Amendment ensures that everyone receives equal protection under the law. It prohibits states from penalizing people on the grounds of race, color, gender, disability, or anything else that may lead to discrimination. This means that when people feel that they have been discriminated against, they can challenge their treatment in court. The fact that people can protest against unequal treatment is central to the protection of civil liberties. Organizations such as the American Civil Liberties Union (ACLU) and the Freedom Forum also exist to monitor, comment on, and help prevent abuses of civil rights from occurring.

Over 200 years after the framing of the Constitution and the Bill of Rights the establishment of equal rights remains an ongoing process. According to the U.S. Courts website, the Internet site of the federal judiciary, the number of lawsuits filed over civil rights abuses more than doubled in the decade between 1990 and 2000. This increase might reflect the effects of legislation introduced during the period specifically to ensure that certain minority groups received more equal treatment by employers and other sectors of society. After the introduction of the Americans with Disabilities Act (1990) and the Civil Rights Act (1991), for example, filings increased in every year between 1990 and 1997, although they rose at a stable rate of just 1 to 2 percent per year.

Race

One of the most discussed areas of inequality lies in the unfair treatment of people on the basis of race. The Civil Rights Movement in the 1960s led to great changes in the way in which minority groups were treated in law. Since then positive discrimination ("affirmative action") policies have also arguably created more equal opportunities for people of different races and sexes in the workplace and in colleges and universities in particular. Positive discrimination is controversial, however, and racial inequality is still an important issue in the United States.

Many people believe that the Constitution itself endorses racism—it is a noted fact that many of the Framers were themselves slave owners, and that slaves did not count as full human beings for the purposes of assessing the populations of the states. Critics argue, however, that the three "Civil War" or "Reconstruction" amendments—Thirteenth, Fourteenth, and Fifteenth—which secured the rights of the newly freed slaves, established equality for all Americans regardless of race. Topic 5 examines this issue in greater detail in extracts by journalist Michael Schwartz and in a State Department report on President George W. Bush celebrating the life of Dr. Martin Luther King, Jr.

Race and inequality are intimately connected with poverty in the United States. According to the Institute of

provide for the "general welfare" of its people. Other people, however, argue that welfare just exacerbates social problems by supporting a culture in which people expect to receive "money for nothing." They also assert that the welfare system itself is unconstitutional, and that the Framers did not envision the welfare state when they used the term "general welfare." Peter B. Edelman and Richard A. Epstein examine the constitutionality of welfare in Topic 6.

Other areas of inequality
Minority racial groups are not the only Americans to have suffered from alleged discrimination. The mentally and physically disabled, homosexuals, and people of different religious

---

"The true civilization is where every man gives to every other every right that he claims for himself."
—ROBERT G. INGERSOLL (1833–1899), POLITICIAN

Race and Inequality, based at the University of Minnesota Law School in Minneapolis, many of the social ills facing the nation today are the result of the increasing concentration of poor people in communities that are "racially, spatially, socially, and economically isolated from mainstream America."

The welfare system helps alleviate some of these problems, but some critics believe that it does not go far enough. They argue that the government has a far-reaching responsibility to look after people who are unable to take care of themselves. They claim that the Constitution places a clear obligation on the government to

denominations also claim to have had their rights overlooked. Justice White and the ACLU discuss whether the Constitution adequately protects the rights of the disabled in Topic 7. Similarly, the right of homosexuals to serve in the military is examined in Topic 8 by journalist Chris Bull and Senator Sam Nunn.

The last topic in this section examines whether the Constitution really does protect the right to religious freedom. As early as 1785 Thomas Jefferson, one of the Framers, called for a law establishing religious freedom. In Topic 9 Justices Kennedy and Frankfurter argue the case.

Topic 5
IS THE CONSTITUTION RACIST?

YES
"CONSTITUTION FURTHERS INSTITUTIONAL RACISM"
UCLA DAILY BRUIN ONLINE
MICHAEL SCHWARTZ

NO
"BUSH CELEBRATES THE LIFE OF MARTIN LUTHER KING AT WHITE HOUSE"
U.S. DEPARTMENT OF STATE PRESS RELEASE, JANUARY 21, 2002
U.S. DEPARTMENT OF STATE

INTRODUCTION

Racism is the belief that someone's particular race or ethnic group is superior to another's. Racism invariably leads to prejudice against other races, prompting discrimination, hatred, and physical and verbal abuse.

The fundamental written laws that govern the United States, collectively called the Constitution, are based on ideals proposed in the 1776 Declaration of Independence. The Constitution was sanctioned in the aftermath of the War of Independence (1775-1783) against British colonial rule. Ten amendments, now called the Bill of Rights, were approved in 1791 to protect the rights of citizens of the new republic. The Constitution does not include the word "race," yet some people have pointed to certain of its sections that they believe express racism. With its emphasis on liberty and equality, many people find it hard to believe that the Constitution could endorse racism. However, others claim that the history and Constitution of the United States are littered with examples that tell a different story.

Racism led to the advent of slavery in the United States. As Europeans began to colonize the Americas in the 16th century, millions of Africans were traded as slaves to work the land. Slavery was later put in the spotlight when the Constitution was forged. Many of the Framers of the United States Constitution opposed slavery—such as Benjamin Franklin, for example—but others owned slaves themselves, and the South was highly dependent on slave labor. Thus, when drafting the Constitution, the Framers decided the safest option was to protect slaveowners' interests. African slaves were given few rights. In the Constitution in 1787, Article I, Section 2, slaves were identified for a state's tax and political representation as "three-fifths of a person." Some people claim this was done by Northerners merely as a way of reducing Southern representation in the government. It was based on state population and therefore tilted unfairly in favor of the South, which included slaves in its count, although slaves had no rights to vote. Others, however, cite this section as proof that racism is written into the Constitution. Yet how does this fit with the Constitution's recognition of liberty and equality?

> *"We hold these truths to be self-evident, that all men are created equal, that they are endowed by their Creator with certain unalienable Rights, that among these are Life, Liberty, and the pursuit of happiness."*
> —THE DECLARATION OF INDEPENDENCE OF THE THIRTEEN COLONIES, JULY 4, 1776

The end of the Civil War (1861–1865) marked the official end of slavery in the United States. Yet the victory created resentment among the defeated white Southerners toward African Americans, who faced discrimination, segregation, and poverty. To address these injustices, the first Civil Rights Act was passed in 1866. It outlawed slavery, guaranteed all African Americans citizenship, and citizens of any color legal rights equal to those of white citizens. But this did not prevent Southern states from enacting "black codes" to limit African Americans' civil rights.

With the advent of World War II (1939–1945) many African Americans moved away from the South to work on northern production lines; others joined the military. This wider experience of playing a larger role in American society helped bring African Americans into the mainstream and kicked off the civil rights movement championed by Dr. Martin Luther King, Jr., and others, which culminated in the Civil Rights Act of 1964. Civil Rights Acts were also passed in 1957 and 1960 to protect African American voting rights—the 1957 act made it a federal crime to interfere with any citizen's right to vote, and the 1960 act called for supervision of voter registration. Yet some cynics have claimed that these acts were merely a ploy by Dwight D. Eisenhower's Republican administration to win the "black vote" at a time when only 20 percent of African Americans had registered to vote (this low percentage was often the result of intimidation by white citizens). The stated purpose of the 1964 act, however, was "… to provide injunctive relief against discrimination." It made racist actions such as hate crimes and segregation criminal offenses. Yet the freedom to speak and distribute racist opinions were not considered to be illegal; in fact, this freedom of expression is protected by the First Amendment of the Constitution.

The Civil Rights Act of 1964 was amended in 1991 mainly "to strengthen and improve Federal civil rights laws" and "to provide for damages in cases of intentional employment discrimination." Some people—including President George W. Bush in his speech honoring Dr. Martin Luther King, Jr., the second of the following articles—see the Civil Rights Act as a true turning point in the struggle against racism. Others, such as Michael Schwartz in the first article, think that there is a "race exception" to the Constitution and that racism is an integral part of law and culture.

CONSTITUTION FURTHERS INSTITUTIONAL RACISM
Michael Schwartz

YES

The author has constructed a very powerful beginning to his article by introducing the element of surprise. He begins with a statement that most people would agree with, then refutes it. This immediate contradiction has the effect of grabbing the reader's attention.

✓ History teaches us that slavery was abolished in the United States after the Civil War. History has taught us wrong.

Slavery was never abolished in the United States. Go ahead; take a look at the Constitution. The 13th Amendment reads as follows: "Neither slavery nor involuntary servitude except as a punishment for a crime whereof the party shall have been duly convicted shall exist within the United States."

Why don't you read that again? Yeah, that means that if you've been convicted of a crime, you are legally allowed to be a slave. At the same time the United States blasts China for the use of prison slave labor, this country is engaging in the same practice. But it goes much deeper than that.

People are constantly talking about how much better things have gotten, but the only thing that has changed is that the practice of slavery today has become modernized. The prison industrial complex is big business in this country, and the U.S. government and big businesses are reaping the rewards.

This article was written in 1999. The legislation for privatizing Tennessee state prisons had not been passed as of August 2002.

Slavery in private prisons and companies

Private companies are not only operating prisons but are also using prisoners as workers without paying wages, a practice known as slavery. The largest private prison operator is called Correction Corporations of America; it operates over 30 prisons nationwide (a number that will double next year when every state prison in Tennessee is supposed to go private). And the number of private companies using slavery is astounding.

Downsize This!, published by Random House in 1996, is a book written by author and filmmaker Michael Moore (1971–) about what he views as the unfair practices of large corporations.

According to sources ranging from Michael Moore in "Downsize This!" to "Business Week" to "Prison Legal News," the following are just a fraction of the companies using slave labor: IBM, Motorola, Compaq, Texas Instruments, Honeywell, Microsoft, Boeing, Revlon, Chevron, TWA, Victoria's Secret, Eddie Bauer, K-Mart, JC Penny and McDonalds.

These companies are using prisoners right here in this country to make their products. Prison bonds are also big business. Goldman Sachs and Company, Prudential Insurance, Smith Barney and Shearson and Merrill Lynch all invest in prison bonds, which provide lucrative return (*ColorLines* magazine, October, 1998).

Products bought by the U.S. government are bought from UNICOR, which is the trade name for the Federal Prison Industries. Yes, prisoners build desks for members of Congress. UNICOR proudly displays on its web site that it's "where the government shops first" (http://www.unicor.gov/homepage.html).

This isn't about making the streets safe; it's about money and a never-ending supply of cheap labor. State corrections agencies are advertising their prisoners to the corporations: "Are you experiencing high employee turnover? Worried about the costs of employee benefits? Unhappy with out-of-state or offshore suppliers? Getting hit by overseas competition? Having trouble motivating your work force? Thinking about expansion space? Then the Washington State Department of Corrections Private Sector Partnerships is for you." (http://www.wa.gov/doc/Content/Industries/psp.html).

For further discussion on the use of prisoners to provide cheap labor see Topic 15 Should prisons be privatized? —pages 190–201 in Volume 9 Criminal Law and the Penal System.

Rising numbers of prisoners and prisons

When Ronald Reagan became president, there were 400,000 prisoners across the United States. In 1992 there were almost 1 million prisoners and today that number stands at over 2 million. Before you start thinking about those "violent" people, listen to some facts. In our federal prisons, only 2.4 percent of prisoners are there for violent crimes …

It took 150 years for California to build 10 state prisons. The state has built 21 prisons in the last 10 years alone (one state university has been built in that time) and this trend isn't stopping. With the three strikes law in effect the state estimates that it will have to build 20 more prisons over the next 10 years.

This statistic and others relating to prisoners can be found on the Department of Justice's Federal Bureau of Prisons National Institute of Corrections website at www.bop.gov/ under "Public Information" and "Quick Facts."

African American majority in prisons

Seventy percent of those being sentenced under the three strikes law are people of color. Thirty-nine percent of African American men in their 20s are in prison, on probation or on parole. African Americans are 17 times more likely to be charged with a third strike than whites. And the majority of those sentenced under the three strikes law are for non-violent offenses (Families to Amend Three Strikes).

Where does the racism come into view? Right now, white people make up 82 percent of our nation's population, yet our nation's prisons house 72 percent people of color (*ColorLines* magazine, October 1998). African Americans make up 12.5 percent of the nation's population, but make

For information on the three strikes law see Topic 3 Is the three strikes law a deterrent? —pages 36–47 in Volume 9 Criminal Law and the Penal System.

A young African American prisoner at Rikers Island correction facility in the Bronx, New York.

up 38.8 percent of our federal prisoner population (http://www.bop.gov/). And of more than 130,000 prisoners in our federal prisons, more than 97,000 are people of color. The numbers don't change state by state either.

In California, where whites make up 68 percent of the population, people of color make up 70.5 percent of our state prisons (http://www.cdc.state.ca.us/factsht.html). In case you're wondering, 69 percent of the people arrested in this country are white (U.S. Department of Justice).

In 1980, 33 percent of all federal prisoners were people of color; today that number is over 73 percent (Coalition for Federal Sentencing Reform, 1997.) Right now an estimated 1,471 African Americans per 100,000 African American residents were incarcerated in the nation's prisons, compared to 207 whites per 100,000 white residents. (Bureau of Justice Statistics, "Prisoners in 1994," 1995.)

The author does a comprehensive job of supplying statistics to support his argument. He reinforces the authority of the statistics he uses by providing their sources as well.

Racist laws

The laws that allowed this to happen are the blatantly racist mandatory sentencing laws concerning crack and cocaine. Right now possession of five grams of crack requires a sentence of five years in prison. It takes 500 grams of cocaine to get the same sentence. According to the American Medical Association, crack and cocaine are essentially the same drug.

Cocaine is the powder form, crack the rock form. The myth that the majority of crack users are African American is about to be shattered: The U.S. Sentencing Commission reported in 1995 that whites account for 52 percent of all crack users. But African Americans account for 88 percent of those sentenced for crack offenses. The number of whites convicted: 4.1 percent (U.S. Sentencing Commission, Cocaine and Federal Sentencing Policy, February 1995.) See any racism? When the United States Sentencing Commission recommended that the sentences be equalized, Congress rejected its recommendation for the first time in history.

To learn more about attempts to equalize drug-related sentences, see the Families Against Mandatory Minimums (FAMM) website at www.famm.org/index2.htm.

The corporations use the prisoners for their labor; cities are dependent on their local prisons and the more prisoners, the higher the profits. You live in a nation where the Constitution specifically makes slavery legal. This shouldn't be surprising since the same document called African Americans three-fifths of a human being.

What you need to do is wake up and realize that there aren't 2 million people in prison for no reason. They're not there to make the country safe; they're there to provide a service: their labor. You can't call them prisoners; call them what they are: slaves.

Whether the Constitution defines African Americans as "three-fifths of a human being" has been debated. To study this issue in more detail, see the National Public Radio (NPR) article "Myths about the Founding" at www.dineshdsouza.com/founding.html.

BUSH CELEBRATES THE LIFE OF MARTIN LUTHER KING AT WHITE HOUSE
U.S. Department of State

NO

During a White House East Room celebration commemorating the life and achievements of the late Dr. Martin Luther King, Jr., [on] January 21, President Bush welcomed Dr. King's widow, Coretta Scott King, two of his children who were present—Bernice and Martin Luther King III—and other family members.

The President acknowledged Dr. King's influence on the Civil Rights Act that was signed by President Lyndon B. Johnson in the summer of 1964 (which came in the wake of the November 22, 1963 assassination of President John F. Kennedy). "Perhaps without Martin Luther King," said Bush, "there might still not have been a Civil Rights Act. There is no doubting that the law came as it did, when it did, because of him."

Making America a better place

Bush recalled that Dr. King "believed that whatever one would change, one must first love—and he loved America. His most powerful arguments were unanswerable, for they were the very words and principles of our Declaration and Constitution."

The President said that "America is a better place because he (Dr. King) was here, and we will honor his name forever."

Mrs. King presented the President with what he called "a beautiful portrait" of the slain Civil Rights leader and Bush told her, "I can't wait to hang it" in the White House.

Following is the White House transcript:
THE WHITE HOUSE, Office of the Press Secretary, January 21, 2002, REMARKS BY THE PRESIDENT DURING THE CELEBRATION AND PROCLAMATION IN HONOR OF DR. MARTIN LUTHER KING JR., The East Room 4:12 P.M. EST

The President's welcome

THE PRESIDENT: "Well, thank you all very much for coming. Mrs. King, thanks for this beautiful portrait. I can't wait to hang it. (Laughter.)

I want to welcome you all to the White House. We've gathered in tribute to Dr. Martin Luther King Jr., to the ideals he held and the life he lived. We remember a man who brought much good into the world by the power of his voice and the truth of his words.

For some of you here this afternoon, Dr. King was, and is, a special part of your life—as a colleague and a friend and a brother. Four call him "dad." And we are pleased that two of his children are here with us today. We welcome Bernice and Martin Luther King III. I know your dad would be incredibly proud of you. (Applause.)

I also welcome Christine King Farris, Dr. King's sister. (Applause.) Alveda King, Isaac Farris Jr., Arthur Bagley and Arturo Bagley, family members are here, as well. Thank you all for coming. (Applause.)

And of course, we're honored to be in the presence of such a distinguished and delightful lady, Coretta Scott King. (Applause.)

I appreciate Secretary Rod Paige for being here. (Applause.) In honor of Dr. King, the Department of Education will soon announce the Martin Luther King Jr., Scholars Program to promising students all across America. (Applause.)

I appreciate all the members of my team who are here, in particular, Condoleezza Rice, the National Security Advisor. Thank you for coming, Condi. (Applause.) It's good to see the Mayor. Mr. Mayor and the First Lady, Diane, are with us today. Thank you all for coming. (Applause.) The Mayor is a good man. I can assure you, Mr. Mayor, we paid our property taxes. (Laughter.)

I appreciate so many members of the diplomatic core for being here. Ambassadors from all across the world are here to say hello to Mrs. King and her family. And thank you all for coming to pay honor to such a great American. Thank you very much. (Applause.)

End of a century of slumber

On a summer night in 1964, right here in the East Room, President Lyndon Baines Johnson signed the Civil Rights Act, and handed a pen to Martin Luther King Jr. The law marked a true turning point in the life of our country. As Dr. King put it, the Civil Rights Act was the end of a century of slumber.

More laws would be needed, and more would follow. But on that day, our federal government accepted the duty of securing freedom and justice for every American. Standing in the White House, marking a national holiday in Dr. King's

The Martin Luther King Jr., Scholars Program is a summer internship that is awarded to up to 10 outstanding undergraduate or graduate students with an interest in education policy or public policy and administration. All Martin Luther King Jr., Scholars are appointed to assist with various projects that will expose them to government and public policy at the Department of Education in Washington, D.C. For further information on the program see www. ed.gov/offices/OMI edjobs.html.

To view the full text of the Civil Rights Act of 1964, go to www.usbr.gov/laws/ civil.html.

Dr. Martin Luther King, Jr.'s work was integral in the creation of the 1964 Civil Rights Act.

King moved to Montgomery, Alabama, in 1954 to be the preacher at the Dexter Avenue Baptist Church and began his civil rights activities there. He registered to vote in Selma, Alabama, in 1965, an act for which he was assaulted by James George Robinson of Birmingham, Alabama. King was arrested for protesting in Birmingham in 1963 and wrote "Letter from a Birmingham Jail" (see the Individual and Society volume, pages 106–109).

memory, we are now two generations and a world away from Montgomery, Selma and Birmingham, as he knew them.

It would be easy to forget the great obstacles he overcame, and the years of effort and the daily courage that turned a cause into a movement. Perhaps without Martin Luther King, there might still (not) have been a Civil Rights Act. There is no doubting that the law came as it did, when it did, because of him.

Civil Rights Law written by many black citizens

Yet, he was not one to claim credit for himself. The civil rights law, he said, was first written in the streets, by many thousands of black citizens, and others who shared their goals. Their movement rose from generations of bitter experience—the slights, the cruelties, the pervasive wrongs that marked the lives of many black Americans.

As a small boy, Martin has seen his father, a gifted and learned man, retain great dignity while being insulted, ordered about, and spoken down to. I don't care how long I have to live with this system, said Martin Luther King Sr., will never accept it. The son would not accept it either.

Putting his mind up in the front seat

Years afterwards, he related the story of going to the back of the bus, day after day, putting his mind up in the front seat. He told himself, one of these days I'm going to put my body where my mind is. (Applause.)

In time, he did so, as did others, some of whose names are also honored in our history. Along the way, he was beaten and stabbed, jailed, and came close to losing his wife and baby daughter when their house was bombed. At a certain point, even a strong man might have yielded. Dr. King never did, and he never gave up on his country.

He believed that whatever one would change, one must first love—and he loved America. His most powerful arguments were unanswerable, for they were the very words and principles of our Declaration and Constitution.

When he came to this capital city and stood before the figure of the great emancipator, it was not to assail or threaten. He had come to hold this nation to its own standards, to live out the true meaning of its creed.

A man of faith

We see Martin Luther King in many ways. Perhaps, above all, we should see him as a minister of the gospel. He said, I decided early to give my life to something eternal and absolute—not for these little gods that are here today and gone tomorrow, but to God, who is the same yesterday, today and forever.

That faith gave Dr. King the grace to forgive, and the strength to love. He refused to answer hatred with hatred, or meet violence with violence. He appealed not to resentment, but to reason; not to anger, but to conscience. He was on this earth just 39 years. On the last night of his life, he did seem to sense that grave danger was lying in wait. But he trusted in the ways of providence, not fearing any man, certain that no man could ever finally prevent the purposes of Almighty God.

Here on all the roads of life, said Dr. King in a sermon, God is striving in our striving. As we struggle to defeat the forces of evil, the God of the universe struggles with us. Evil dies on the seashore, not merely because of man's endless struggle against it, but because of God's power to defeat it. Martin Luther King Jr., lived in that belief, and died in that belief.

Some figures in history, renowned in their day, grow smaller with the passing of time. The man from Atlanta, Georgia, only grows larger with the years. America is a better place because he was here, and we will honor his name forever. (Applause.)

It is now my honor to sign the proclamation (Applause.)

(The proclamation is signed.) (Applause.)

King's Montgomery house was bombed in 1956 while he was leading a boycott against segregation on buses. Alabama's segregation laws were later declared unconstitutional by the Supreme Court. In 1958 an African American woman stabbed King in a Harlem, New York, bookstore while he was promoting his memoir of the bus boycott, Stride toward Freedom.

The "figure of the great emancipator" is a reference to the statue of Abraham Lincoln in the Lincoln Memorial in Washington, D.C.

Do you agree with the president that Dr. Martin Luther King, Jr., grows larger with the years? What do you think Dr. Martin Luther King, Jr., stands for in our present society?

Summary

The principles of liberty and equality lie at the heart of the Constitution. But when the Framers drafted this important document, did they ensure that all members of American society benefited from these principles?

In the first article Michael Schwartz argues that prisoners are the modern equivalent of slaves. He uses statistical evidence to show that ethnic minorities, particularly African Americans, are overrepresented in the prison population. Schwartz claims that racism is prevalent in the United States because sentencing laws, particularly those concerning crack cocaine, discriminate against African Americans. He concludes that American society endorses the use of prisoners as slaves because their labor is economical, and corporations depend on this cheap labor to boost their profits.

In the second article President George W. Bush honors Dr. Martin Luther King, Jr., during a White House celebration of King's life and work. Bush gives recognition to King's vital contribution to the passage of the Civil Rights Act of 1964, which made physical racial intimidation a crime. After acknowledging the racism in America's past, Bush suggests that the Civil Rights Act marked the beginning of equality for all Americans and that the efforts of Dr. Martin Luther King, Jr., and others in the civil rights movement of the 1950s and 1960s prompted this important piece of legislation in the fight against racism in the United States. President Bush proclaims that King's arguments were "the very words and principles of our Declaration and Constitution" and praises King for holding "this nation to its own standards" and for living out "the true meaning of its creed."

FURTHER INFORMATION:

Books:

Berry, Mary Frances, *Black Resistance White Law: A History of Constitutional Racism in America*. New York: Penguin, 1995.

Bell, Derrick A., *Race, Racism, and American Law*. New York: Aspen Publishers, 2000.

Useful websites:

www.congresslink.org/civil/essay.html
"Major Features of the Civil Rights Act of 1964" article.
www.constitutioncenter.org/sections/work/2c asp
"Conflicting Perspectives on Race, Equality, and Affirmative Action" from the National Constitution Center's "The Constitution at Work" site.
www.sodabob.com/Constitution/Census.asp
"The 'Race' Question on the U.S. Census Is Racist: Why This Is So and What To Answer Instead" by Bob Curtis.

The following debates in the Pro/Con series may also be of interest:

In this volume:
Topic 1 Does it matter what the original intentions of the Framers were?

Topic 10 Should the government be able to prohibit hate speech?

In *Criminal Law and the Penal System*:
Topic 1 Is the criminal justice system racist?

IS THE CONSTITUTION RACIST?

YES: Physical expressions of racism are crimes, but freedom of speech is a civil right that forms the backbone of democracy

YES: Many of the leading American corporations rely on the prison system as a never-ending supply of cheap labor. They endorse constitutional racism by placing their profits before people.

YES: The Thirteenth Amendment to the Constitution states that it is perfectly legitimate for slavery or involuntary servitude to be used as "punishment for crime whereof the party shall have been duly convicted"

MIXED MESSAGES
The Constitution penalizes physical expressions of racism but protects hate speech. Is this right?

MODERN SLAVERY
Is prison labor the modern form of slavery?

NO: All forms of racism should be penalized because they are damaging to people and could incite more extreme racial behavior

NO: People choose to commit criminal offenses and realize the consequences of their actions, whereas slavery is involuntary

IS THE CONSTITUTION RACIST?
KEY POINTS

NO: History has shown that the Constitution has failed to protect ethnic minorities in the past, so there is certainly no guarantee that future policies will do so

AN END TO RACISM
Has the 1964 Civil Rights Act finally put an end to constitutional racism?

YES: The law makes certain acts of intimidation, such as segregation and racially motivated violence, crimes that are punishable by imprisonment

NO: Statistics show that the Constitution promotes racism by institutions such as the judiciary, since ethnic minorities are over-represented in the prison system

Topic 6
IS WELFARE CONSTITUTIONAL?

YES

FROM "THE NEXT CENTURY OF OUR CONSTITUTION: RETHINKING OUR
DUTY TO THE POOR"
HASTINGS LAW JOURNAL, NOVEMBER 1987
PETER B. EDELMAN

NO

FROM *TAKINGS: PRIVATE PROPERTY AND THE POWER OF EMINENT DOMAIN*
RICHARD A. EPSTEIN

INTRODUCTION

American democracy, Abraham Lincoln famously remarked, is "that form, and substance of government, whose leading object is, to elevate the condition of men—to lift artificial weights from all shoulders—to clear the paths of laudable pursuit for all—to afford all, an unfettered start, and a fair chance, in the race of life." He thus thought it best "for all to leave each man free to acquire property as fast as he can." But he also included "providing for the helpless young and afflicted" within "the legitimate object of government," which is "to do for the people what needs to be done, but which they can not, by individual effort, do at all, or do so well, for themselves."

In the century and a half since Lincoln expressed those sentiments, American democracy has come to accept an obligation to provide food, shelter, jobs, education, pensions, medical care, child support, and other goods to every member of society who meets the qualification requirements. Indeed, this so-called welfare state, despite public perceptions to the contrary, does not consist solely of aid to the poor. One way or another it touches the lives of virtually every American through a vast array of programs at all levels of government. The rise of the modern welfare state marks a historic change in our understanding of government's proper role in society. It is worth reflecting, then, on whether the modern welfare state is consistent with the notion of constitutionally limited government.

Today, Lincoln's words would be understood as justification of expansive government programs to ensure economic security. But they were not understood by his contemporaries in this way. In the 19th century Americans held firm to the belief that limited government would best allow people to better themselves, and the general rule was that each citizen should, as one senator put it, "look to himself" to provide for his or her own well-being.

Those who believe that today's welfare state is unconstitutional would side with this view, arguing that the Framers did not place the provision of social security within the powers of Congress. These powers are enumerated in Article I, Section 8, of the Constitution. Nor, they would assert, does the provision of welfare fall within the "necessary and proper" clause (clause 18) of that section, which allows for the making of laws "for carrying into execution" these enumerated powers.

"Congress shall have power 1) To lay and collect taxes, duties, imposts, and excises, to pay the debts and provide for the common defence and general welfare of the United States...."

—ARTICLE I, SECTION 8, THE CONSTITUTION

This limited-government view regarding welfare was the prevalent one well into the 20th century. However, the Great Depression changed everything. President Franklin D. Roosevelt's efforts to lead the American people through the worst economic crisis in American history marked the beginning of the modern welfare state. In sharp contrast to the traditional idea that rights embody only guarantees against government oppression, Roosevelt expanded the notion of rights to encompass government responsibility to ensure economic security. As he explained in his 1944 State of the Union Address, ensuring economic security meant that the

inalienable rights secured by the Constitution—free speech, a free press, trial by jury, and protection against unreasonable search and seizure—had to be supplemented by a "second bill of rights … under which a new basis of security and prosperity can be established for all—regardless of station, race, or creed." He added that "… true individual freedom cannot exist without economic security and independence. Necessitous men are not free men."

Roosevelt's belief that government has a responsibility to provide for the well-being or welfare of the American people was, in his view, perfectly consistent with both the letter and spirit of the Constitution. During Roosevelt's tenure as president a variety of government programs were established to assist those in need. The most significant of them was the Social Security Act of 1935, which invoked the reference to the "general welfare" in Article I, Section 8 (also in the Preamble) as its constitutional vindication. The Supreme Court upheld this authority in *Helvering v. Davis* (1937), and welfare became a fact of American life. Even so, those who question the validity of Social Security maintain that the Framers' meaning of "general welfare" has been misconstrued.

The following articles provide two very different answers to the question of whether welfare is constitutional. Peter Edelman finds a constitutional imperative for government assistance to the poor under the due process or the Equal Protection clauses, while Richard Epstein argues that government programs that redistribute wealth among citizens are fundamentally at odds with the notion of constitutionally limited government.

THE NEXT CENTURY OF OUR CONSTITUTION ...
Peter B. Edelman

YES

President Lyndon B. Johnson (1908–1973) declared the War on Poverty in the State of the Union address on January 8, 1964. The following August he signed into law the Economic Opportunity Act, whose provisions included the creation of the Job Corps and the extension of loans to small businesses.

Poverty and inequality in the United States

For all the injustices and inequalities that persist in American society, none is more serious than the continuing poverty of millions in the midst of the greatest affluence any country has ever known. This injustice continues despite a national declaration more than two decades ago of a "War on Poverty." It is therefore appropriate in celebrating our constitutional bicentennial to consider anew the existence of a constitutional right to some form of minimum income.

The question received attention from scholars in the late 1960s and the 1970s, but is worth reexamining because the condition of the poor has deteriorated alarmingly since 1978. It was perhaps arguable then, as Robert Bork in fact did argue, that the poor had done pretty well legislatively and needed no special judicial protection. But what has occurred since demonstrates pointedly the poor's continuing political powerlessness and suggests again the value of considering judicial intervention.

Subsistence income

The argument I make in this essay is for a constitutional right to a "survival" income, or if that term seems too elementally biological, the idea of a "subsistence" income may communicate my meaning more clearly. I have chosen this terminology to indicate that I am not arguing for a court-ordered end to "poverty." The latter would raise difficult definitional and remedial questions, as the following discussion will show. On the other hand, I do not mean survival in the literal sense of confining the claim to people who will starve or die of exposure without a court order. If there is a societal obligation to assure survival, I believe it is at a more generous level than a bed in a homeless shelter and meals at a soup kitchen.

My basic point is that the past half century has brought us to a need for a new constitutional era, one presaged by intimations in existing doctrine but admittedly a step or more beyond where we have been, an era which involves

Rosa Garza sits outside her home in Ontario, Oregon, with five of her family's nine children. She receives welfare in a new program under which she must work to keep her benefits.

judicial recognition of certain affirmative obligations on the part of the state to its citizens.

There are two lines of theoretical justification for this: one, that it is an obligation which has been implicit in our constitutional structure all along, or at least since the American polity has had enough resources to share its wealth more equitably; and two, that it is an obligation which has been acquired as a consequence of the government's historic and continuing complicity in economic arrangements that foreseeably resulted in the current maldistribution. The first is a substantive due process argument; the second is an equal protection theory.

The Framers surely did not contemplate any constitutional right to any degree of redistribution, however modest. They thought of themselves as protecting property rights and interests as distributed at the time. Any notion that effective political participation required economic fairness was irrelevant because suffrage was limited to the propertied.

The "due process [of law]" clauses are found in the Fifth and Fourteenth Amendments to the Constitution. The Fourteenth Amendment also contains the "Equal Protection" clause, which states that "No state shall ... deprive any person of life, liberty, or property, without due process of law; nor deny to any person within its jurisdiction the equal protection of the laws."

Indeed, it is precisely this recognition of the economic and therefore the political realities of the late eighteenth century that underscores why a narrow jurisprudence of original intent is unacceptable and unworkable.

Income distribution and the Constitution

Can we find a right to minimum income in the Constitution? Those who reject the idea at the moral level will probably go no further, although it is certainly possible that one who rejects the idea of a moral requirement might still find it to be constitutionally required, on positivistic grounds. And many who accept the notion of a moral obligation do not agree that it is embodied in the Constitution.

I am hardly writing on a clean slate. For example, Judge Richard Posner recently wrote that "the Constitution is a charter of negative liberties; it tells the state to let people alone; it does not require the federal government or the state to provide services, even so elementary a service as maintaining law and order."

This position is also represented in a recent brief essay by then Judge Antonin Scalia. He wrote that "the moral precepts of distributive justice ... surely fall within the broad middle range of moral values that may be embodied in law but need not be. It is impossible to say, he continued, "that our constitutional traditions mandate the legal imposition of even so basic a precept of distributive justice as providing food to the destitute."

Surely fall within the middle range? Impossible to say? Why surely? Why impossible? That is Scalia's view. Others say differently, and defend their position with elaborate philosophical justifications. It depends on one's view as to the basic obligations of government and their inclusion in the Constitution. But Scalia is now in a position to have his view on the subject count more heavily.

So those who insist on narrow devotion to original intent will not be convinced. But then I think our constitutional history proves them wrong in any case. The Constitution has acquired new meaning as times have changed, and properly so.

One Rubicon in American constitutional law, as Judge Posner's comment illustrates, has been the idea of inferring affirmative rights to invoke state action. Our constitutional rights are primarily negative, involving protection against state action rather than any state obligation to "provide."

It is time we crossed that Rubicon, and I think it justifiable doctrinally to do so. I say this reluctantly because, as I have indicated and will discuss in more detail later, the primary

Richard A. Posner (1939–) is a judge on the Seventh Circuit Court of Appeals and senior lecturer at the University of Chicago Law School. Antonin Scalia (1936–) was a judge on the Court of Appeals for the District of Columbia Circuit. He has been an associate justice of the Supreme Court since 1986.

For a more complete picture of Scalia's views on the Constitution's role in the obligations of government see the court case on pages 28–31 of this volume.

A "Rubicon" is a bounding or limiting line that, if crossed, fully commits those who cross it to pursue a course of action.

public policy impetus regarding poverty has to be legislative. And I certainly do not advocate going much beyond the other side of the divide in terms of what I would have the courts do. But we have come to a legislative impasse on the problem of poverty that the poor are powerless to break, so if there is a justifiable constitutional claim it should be vindicated.

A fundamental right to survive?

In that regard I want to explore two ideas, which I introduced earlier. One idea is that there is a fundamental right to enough income to survive. This is, for lack of a better term, a substantive due process argument. If there are certain fundamental rights with which the government cannot interfere, and if these rights are guaranteed under the due process clauses, then, if the right to subsist is fundamental and if failure to assure subsistence constitutes interference with the right, the right to governmental assistance in order to "survive" can properly be termed one of substantive due process. The other idea is that government has been guilty of complicity in the persisting poverty. This is an equal protection argument. If government policy has created conditions which have helped some to prosper mightily and left others in a state of total and absolute deprivation, it has denied the latter the equal protection of the laws, and steps must be taken to remedy that denial.

"Substantive due process" deals not with matters of legal procedure (that is "procedural due process") but with infringement of fundamental rights guaranteed by the Constitution.

TAKINGS: PRIVATE PROPERTY AND THE POWER OF EMINENT DOMAIN
Richard A. Epstein

X Welfare transfers, whether in cash or in kind, aid the poor at the expense of the rich, within the limits of practical measurement. Even if welfare payments to the poor were completely proper in principle, there is nothing to warrant the capricious redistributions, whether they are to tenants at the expense of landlords, to residents at the expense of outsiders, to debtors at the expense of creditors, to consumers of oil and gas at the expense of producers, or to women at the expense of men (or neither at the expense of both).

Epstein states the heart of a dilemma in politics about the duty of the government to redistribute wealth to poorer citizens.

Welfare and the poor

The case for welfare rights within a system of private property must rest upon implicit in-kind compensation to those who have paid the taxes. One form of that argument traces the police power point. The compensation to the rich is that they are spared the violence that would overcome them if the poor were shut out from the social gains. The peace obtained is worth more than the money paid to obtain it. So viewed, the welfare payment is little more than a strategic bribe that spares the payers the greater costs of police enforcement and control. Yet where the opportunities for individual advancement are left as open as a system of limited government would leave them (for example, without barriers, such as the minimum wage, to entry in labor markets), there is less reason to fear that some permanent underclass will remain a constant threat to the social order. Because individual initiative promises relatively higher returns the propensity for violent activity should be reduced. The proper constitutional response, therefore, is to insist upon the usual level of means scrutiny to justify transfer payments. The first defense against violence should be police measures, which can be modified as exigencies arise. Transfer payments are rarely a suitable means to counteract violence; they are best justified by showing a clear and present danger of social unrest that cannot be handled by conventional techniques. It is hard to quarrel with providing free food in a

The author cites the minimum wage as a disincentive to employment. Can you think of any other "barriers to entry in labor markets"?

COMMENTARY: Origins of welfare

If one of the cornerstones of social security is assistance to families in need, then the origins of welfare can be traced back to the orphanage system. The first orphanage to be founded in the United States was a private charity that opened in 1729 in New Orleans, and only seven existed nationwide by the end of the 18th century. Yet during the 1800s children's homes quickly grew in number as more and more Americans moved to the cities, and the perils of urban life, such as crime and disease and then the Civil War swelled the total of unattached children. By 1880 the United States was home to more than 600 orphanages, and the figure eventually peaked at about 1,100 with a population of perhaps as many as 200,000 children. Orphanage funding came from church, private, and public sources, with the former two categories providing the lion's share of the support.

The birth of welfare

By the early 20th century orphanages were taking in not only the parentless but also the children of single parents and the victims of abuse. Parents struggling with poverty also often saw the orphanage as a (sometimes temporary) refuge for children they could not support. At around the same time a shift occurred in government thinking on child care. At the first White House Conference on Dependent Children, which took place in 1909, President Theodore Roosevelt opined that "mothers should raise their own children." Over the next few years the states passed mother's pension laws under which widowed mothers received cash to enable them to keep their children at home.

The Social Security Act and onward

With the coming of the Great Depression in the 1930s the administration of Franklin D. Roosevelt intervened to aid the poor, introducing the first federal welfare program—the Social Security Act of 1935. Under this act mother's pensions were replaced by Aid to Dependent Children (ADC), also called Aid to Families of Dependent Children (AFDC). AFDC entitled needy families to cash payments and remained in force until the arrival of the Personal Responsibility and Work Opportunity Reconciliation Act (PWRORA) of 1996. Under this act the cash entitlement of AFDC was replaced with Temporary Assistance for Needy Families (TANF) in an attempt to reduce welfare dependency. TANF may, but does not necessarily, take the form of cash payments and has a strict work requirement.

The existence of welfare and changed attitudes to child care have caused the orphanage system to shrink. But in a period in which concern over welfare spending remains high, some politicians and commentators have suggested a remedy that would bring the United States full circle—the reintroduction of orphanages.

A charity box hangs below a plaque asking for contributions from passersby for the upkeep of of the orphans residing in this old orphanage in New Orleans, Louisiana.

flood-torn town to reduce the chances of looting, even if that were characterized as a transfer scheme. It is equally hard to see how the same argument justifies the Food Stamp Program as an antidote to revolution.

Intolerable complications

The basic rules of private property are inconsistent with any form of welfare benefits. One way to avoid failure is to throw the baby out with the bath water, to get out of the welfare business entirely. That judgment is not based simply upon some narrow sense of egoism or a belief that private greed is the highest form of social virtue. Nor does it rest on the hidden pleasure of watching small children starve or derelicts freeze on the street. To the contrary, it rests on the belief that once the state runs a transfer system, it can never extricate itself from the intolerable complications that follow. The higher the level of benefits, the greater the demand, until the political dynamic—rent seeking again—produces an aggregate demand that the system itself can meet only with great cost to its productive capacities. Rather than become mired in the quicksand, do not start down that path at all. If it is said that no system of private support could handle the current level of demands, the proper answer is that no system of private support would ever have spawned the current levels of demand.

Need would be reduced by better policing, and the means to satisfy it would be larger, because the overall levels of wealth would be greater. A private welfare system becomes conceivable in principle once it is realized that the system would be much more modest than it is today. Charitable activities were common in the nineteenth century before the income tax, not only for the support of great universities and hospitals, but also for the relief of victims of tragedies. Many programs for the poor were in place before the New Deal, but they were replaced by government programs that exhausted the public willingness to make welfare payments. Reduce government involvement and private benevolence will again increase.

The Food Stamp Program was introduced in 1964 by the Johnson administration. To find out more, see www.law.cornell. edu/topics/food_ stamps.html.

The "New Deal" was the name given to the domestic program begun in 1933 by the administration of President Franklin D. Roosevelt. The subject is covered in depth at http:// newdeal.feri.org.

Summary

Peter Edelman concedes that "our constitutional rights are primarily negative, involving protection against state action rather than any state obligation to 'provide.'" But he also points out that "the Constitution has acquired new meaning as times have changed." Since 1978, he asserts, the conditions of the poor have deteriorated so much—while political institutions have proved incapable of addressing poverty—that Americans should alter the way they have traditionally interpreted the government's constitutional obligations to the poor. He suggests a look at the equal protection or due process clauses. Concerning the latter, he argues that the Constitution's guarantee that no one is deprived of life, liberty, or property except by a suitable or appropriate process should now be interpreted to encompass a right to a minimum income. As Edelman explains, "If the right to subsist is fundamental and if failure to assure subsistence constitutes interference with the right, the right to governmental assistance in order to 'survive' can properly be termed one of substantive due process."

Richard Epstein would strongly reject such reasoning. He denies that we have a constitutional right to be taken care of by government or that it is constitutional to take money from some to provide for others. Ours is "a system of private property," he argues, and "the basic rules of private property are inconsistent with any form of welfare benefits." As Epstein would argue, constitutionally limited government provides the basic freedoms necessary to allow individuals to live their own lives, meet their own needs, and dispose of the material resources they have acquired by their own efforts. Welfare, on the other hand, undermines personal responsibility and self-reliance by conferring benefits independent of the process of earning them. Epstein does not advocate leaving the poor to suffer. "Reduce government involvement," he argues, "and private benevolence will again increase."

FURTHER INFORMATION:

Books:

Katz, Michael B., *The Price of Citizenship: Redefining America's Welfare State*. New York: Metropolitan Books, 2001.

Trattner, Walter I., *From Poor Law to Welfare State: A History of Social Welfare in America*. New York: The Free Press, 1999.

Useful websites:

www.ssa.gov/history/history.html
Social Security history page, including a timeline.
www.policyalmanac.org/social_welfare/poverty.shtml
Almanac of poverty with related links.

The following debates in the Pro/Con series may also be of interest:

In this volume:
Topic 1 Does it matter what the original intentions of the Framers were?

In *Economics*:
Topic 6 Should welfare be abolished?

IS WELFARE CONSTITUTIONAL?

YES: *The Social Security Act of 1935 was authorized by the "general welfare" clause*

YES: *In a wealthy society it is a scandal that some are very rich while others live in deprivation*

INTERPRETATION
Was the New Deal in accordance with the Constitution?

MORALITY
Shouldn't the government help the poor with cash?

NO: *The "general welfare" clause was misconstrued. It has nothing to do with social security.*

NO: *Social Security and wealth redistribution have no place in a private property society and risk creating welfare dependency*

IS WELFARE CONSTITUTIONAL? KEY POINTS

YES: *The Constitution is a "living document" and its meaning has often changed over the years*

YES: *The Constitution may allow welfare on due process or equal protection grounds*

FLEXIBILITY
Should Americans be allowed leeway in interpreting the Constitution?

NO: *We should remain faithful to the Framers' original intent*

NO: *The Constitution tells government to leave its citizens alone. We cannot "infer affirmative rights."*

Topic 7

DOES THE CONSTITUTION ADEQUATELY PROTECT THE RIGHTS OF THE DISABLED?

YES

FROM *CITY OF CLEBURNE, TEXAS V. CLEBURNE LIVING CENTER,* 473 U.S. 432
JULY 1, 1985
JUSTICE BYRON R. WHITE

NO

FROM "DISABILITY RIGHTS"
ACLU BRIEFING PAPER NO. 21, WINTER 1999
AMERICAN CIVIL LIBERTIES UNION

INTRODUCTION

The Constitution is supposed to protect all citizens, the Equal Protection clause of the Fourteenth Amendment commanding that no state "deny to any person within its jurisdiction the equal protection of the laws." In practice, however, disabled people have often found that protection lacking, and critics argue that the civil rights of disabled people have rarely been upheld.

The United States, like many countries, has a poor record when it comes to its disabled citizens. Before and immediately after the American Revolution disabled people were routinely labeled as defective, many disabled children being abandoned to orphanages, and adults locked away in asylums or poorhouses. The situation improved a little in the 1790s, when pioneers such as the Tukes began to promote humane treatment, but state institutions still tended to use their inmates as a poorly paid workforce.

The situation deteriorated again in the early 1900s, when many middle- and upper-class white Americans embraced the concept of eugenics. The term came from the Greek for "good origin" and was coined in 1883 by the English mathematician Francis Galton, who proposed that defects could be "bred out" of society. Soon eugenics became a major part of U.S. thinking, and disabled people were demonized as a drain on national resources and the cause of social ills. State-sponsored fairs held competitions to find "fitter families" and "better babies," while new laws banned disabled people from moving to America or from marrying or having children.

In 1916 Margaret Sanger opened the first birth-control clinic "to limit and discourage the over-fertility of the mentally and physically defective." Meanwhile, biologists Harry Laughlin and Charles Davenport led scientists in justifying forced sterilizations. Soon 30 states had passed sterilization laws targeting "defective strains" such as the blind, deaf, epileptic, and feebleminded.

By 1939 about 60,000 to 100,000 people had been sterilized in an attempt to rid the United States of the feebleminded.

After the atrocities of World War II eugenics began to lose some of its luster as various independent scientists disproved the eugenicists' claims and revealed much of their data to be biased. But although most eugenicists tried to cover up their previous collaboration with England and Germany, the movement continued to operate under the umbrella of organizations such as the International Planned Parenthood Federation. A dominant figure was Major General Frederick Osborn, who, in 1956, said, "people won't accept the idea that they are in general, second rate. We must rely on other motivation ... a system of voluntary unconscious selection." Sterilizations were still commonplace even in 1979.

"There has to be positive action that allows the most disadvantaged people to get their fair share...."

—PAUL BURTON,

PLANNED GIVING COMMITTEE,

WHITMAN COLLEGE

Attitudes to disabled people only really began to change during the civil rights movement of the 1960s, which prompted numerous disabled activists to campaign for legal equality. One of the earliest laws that tried to provide more rights for disabled people was the Rehabilitation Act of 1973, which required federally funded organizations to provide access and remove obstacles to services. But even these regulations were not signed into law until a group of disabled people staged a month-long sit-in at the Department of Health, Education, and Welfare in San Francisco.

The Americans with Disabilities Act (ADA) of 1990, which bars job discrimination and requires disabled access to buildings, transportation, and telecommunications, is the culmination of all these laws, giving disabled people legal recourse should they feel discriminated against. But even the ADA is controversial. Research certainly suggests that it has made life easier for many disabled people, but critics have argued that it is unconstitutional and can even harm the very people it is meant to help by requiring them to prove in court that their disability "substantially limits one or more major life activities...." Thus a person has to be disabled enough to qualify for protection but not disabled enough to do a job, which for many is virtually impossible—especially since subsequent Supreme Court decisions have narrowed the ADA's reach, making it even more difficult for disabled workers to claim special protection.

In the following articles the case of the *City of Cleburne, Texas v. Cleburne Living Center* is cited as an example of the Supreme Court upholding the rights of disabled people. In an important victory the court overturned the city's decision to refuse a special permit for a proposed home for the mentally retarded after they deemed it to be based on irrational prejudice. In contrast, the ACLU Briefing Paper argues that despite the recent laws passed to try to improve the lives of disabled people, there is still too little being done to uphold their constitutional rights.

CITY OF CLEBURNE, TEXAS V. CLEBURNE LIVING CENTER
Justice Byron R. White

☑ …In July 1980, respondent Jan Hannah purchased a building at 201 Featherston Street in the city of Cleburne, Texas, with the intention of leasing it to Cleburne Living Center, Inc. (CLC), for the operation of a group home for the mentally retarded. It was anticipated that the home would house 13 retarded men and women, who would be under the constant supervision of CLC staff.… CLC planned to comply with all applicable state and federal regulations. The city informed CLC that a special use permit would be required for the operation of a group home at the site, and CLC accordingly submitted a permit application.… the city explained that under the zoning regulations applicable to the site, a special use permit, renewable annually, was required for the construction of "[hospitals] for the insane or feebleminded, or alcoholic [sic] or drug addicts, or penal or correctional institutions." The city had determined that the proposed group home should be classified as a "hospital for the feebleminded." After holding a public hearing on CLC's application, the City Council voted 3 to 1 to deny a special use permit.

CLC then filed suit in Federal District Court against the city … alleging that the zoning ordinance was invalid … because it discriminated against the mentally retarded in violation of the equal protection rights of CLC and its potential residents. The District Court found that "[if] the potential residents of the Featherston Street home were not mentally retarded, but the home was the same in all other respects, its use would be permitted under the city's zoning ordinance.…" Even so, the District Court held the ordinance and its application constitutional… and … to be rationally related to the city's legitimate interests in "… the safety and fears of residents in the adjoining neighborhood"…. The Court of Appeals for the Fifth Circuit reversed, determining that mental retardation was a quasi-suspect classification.… The court considered heightened scrutiny to be … appropriate … because the city's ordinance withheld a benefit which, although not fundamental, was very important to the mentally retarded. Without group homes, the court stated, the retarded could

The term "feebleminded" was once a polite alternative to words such as imbecile and moron, and it is still listed in many dictionaries. But it is now considered to be largely unacceptable, a suggested alternative being "a person who has an intellectual disability." See www.vrri.org/rhb0897.htm for more on the history of unacceptable terms.

Discrimination is considered constitutional in some cases if the state has a rational reason for making a distinction that is in its own interests.

never hope to integrate themselves into the community.
…the court held that the ordinance was invalid on its face
because it did not substantially further any important
governmental interests.…

The Equal Protection clause of the Fourteenth Amendment
commands that no State shall "deny to any person within
its jurisdiction the equal protection of the laws," which is
essentially a direction that all persons similarly situated
should be treated alike.… The general rule is that legislation is
presumed to be valid and will be sustained if the classification
drawn by the statute is rationally related to a legitimate state
interest. When social or economic legislation is at issue, the
Equal Protection Clause allows the States wide latitude and
the Constitution presumes that even improvident decisions
will eventually be rectified by the democratic processes.…

The decision of the Court of Appeals
We conclude … that the Court of Appeals erred in holding
mental retardation a quasi-suspect classification calling for
a more exacting standard of judicial review.… First, it is
undeniable, and it is not argued otherwise here, that those
who are mentally retarded have a reduced ability to cope
with and function in the everyday world. Nor are they all
cut from the same pattern:… they range from those whose
disability is not immediately evident to those who must be
constantly cared for. They are thus different, immutably so,
in relevant respects, and the States' interest in dealing with
and providing for them is plainly a legitimate one. How this
large and diversified group is to be treated under the law
is … very much a task for legislators guided by qualified
professionals and not by the perhaps ill-informed opinions
of the judiciary. Heightened scrutiny inevitably involves
substantive judgments about legislative decisions, and we
doubt that the predicate for such judicial oversight is present
where the classification deals with mental retardation.

Second, the distinctive legislative response, both national
and state, to the … mentally retarded demonstrates not only
that they have unique problems, but also that the lawmakers
have been addressing their difficulties in a manner that belies
a continuing antipathy or prejudice and a corresponding
need for more intrusive oversight by the judiciary.…..

Third, the legislative response, which could hardly have
occurred and survived without public support, negates any
claim that the mentally retarded are politically powerless in
the sense that they have no ability to attract the attention of
the lawmakers. Any minority can be said to be powerless to

Since the 1970s the Supreme Court has held that "suspect classes" receive strong judicial protection under the equal protection clause, and that "quasi-suspect classes" receive medium levels of protection. Courts rarely tolerate laws that discriminate against groups in either of these classes. Laws that discriminate against excluded groups such as the elderly, however, are usually upheld as long as there is a "rational basis" for the laws.

A "substantive judgment" is one that creates or defines the legal rights of a person or group.

The Court of Appeals cited lack of political power as one of the reasons that cases involving the "mentally retarded" required higher levels of judicial scrutiny.

assert direct control over the legislature, but if that were a criterion for higher level scrutiny by the courts, much economic and social legislation would now be suspect.

Fourth, if the large and amorphous class of the mentally retarded were deemed quasi-suspect for the reasons given by the Court of Appeals, it would be difficult to find a principled way to distinguish a variety of other groups who have perhaps immutable disabilities setting them off from others … and who can claim some degree of prejudice from at least part of the public at large. One need mention in this respect only the aging, the disabled, the mentally ill, and the infirm.….

We turn to the issue of the validity of the zoning ordinance insofar as it requires a special use permit for homes for the mentally retarded. We inquire first whether requiring a special use permit for the Featherston home … deprives respondents of the equal protection of the laws.

The constitutional issue is clearly posed. The city does not require a special use permit in an R-3 zone for apartment houses, multiple dwellings, boarding and lodging houses … hospitals, sanitariums, nursing homes for convalescents or the aged (other than for the insane or feebleminded or alcoholics or drug addicts) … and other specified uses. It does, however, insist on a special permit for the Featherston home … because it would be a facility for the mentally retarded. May the city require the permit for this facility when other care and multiple-dwelling facilities are freely permitted?

It is true … that the mentally retarded as a group are … different from those who would occupy other facilities that would be permitted in an R-3 zone without a special permit. But this difference is largely irrelevant unless the Featherston home and those who would occupy it would threaten legitimate interests of the city in a way that other permitted uses such as boarding houses and hospitals would not. Because in our view the record does not reveal any rational basis for believing that the Featherston home would pose any special threat to the city's legitimate interests, we affirm the judgment … insofar as it holds the ordinance invalid as applied in this case.

The District Court found that the City Council's insistence on the permit rested on several factors. First, the Council was concerned with the negative attitude of … property owners located within 200 feet of the Featherston facility, as well as with the fears of elderly residents of the neighborhood. But mere negative attitudes, or fear, unsubstantiated by factors which are properly cognizable … are not permissible bases for treating a home for the mentally retarded differently from apartment houses, multiple dwellings, and the like. "Private biases may be outside the reach of the law, but the law cannot, directly or indirectly, give them effect."

Second, the Council … was concerned that the facility was across the street from a junior high school, and it feared that the students might harass the occupants of the Featherston home. But the school itself is attended by about 30 mentally retarded students, and denying a permit based on such vague … fears is again permitting some portion of the community to validate what would otherwise be an equal protection violation. The other objection to the home's location was that it was located on "a five hundred year flood plain." This concern … however, can hardly be based on a distinction between the Featherston home and, for example, nursing homes, … sanitariums or hospitals, any of which could be located on the Featherston site without obtaining a special use permit. The same may be said of another concern of the Council— doubts about the legal responsibility for actions which the mentally retarded might take. If there is no concern about legal responsibility with respect to other uses that would be permitted in the area … it is difficult to believe that the groups of mildly or moderately mentally retarded individuals who would live at 201 Featherston would present any different or special hazard.

Fourth, the Council was concerned with the size of the home and the number of people that would occupy it.… In the words of the Court of Appeals, "[the] City never justifies its apparent view that other people can live under such 'crowded' conditions when mentally retarded persons cannot."

… the City also urged that the ordinance is aimed at avoiding concentration of population.…These concerns obviously fail to explain why apartment houses, fraternity and sorority houses, hospitals and the like, may freely locate in the area without a permit. So, too, the expressed worry about fire hazards, the serenity of the neighborhood, and the avoidance of danger to other residents fail rationally to justify singling out a home such as 201 Featherston for the special use permit, yet imposing no such restrictions on the many other uses freely permitted in the neighborhood.

The short of it is that requiring the permit … appears to us to rest on an irrational prejudice against the mentally retarded … who would occupy the Featherston facility and who would live under the closely supervised and highly regulated conditions expressly provided for by state and federal law. The judgment of the Court of Appeals is affirmed insofar as it invalidates the zoning ordinance …[but] is otherwise vacated.…

Do you think the law is always outside the reach of private biases, or is it possible that the private biases of the judiciary might influence legal decisions on some occasions?

Does this imply that there might be other circumstances in which a prejudiced judgment might be deemed rational?

DISABILITY RIGHTS
American Civil Liberties Union

NO

…People with disabilities are the poorest, least employed, and least educated minority in America. At the end of 1995, it was estimated that one out of five people in the U.S. had some level of disability, one of ten, severe. Too often, people with disabilities have been treated as second class citizens, shunned and segregated by physical barriers and social stereotypes. They have been discriminated against in employment, schools, and housing, robbed of their personal autonomy, and too often, hidden away and forgotten by the larger society.

By and large, people with disabilities continue to be excluded from the American dream:

There is a strong correlation between disability and low income. According to 1995 census data, the percentage of people between 22 and 64 years of age who live in poverty was 13.3%. But among the disabled it was 19.3%. And among the severely disabled, it was 42.4%. The correlation between disability and poverty worsens with age.

Two-thirds of Americans with disabilities between the ages of 16 and 64 were unemployed. A 1994 Harris poll revealed that 79% of these Americans wanted to work.

In 1995, 9.6% of disabled people aged 16–64 had completed college. This was one-third the rate of non-disabled people in the same age group.

A history of discrimination

America has a shameful history of cutting off people with disabilities from the rest of society by sequestering them inside their homes, or consigning them to isolated, often squalid institutions. In Hawaii, for example, thousands of people with Hansen's Disease (leprosy) were permanently quarantined to isolated islands, cut off from their families and their livelihood. This forced separation, which had no public health justification, continued well into the 1950s. In 1972, the nation was shocked by film footage showing the filthy and dehumanizing conditions endured by 5,400 mentally disabled children at New York's Willowbrook "School."

Historically, people with disabilities have had little success in vindicating their rights in court. In 1927, the U.S. Supreme

Court upheld the forced sterilization of a woman whose mother and daughter were both mentally retarded. People with mental disabilities were, the Court said, a "menace" who "sap the strength of the state." Society would be wise to "prevent those who are manifestly unfit from continuing their kind....Three generations of imbeciles are enough."

Celebrity influence

Finally, and thanks in part to the inspiration provided by the civil rights struggles of the 1960s, disability rights advocates began to press for full legal equality and access to mainstream society. Through lobbying and litigation, laws were passed and rights established; public education and advocacy were used to promote reason and inclusiveness rather than fear and pity.

National heroes and celebrities joined grassroots activists to force disability rights issues onto the public agenda. World famous classical violinist Itzhak Perlman, who has polio, will perform only in concert halls that are fully accessible. Former "mouseketeer" Annette Funicello has become a vocal spokesperson for people with multiple sclerosis. But while significant progress has been made to protect the legal rights of people with disabilities, there are still many battles ahead in the struggle for equal rights. Too many disabled people are still institutionalized, despite the fact that the care they need can be provided within their communities. Too much discrimination, fear and even hatred prevail. The ACLU and other advocacy organizations will continue to fight for the rights of people with disabilities, in the courts, in Congress, and elsewhere.

Congress defines disabilities

Current disabilities are physical or mental impairments that "significantly limit one or more major life activities." The previously disabled are people who have been diagnosed with conditions like cancer or manic depression, but are either fully recovered from or functioning with the condition. Finally, there are those who are perceived as having a disability but who are fully abled, such as burn victims and obese people. This third group is often discriminated against based on "lookism." People whose mental disorders are associated with criminal behavior, and drug addicts and alcoholics who are still engaged in substance abuse are not protected under the Americans with Disabilities Act.

The ADA can be considered the cumulation of several laws that have enhanced the civil rights of people with disabilities. Improved access and mobility were guaranteed

Despite the fact that Carrie Buck had given birth out of wedlock after she was sexually assaulted, Justice Oliver Wendell Holmes judged her to be both feebleminded and promiscuous. She was given little in the way of defense, and no one spoke in her favor.

Born in 1942, Annette Funicello was discovered by Walt Disney at the age of 12 and went on to become a popular star of the Mickey Mouse Club. She went on to star in various Disney and beach party movies, carving out a successful career in TV, music, and film over three decades. She was diagnosed with multiple sclerosis in 1987. Vowing to use her own experience for good, she founded a research fund for neurological diseases.

by the Architectural Barriers Act of 1968; the Urban Mass Transportation Act of 1964 (amended in 1970); the Amtrak Improvement Act of 1973 and the Air Carrier Access Act of 1986. Equity in education, housing and civic life were boosted by the Individuals with Disabilities Education Act of 1975; the Developmental Disabilities Assistance and Bill of Rights Act of 1975; the Civil Rights of Institutionalized Persons Act of 1980; the Voting Accessibility for the Elderly and Handicapped Act of 1984; the Protection and Advocacy for Mentally Ill Individuals Act of 1986; the Fair Housing Act Amendment of 1988 and the Civil Rights Restoration Act of 1989.

Along with Section 504 of the 1973 Rehabilitation Act requiring nondiscrimination on the basis of disability in all aspects of programs or activities receiving federal funds, the above-mentioned laws were stepping stones to the landmark 1990 Americans with Disabilities Act.

Do you think that the number of laws passed relating to disability might give some indication of the extent to which disabled people are discriminated against in spite of the Fourteenth Amendment?

Focus on ADA

The 1990 Americans with Disabilities Act (ADA) represents the most comprehensive civil rights law in a generation. Based on Congress' finding that people with disabilities have been "subjected to a history of purposeful unequal treatment, and relegated to a position of political powerlessness," its purpose is to extend to people with disabilities the same legal protections against discrimination available to women and racial and religious minorities under the 1964 Civil Rights Act. The ADA outlaws discrimination in public and private employment, public services, transportation, communications technology and public accommodations (hotels, restaurants, stores, museums, etc.).

The ADA also requires employers to make reasonable modifications in facilities and equipment (depending on the size and resources of the employer) that will enable people with disabilities to perform their jobs. In addition, the Act prohibits private businesses from discrimination against customers with disabilities and requires them to build all new buildings in an accessible manner. The ADA requires private businesses to provide modifications that will enable people with disabilities to enjoy the goods and services being offered.

The Yeskey case involved a prisoner who was denied access to a motivational boot camp program— completion of which would have resulted in his parole—because of a history of hypertension. The court held that state prisons were included in the ADA's definition of public services, and that disabled prisoners were thus entitled to equal access to facilities such as medical services and recreational activities. To read about related cases, go to www.aclu.org/ court/pennsylvania vyeskey.html.

In 1998, the Supreme Court extended the scope of the ADA. In *Pennsylvania Department of Corrections v. Yeskey*, it recognized that prisons were not exempt from ADA compliance, disavowing the claim of 36 states that were resisting equal access accommodations for incarcerated people with disabilities. And in *Bragdon v. Abbott*, the Court established that people with HIV—even if asymptomatic—were entitled to ADA protection from discrimination.

Under the protection of the ADA, millions of disabled people can now seek legal recourse. A 1996 study by the United Cerebral Palsy Association showed that 96% of a sample of disabled Americans surveyed said the ADA had made a positive difference in their lives.

People with mental disabilities

Some of the earliest legal challenges to unfair discrimination and involuntary confinement were won by people with mental disabilities. This group numbers in the tens of millions in this country, and includes both the mentally retarded and people with psychiatric disorders. Objects of both fear and contempt, the mentally disabled have had to fight long and hard for recognition of their civil rights. A mere generation ago, the mentally ill could be involuntarily committed to state institutions for long periods of time—sometimes decades—with no right to court review of their confinement, and with no right to treatment. On any given day in the 1950s, the institutionalized population in America numbered some 559,000 people (today the number is about 100,000). While hospitalized, mental patients were robbed of their right to personal autonomy. They could be forced to work and to submit to unwanted medical procedures, including medical experiments. Their contact with the outside world could be completely curtailed. They could be placed in seclusion or subjected to physical restraints on an attendant's whim.

People with mental retardation did not fare any better. They were viewed as untrainable and as a potential danger to society because if permitted to propagate, they would beget more "imbeciles." People with mental retardation were also confined by the millions in large custodial institutions.

Today, as a result of the self-advocacy movement and a series of constitutional test cases, people with mental disabilities have many more rights than they used to, including: the right not to be confined unless they constitute a danger to themselves or others; the right to a court hearing to contest an involuntary commitment; the right to a lawyer during commitment hearings; the right to refuse medication; the right to "minimally adequate" treatment and training; the right to safe and secure conditions, including food, shelter, clothing and medical care.

But in spite of much progress, people with mental disabilities still face abuse, coercion, and discrimination based on stereotypes and misconceptions.

Improvements cited in the study included better access to buildings and transportation, greater acceptance in the community, and increased employment. See www.pacer.org/pride/snapshot.htm for more details.

The self-advocacy movement began in Europe in the 1960s, spreading to Canada in 1972. A group from Oregon formed the first self-advocacy group in the United States in 1973, calling it "People First." See web.syr.edu/~thechp/selfadvm.htm for more information.

Summary

In the first article Justice White sets out the Supreme Court's opinion in the case of *City of Cleburne, Texas v. Cleburne Living Center* (CLC), providing an example of the rights of disabled people being upheld. The case took place after Jan Hannah purchased a building in the city of Cleburne, intending to lease it to CLC for use as a group home for the mentally retarded. CLC was forced to go to court after the city told them to apply for and then denied them a special use permit. Following a ruling by the District Court and a reversal by the Court of Appeals, the Supreme Court eventually judged the city to have shown an irrational prejudice against the mentally retarded by deciding that a special use permit was necessary. The Equal Protection clause of the Fourteenth Amendment is essentially a direction that all persons similarly situated should be treated alike, and the court concluded that the city had violated the rights of CLC because other facilities such as hospitals and nursing homes would not have been required to apply for such a permit.

The American Civil Liberties Union (ACLU) argues that despite the Constitution's promise of equal rights for all, America has a shameful history of ill-treating disabled people. The ACLU acknowledges that things have improved since the civil rights struggles of the 1960s, which led to a series of acts supporting disabled people, culminating in the Americans with Disabilities Act of 1990. But despite these improvements, the ACLU argues that the Constitution still does not adequately protect the rights of disabled people. Congress defines disability as current, previous, or perceived, and according to this definition disabled people are still the poorest, least-employed, and least-educated people in America. This is particularly apparent in the case of people with mental disabilities: They may have won some of the earliest legal battles for civil rights, but they still face "abuse, coercion, and discrimination."

FURTHER INFORMATION:

Books:

Dybwad, Gunnar, Hank Jr. Bersani, and Bob Williams, *New Voices: Self-Advocacy by People with Disabilities* Cambridge, MA: Brookline Books, 1996.

Herr, Stanley S. and Germain Weber, *Aging, Rights, and Quality of Life: Prospects for Older People with Developmental Disabilities*. Baltimore, MD: Brookes Publishing, 1999.

Useful websites:

www.mrsc.org/legal/ada/adainfo.htm
Americans with Disabilities Act site with other web links.
www.brooklinebooks.com/disabilities/disindex.htm
Disability index for Brookline Books.

The following debates in the Pro/Con series may also be of interest:

In *Health*:
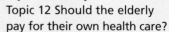
Topic 14 Should psychiatric patients be forced to take medications that have harmful side effects?

In *Family and Society*:
Topic 12 Should the elderly pay for their own health care?

DOES THE CONSTITUTION ADEQUATELY PROTECT THE RIGHTS OF THE DISABLED?

YES: The courts have passed many laws reinforcing disabled people's rights to equal treatment

YES: America has a history of ill-treating disabled people, and things have barely improved

EQUAL RIGHTS
Does the Fourteenth Amendment guarantee equal protection to all?

HISTORY
Has history shown that the Constitution seldom protects disabled people?

NO: Equal protection only applies to groups that are similarly situated, which leaves plenty of room for dispute over what that means

NO: Although not perfect, things have improved vastly for disabled people since legal developments began in the 1960s, and the situation can only get better

DOES THE CONSTITUTION ADEQUATELY PROTECT THE RIGHTS OF THE DISABLED?
KEY POINTS

YES: If racial minorities and women are considered to need extra legal protection against discrimination, it is likely that disabled people need similar levels of protection

YES: Without the higher levels of scrutiny awarded to suspect classes states can enforce laws that discriminate against disabled people by declaring a rational vested interest

SUSPECT CLASSES
Do disabled people need to be labeled as a suspect class to ensure they receive adequate protection in court?

NO: Any improvident decisions made by the local courts will ultimately be rectified through the democratic process

NO: The courts can usually determine whether a law is fair and has a rational grounding without higher levels of scrutiny

Topic 8

SHOULD HOMOSEXUALS BE ALLOWED TO SERVE IN THE MILITARY?

YES

"BROKEN PROMISE: LAWSUITS, PROTESTS, CONFUSION, AND CONDEMNATION FOLLOW
THE PRESIDENT'S COMPROMISE ON GAYS IN THE MILITARY"
THE ADVOCATE, AUGUST 24, 1993
CHRIS BULL

NO

FROM "GAYS AND LESBIANS IN THE ARMED FORCES"
DELIVERED TO THE U.S. SENATE, JULY 16, 1993
SENATOR SAM NUNN

INTRODUCTION

Current estimates suggest that anywhere between 5 and 15 percent of the population of the United States is homosexual. Although there are no official statistics, it seems reasonable to suppose that a similar proportion of homosexuals serve in the armed forces. But gays are officially forbidden from serving in the military, and senior military figures refuse to acknowledge their presence in the services.

Military opposition is based on the argument that open homosexuality within the armed forces would prove disruptive. Those who believe this argue that since service personnel live in such close quarters, acceptance would leave homosexuals free to invade the privacy of heterosexual colleagues. Military leaders say that this would undermine morale.

The military opinion reflects wider historical and social beliefs. Until the middle of the 20th century same-sex intercourse was treated as a criminal offense. Attitudes began to alter somewhat in the 1940s, when the psychiatric profession began classifying homosexuality as a mental illness. The military's ban on homosexuals became law during World War II (1939–1945).

In the decades following the war military opposition to homosexuality intensified. During the Cold War senior military figures believed that homosexual servicemen were espionage risks because they were vulnerable to blackmail by enemy agents. In the 1980s the appearance of the AIDS virus added to their concerns.

The military's opposition to gay service personnel is contested by gay-rights activists and civil-liberties organizations. Since the Constitution protects the civil rights of different cultural and ethnic groups, they argue that it should also protect the right of homosexuals to serve their country.

Gay-rights activists and others who support lifting the ban thought they had found a champion in Bill Clinton. Shortly after entering the White House in January 1993, Clinton announced his intention of ending the ban on homosexuals serving in the military. But Clinton faced such overwhelming opposition from senior military figures and conservative politicians and lawmakers that he was unable to implement his policy.

> *"It is hard to imagine why the mere holding of hands off base and in private is dangerous to the mission of the armed forces if done by a homosexual but not if done by a heterosexual."*
> —JUDGE EUGENE NICKERSON,
> U.S. DISTRICT JUDGE, NEW YORK

A compromise was eventually reached, popularly entitled "Don't ask, Don't tell." Gays and lesbians could serve in the armed forces as long as they did not broadcast their sexual preference or engage in homosexual activity. While provision was made to keep military recruiters from asking questions about sexual orientation, proven homosexual activities still constituted grounds for discharge.

Clinton's compromise did not resolve the argument. Military leaders and their allies saw the new law as a shift toward accepting homosexuals in the military. They argued that the unique role of the military set it apart from civilian society. The job of running the military, they argued, should be left to the expertise of military leaders, not politicians.

Gay-rights groups and their allies argued that the compromise continued to penalize people on the grounds of their sexual orientation. Further, they claimed that the compromise violated the constitutional rights to free speech by forcing homosexuals not to talk about their sexuality.

Civil rights groups, such as the American Civil Liberties Union (ACLU), have supported legal challenges to the policy. Gay-rights activists say that the policy encourages "witch hunts" to oust suspected homosexuals from military service. In 1998, for example, the military discharged 1,145 homosexuals—a 92 percent increase since "Don't ask, Don't tell" was introduced. Military officials believe the increase simply reflects an increase in personnel openly declaring their sexual orientation.

The following articles present the arguments for and against accepting homosexuals in the military.

In the first article Chris Bull discusses the political fallout from "Don't ask, Don't tell." Bull accepts that the law falls far short of lifting the ban on homosexuals and concedes that politics remains the best way in which to move the debate forward.

The second contribution is a speech made by Sam Nunn, chairman of the Senate Armed Services Committee, in the run up to President Clinton's announcement of the "Don't ask, Don't tell" policy. Nunn argues that military life cannot be compared with civilian society. He concludes that homosexuals are not suited to military life because they would disrupt morale.

BROKEN PROMISE: LAWSUITS, PROTESTS, CONFUSION, AND CONDEMNATION FOLLOW THE PRESIDENT'S COMPROMISE ON GAYS IN THE MILITARY
Chris Bull

YES

✓ Angry protests, legal challenges, and widespread condemnation greeted President Clinton's unveiling of a military policy that keeps much of the Pentagon's ban on gay and lesbian service personnel in place and falls far short of filling his campaign pledge to lift the ban.

Announcing the policy July 19 at Fort McNair, Va., Clinton acknowledged that the plan "certainly will not please everyone, perhaps not anyone," and among gay rights activists, his assessment was correct. The policy sparked protests in cities throughout the country, and gay legal groups vowed to quickly prepare lawsuits to challenge it in court.

Clinton accused of backing down

Heads of gay political groups that had led the effort to overturn the ban through political means accused Clinton of abandoning his principles and betraying gays and lesbians who had worked for his election. "The president could have lifted up the conscience of the country," said Tom Stoddard, coordinator of the Campaign for Military Service (CMS). "Instead, he acceded without a fight to the stereotypes of prejudices he himself had disparaged." Torie Osborn, executive director of the National Gay and Lesbian Task Force (NGLTF), said the plan is "simply a repackaging of discrimination," while Tim McFeeley, head of the Human Rights Campaign Fund, called it a "shattering disappointment."

Acknowledging that the plan's specifics are "not identical with some of my own goals," Clinton nonetheless called it an "honest compromise" on an issue that had "diverted our attention from other matters for too long." The policy, which is scheduled to take effect Oct. 1, bars military recruiters from asking if prospective enlistees are gay or lesbian, but it forbids same-sex intercourse and myriad other actions detailed in a four-page policy statement, making them

In both 1992 and 1996 Clinton received overwhelming support from gay and lesbian voters.

NGLTF emerged in the early 1970s as a high-profile lobby group for gay and lesbian rights.

grounds for discharge. It was prepared by Secretary of Defense Les Aspin and Joint Chiefs of Staff chairman Colin Powell after the Administration had endured months of sniping from Senate armed services committee chairman Sam Nunn over the issue.

Political analysts said that in the face of intense congressional and military opposition to lifting the ban, the policy was the closest Clinton could come to fulfilling his campaign promise, and they warned that Clinton is likely to be wary of gay rights issues in the future. "Clinton has become a devil figure on both sides of this debate," said Larry Sabato, a professor of political science at the University of Virginia. "He has spilled so much blood on this issue that you can be sure that he will stay away from gay and lesbian political issues, especially those involving the military, for a while. That doesn't leave the gay groups with many options. They can either continue to work within the Democratic party or they can go fishing."

Can you think of other examples when a politician has managed to offend both parties in a debate?

But demonstrators protesting the policy in the streets showed little interest in either working within the Democratic Party or fishing. In Los Angeles more than 1,000 people attended a protest that meandered past hotels where Clinton's wife, Hillary, was rumored to be staying. There were no arrests. In San Francisco 800 people turned out for a protest at the federal building; 41 protesters were arrested for attempting to enter the building, which was closed. In Washington, D.C., 100 protesters demonstrated in front of the White House; ten of them were arrested.

McFeeley said gay rights groups hoped a confrontational stance would make Clinton understand that he would pay a political price for his decision. "You have to play hardball with the guy," he said. "You have to make it clear to him what your bottom line is, and when it isn't delivered, you have to call him on it. The people who were toughest on this issue got their way. The Joint Chiefs of Staff and Sam Nunn hung tough and got what they wanted."

Representatives Studds and Frank, both from Massachusetts, have actively campaigned for gay and lesbian rights since the 1980s. Studds did not seek reelection in 1997.

Measured opposition

U.S. representatives Gerry Studds and Barney Frank, the only two openly gay members of Congress, both said they opposed the policy but struck a more conciliatory tone. "I understand and share the intense disappointment that it was not possible for the president to fulfill his campaign pledge," Studds said. "But we have to focus on the big picture, which is that many of the issues gays and lesbians care about rise and fall on the ability of Bill Clinton to be a successful president." Added Frank: "If the legacy of this difficult, disappointing struggle is that denouncing Bill Clinton becomes the major activity for many gay and lesbian leaders, our chances of keeping and expanding our political alliances will not be helped."

Studds said gay political groups had failed to provide Clinton with enough "political cover" to allow him to lift the ban completely. "At this point we don't have the political strength, the numbers, to win a campaign like this," he said. "We have to win on moral principles, and moral principles alone will not win you a lot of political battles."

But Osborn said much of the blame is Clinton's. "We must recognize that the president sparked a very important debate that helped move the country out of the monumental state of denial that surrounded gays and lesbians in the military," she said. "But it says something about his character that he sparked the debate and then ran."

Clinton was frequently criticized for not having the political courage to back his liberal principles.

Clinton's announcement of the plan sent Osborn and the heads of other gay groups back to the drawing board to devise new strategies for dealing with the military issue. Stoddard said CMS planned to cease operations Aug. 13 and spend its final days lobbying members of Congress to reject Nunn's attempt to codify Clinton's plan, which was in the form of an executive order, into law. "Codification would make the policy even harder to overturn in the long run," Stoddard said.

Nunn convened committee hearings on Clinton's plan the day after it was announced, bristling especially at White House aide George Stephanopoulos's assertion that the policy would create a "zone of privacy" for gay and lesbian service personnel. Aspin told the committee that the new plan would be "more enforceable" than the current one and assured Nunn that under it, gays and lesbians would still "be much more comfortable pursuing a profession other than the military."

Does it matter if gays do not feel "comfortable" in the military? If the military admits them, does it also have to make them feel welcome?

Nunn complained that the specifics of prohibited behavior must be "pinned down. We can't have a commander out there saying 'What do I do?' and somebody says, 'Call the attorney general,'" he said. Within days Nunn's committee had voted to codify the plan along with a provision that would make it easier for commanders to initiate investigations of those suspected of engaging in forbidden conduct.

The American Civil Liberties Union (ACLU) and the gay legal group Lambda Legal Defense and Education Fund (LLDEF) each said they would continue their pending legal challenges to the ban and file lawsuits challenging the new policy as soon as it takes effect. CMS legal adviser Chai Feldblum said the announcement of the new policy makes winning the court challenges already in place "more difficult but not impossible."

A constitutional question?

Meanwhile, William Rubenstein, director of the ACLU's lesbian and gay rights project, said the new policy is vulnerable on both equal-protection and free-speech grounds. "People are going to be penalized for being open about who they are," he said. "The new policy actually puts the prohibition on speech in writing." Added LLDEF executive director Kevin Cathcart: "This policy asks gays and lesbians to take a perpetual vow of silence and chastity if they want to serve in the military."

In 2001 the Army dropped its dismissal case against Arizona state Rep. Steve May, a reserve lieutenant who was openly and defiantly gay.

The *Baltimore Sun* reported that announcement of the new policy had been delayed by at least a day because attorney general Janet Reno had argued strongly during a cabinet meeting that it would be hard to defend in court. Reportedly, the policy was changed slightly to assuage some of her concerns, but Rubenstein said the revisions did not go far enough.

"It's disappointing that Reno wasn't really listened to," he said. "She was trying to tell the Administration that the policy is unconstitutional. It's going to be sickening to see the justice department trying to defend this in court."

But New York Law School professor Arthur S. Leonard warned that judges traditionally defer to the military in cases involving personnel policies. "The courts have almost always bowed to the expertise of professional military leaders," he said. "I don't see any real sign of that changing."

Do you agree with Leonard that the political arena is better than the military one for continuing the battle for gay and lesbian rights?

Despite the setback that the new policy represents, he said, the best chance for eventually lifting the ban completely probably remains in the political arena. "The main road should continue to be politics," he said. "The gay and lesbian community has to show some more political strength in other areas, like overturning state sodomy laws and fighting off antigay initiatives, before we can make a strong case in Congress for lifting the ban."

GAYS AND LESBIANS IN THE ARMED FORCES
Senator Sam Nunn

NO

X Mr. President, the media is filled with accounts as to what may or may not be happening in the White House and Pentagon and the executive branch with respect to the issue of the restrictions on the service of gay men and lesbians in the Armed Forces.

As my colleagues will recall, the President issued an interim policy on January 29, 1993, which basically retained the longstanding restrictions on the service of gays and lesbians while eliminating questions on sexual orientation from the enlistment application. Part of that interim policy was a very important provision, which the President put in his interim order and which I felt strongly needed to be in that order, which said that even though the questions were not being asked, every new recruit would have explained to him or her the expectations of the Uniform Code of Military Justice relating not only to homosexual conduct but also to the other standards relating to sexual conduct, including the problems of sexual harassment.

> *In effect, the military will accept gays and lesbians as long as they keep quiet about their orientation.*

So every new recruit, under the interim policy, is being acquainted with the expectations of conduct in general and also in terms of sexual conduct.

> *Do you think it is fair to make a point of telling new recruits that homosexual behavior is grounds for dismissal?*

Mr. President, the President directed the Secretary of Defense to prepare a draft policy on this issue by July 15, 1993. It is my understanding that in recent days the Secretary of Defense, after detailed review and consultation with the civilian and military leadership of the Department of Defense, has presented a proposal to the President and that that proposal is now under review at the White House.

On February 4, 1993, the Senate agreed to an amendment which directed the Armed Services Committee to conduct hearings on this issue. In addition, the Senate agreed to an order which precluded amendments on this issue until July 15, 1993.

I believe that moratorium on legislation through July 15, 1993, was very helpful in providing the opportunity for our Armed Services Committee to have a fair, objective, and thorough set of hearings without the disruption of constant amendments on the floor that would have had really no legislative history in terms of committee deliberation.

Mr. President, it is my hope that any order issued by President Clinton on this subject will have a delayed effective date of sufficient length to permit congressional review and action if the Congress decides that legislative action is necessary.

Therefore, I urge my colleagues on both sides of the aisle to withhold any amendments on this issue until the Armed Services Committee has completed our action on what I think is a very important issue in the military services. …

The necessity for clear guidelines

Regardless of what action is taken by the Clinton administration in the executive branch, however, we will have to consider and act on this issue because our bill is expected to be considered by the Senate prior to the August recess. So next week is the time we are going to have to act legislatively, notwithstanding any delay that may take place in the executive branch. We have to get this in our bill if we are going to have the kind of findings that I believe are necessary as we move from the legislative area to the executive branch in terms of implementation, and we need to give policy guidelines. And I am certain there will be legal challenges. So what we do in committee will also be important to the judicial branch of Government when this matter is brought before them in the proper forum.

Mr. President, I believe it is essential that the Congress codify the policies regarding homosexuality in the Armed Forces by adopting legislative findings and by providing clear legislative direction to the executive branch and to the leadership and the men and women in the Armed Forces.

Based upon the hearings held in our committee, it is my view that any policy issued by the executive branch as well as any legislation enacted by the Congress must at a minimum be consistent with the following principles. These are broad principles, and they are not meant to be exclusive because the issue is much too complex to be summarized. …

The first principle I would articulate today is that military service is a unique calling which has no counterpart in civilian society. The primary purpose of our Armed Forces is to prepare for and to prevail in combat should the need arise. The conduct of military operations requires members of the Armed Forces to make extraordinary sacrifices including, if need be, the ultimate sacrifice to provide for the defense of our Nation.

Senator Nunn was correct in anticipating legal challenges to the policy. For a comprehensive report on how "Don't ask, Don't tell" has fared in the courts visit http://dont.stanford.edu/

No. 2, the foundation of combat capability is unit cohesion. Unlike our civilian society, in the military the mission is the No. 1 priority. The unit is the second priority, and the individual is the third priority.

Mr. President, in society the individual comes first. In the military, the mission comes first. If in a quest for full societal constitutional rights in the military, which have never existed in the military, if in that quest we end up placing consideration of the individual before consideration of the mission, we are going to have an awful lot of people killed in combat, and we are going to have an awful lot of people wounded in combat. And we are going to have questionable military performance by many of our units if we replace the standing principles for years and years that have been part of our military history—that the mission comes first, not the individual.

That is what so many people do not understand about the military. But it is a cardinal principle, and it is a distinction between the military and our civilian society.

Mr. President, the third principle is that military personnel policies must facilitate the assignment and the worldwide deployment of service members who frequently must live and must work under close conditions affording minimal privacy. There is an awful lot that can be said on this subject. But another fundamental distinction between the military and civilian society is that people in civilian society, by and large, go home at night and they have the privacy of their homes. In many tens of thousands of military assignments, the home is the ship or the home is the tent or the home is the barracks. That is a fundamental distinction.

The fourth principle is that because of the factors that I have already enumerated, the presence in military units of persons who, by their acts or by their statements demonstrate a propensity to engage in homosexual acts, would cause an unacceptable risk to the high standards of morale, good order, and discipline, and unit cohesion that are absolutely essential to effective combat capability. There should be no change in the current grounds for discharge— homosexual acts, statements, or marriages.

The fifth principle is that while DOD [Department of Defense] policies on investigations may be subject to commonsense limitations because of the need to allocate scarce resources and to establish investigative priorities, these policies should not preclude investigations based upon any information relevant to an administrative or disciplinary proceeding.

Do you agree that individual rights count for less in military life than they do in civilian life? If so, why?

What difference would a person's sexuality make in conditions with a lack of privacy?

Has Nunn provided enough evidence to support his conclusion? Or does it reflect his own opinions and values?

Mr. President, despite recent media stories attributing certain statements to the Justice Department—and I have no idea whether they are accurate or not, whether someone in the Justice Department really made these statements or whether this is invented out of whole cloth; but despite these media stories and despite the statements that have been attributed to certain Justice Department people who are unnamed, about the constitutionality of various proposals in this arena, I am convinced that the principles I have enunciated are constitutionally sound and will be upheld by the Supreme Court of the United States.

Do you think the Framers intended the Supreme Court to become involved in such personal matters as an individual's sexuality?

No one can say what some Federal court may do in one case or the other. What we have to be guided by in terms of our deliberations is what we believe the Supreme Court will uphold on appeal.

Putting faith in the Supreme Court

The U.S. Supreme Court has repeatedly held that the application of constitutional rights to members of the Armed Forces is necessarily different from the rights of persons in civilian society.

Mr. President, there are many lawyers who speak on this subject and are quoted in the newspapers that I do not believe have read a number of these Supreme Court cases. It is the fundamental principle of the Supreme Court decisions on the military that there is a distinction, a significant distinction, between the individual rights in society and the individual rights when they wear a military uniform. The Federal courts on many different levels have ruled on numerous occasions that restrictions on the service of gay men and lesbians, including restrictions on acts and statements, do not violate the constitutional rights of military personnel.

Should people who join the military have to surrender some rights? What kind of rights might they need to sacrifice?

Mr. President, I have come to these conclusions based upon the committee's extensive review of this matter over the last 6 months. During the Armed Services Committee markup next week of the National Defense Authorization Act for fiscal year 1994, I will be proposing, along with others, legislation that embodies these general principles....

Summary

Much debate has centered on the legal implications of President Clinton's "Don't ask, Don't tell" law. In the first article Chris Bull presents the views of those who argue that "Don't ask, Don't tell" is unfair and unconstitutional. A law that forces homosexuals to conceal their sexual orientation if they want to serve in the military, such critics say, negates their constitutional right to free speech. Bull accepts that the courts will probably come down in favor of the military, yet he concludes with a quote suggesting that opponents of the ban on gay service personnel should concentrate their energies to fight antigay state laws before tackling the bigger military issue.

In the second article Senator Sam Nunn argues in a Senate speech that allowing gay and lesbian recruits to be open about their sexuality would undermine morale, especially in light of the intimacy of military life in combat conditions. Nunn expresses confidence in the judiciary and claims that the courts have repeatedly affirmed that there are differences between the constitutional rights of civilians and military personnel.

FURTHER INFORMATION:

Books:

Cammermeyer, M., *Serving in Silence*. New York: Viking, 1994.

Halley, Janet E., *Don't: A Reader's Guide to the Military Anti-Gay Policy*. Durham, NC: Duke University Press, 1999.

Humphrey, M. A., *My Country, My Right to Serve: Experiences of Gay Men and Women in the Military, World War II to the Present*. New York: HarperCollins, 1990.

Articles:

Benecke, M., and K. Dodge, "Military Women in Nontraditional Job Fields: Casualties of the Armed Forces' War on Homosexuals." *Harvard Women's Law Journal* (13), 1990.

Blacker, Coit, and Lawrence J. Korb, "Military Tolerance Works." *The New York Times*, January 3, 2000.

Davis, J. S., "Military Policy toward Homosexuals: Scientific, Historical and Legal Perspectives." *Military Law Review* (55), 1991.

Lara, A., "The Trial of Sergeant-Major McKinney: An After Action Report," *Journal of Gender and the Law*, 3 Geo. (1), 2001. The same issue contains six other papers on gender and sexual orientation in the military.

Useful websites:

www.aclu.org
The American Civil Liberties Union. Gay and lesbian rights are one of many civil rights issues of concern.

www.glbva.org
American Veterans for Equal Rights (specifically devoted to gay and lesbian and transgender issues).

www.gaymilitary.ucsb.edu/index.htm
The Center for the Study of Sexual Minorities in the Military. Large site with many interesting links.
National Gay and Lesbian Taskforce. An activist political pressure group promoting gay and lesbian rights.

www.california.com/~rathbone/gw400004.htmwww.ngltf.org
"And the Flag Was Still There: Straight People, Gay People, and Sexuality in the U.S. Military" by Lois Shawver.

The following debates in the Pro/Con series may also be of interest:

In this volume:
Topic 2 Is the Supreme Court too powerful?

SHOULD HOMOSEXUALS BE ALLOWED TO SERVE IN THE MILITARY?

YES: Banning gays from the military violates their rights to free speech and equal protection

YES: The military has no equivalent in civilian society. Making the right decision can mean the difference between life and death.

CONSTITUTION
Is banning gays from the military unconstitutional?

MILITARY MATTERS
Do only military leaders have the expertise to make military personnel decisions?

NO: Military personnel do not enjoy the same constitutional rights as civilians, since they have a unique role in maintaining national security

YES: While individual homosexuals may be good soldiers, their sexual orientation diminishes morale and reduces the effectiveness of the troops as a whole

NO: The military is a conservative institution that embraces outdated attitudes toward homosexuality

YES: Statistics show that there has been a huge increase in discharges for homosexuality since the introduction of Clinton's policy

SHOULD HOMOSEXUALS BE ALLOWED TO SERVE IN THE MILITARY?
KEY POINTS

UNIT COHESION
Would homosexuality harm effective military combat?

WITCH HUNTS
Does Clinton's compromise encourage the military to oust suspected homosexuals?

NO: Being gay does not keep someone from being a good soldier

NO: The compromise policy states that investigations concerning a person's sexual orientation can only be made if there are reasonable grounds to do so. The discharge statistics simply reflect the increasing number of serving homosexuals declaring their sexual orientation.

GAYS AND LESBIANS IN THE MILITARY

"I have learned that 'if I am uncomfortable, it is where I need to be.' It is only by challenging others with our humanity that we will become human in their eyes. I will continue to speak out."
—COLONEL MARGARETHE CAMMERMEYER, JULY 2002

1916 The Articles of War address the issue of homosexual conduct for the first time. Assault with the intent to commit sodomy is listed as a capital crime.

1919 In a revision to the Articles of War consensual sodomy is considered to be a felony and punishable by imprisonment.

1920–1930s Homosexuality is treated as a criminal act; thousands of gay soldiers and sailors are imprisoned. The military's move to transform homosexuality from a crime to an illness does not take place until World War II.

1941–1945 Nearly 10,000 members of the armed forces receive dishonorable or "blue discharges" for homosexuality, so called because they are typed on blue paper.

1942 The armed forces release the first regulations instructing military psychiatrists to state that those engaged in "homosexual or other perverse sexual practices" are unsuitable for military service.

1943 Final regulations are issued banning homosexuals from all branches of military service. They have remained in effect with only slight modifications.

1950 Congress establishes the Uniform Code of Military Justice, which sets down the basic policies, discharge procedures, and appeal channels for homosexual service members.

1953 President Eisenhower signs Executive Order 10450, which makes "sexual perversion" sufficient grounds for dismissal from federal employment.

1957 The Navy's Crittenden Report concludes that there is "no sound basis" for the charge that homosexuals in the military pose a security risk. The Pentagon denies the existence of this report for nearly 20 years. Federal courts rule that lesbians and gay men discharged from the military for homosexuality may appeal to civil courts.

1975 Sergeant Leonard Matlovich sues the Air Force after being dismissed for homosexuality. *Time* magazine features him on the cover with the headline "I Am a Homosexual: The Gay Drive for Acceptance."

1980 A federal judge orders the Air Force to reinstate Matlovich. He accepts a settlement of $160,000 instead.

1981 Deputy Secretary of Defense Graham Claytor issues a revision to the department's policy to state that "homosexuality is incompatible with military service." The directive eliminates loopholes that allowed some to stay in the military.

1989 Two studies by the Department of Defense find no reason to ban lesbians and gays from the military. Openly bisexual veteran Cliff Arnesen testifies before Congress.

1992 The General Accounting Office reports that almost 17,000 service men and women were discharged for homosexuality between 1981 and 1990, at a cost of $493,195,968 to replace them. During the presidential campaign Bill Clinton vows to lift the ban on sexual minorities serving in the military. **June**: Colonel Margarethe Cammermeyer, a high-ranking 27-year-veteran, is discharged from the military after she discloses her sexual orientation during an interview for top security clearance.

1993 President Clinton issues an interim policy that preserves all existing restrictions on homosexuals in the military but ends the practice of questioning recruits about their sexual orientation. The final policy, termed "Don't Ask, Don't Tell; Don't Pursue," was intended to ease restrictions against homosexual members of the armed forces without removing the ban outright.

1994 March: Lamda Legal Defense and Education Fund and the American Civil Liberties Union bring a lawsuit (*Able v. USA*) to federal court on behalf of six lesbian and gay service members, the first direct constitutional challenge to the military's policy. Judge Eugene Nickerson grants the plaintiffs' preliminary injunction preventing the military from initiating discharge proceedings while the case is active. **April**: District Court Judge Thomas S. Zilly orders the army to reinstate Colonel Cammermeyer to the National Guard. Zilly finds the old version of the military ban barring service by lesbians and gay men unconstitutional.

1995 In *Able v. USA* Judge Eugene Nickerson strikes down the antigay ban as unconstitutional for violating the First and Fifth Amendments, and rules that the law is based solely on discrimination, calling it "Orwellian" and "inherently deceptive." President Clinton signs an executive order forbidding the denial of security clearances on the basis of sexual orientation.

1997 January: Former Senator William Cohen replaces William Perry as defense secretary. **February**: Cohen states his opposition to the "active pursuit and prosecution" of gays and lesbians. **March**: The Pentagon issues a memo assuring personnel that they can report harassment and abuse without fear of being targeted for investigation of being homosexual.

1998 April: CNN reports that the Pentagon discharged a record 997 service members for homosexuality in 1997. **October**: The *Air Force Times* reports growing tolerance for gays and lesbians in the military.

1999 Democrat Al Gore and Republican George W. Bush support the Pentagon policy under which gays and lesbians are allowed to serve in the military if they do not openly discuss their sexual orientation.

2001 April: Stephen Herbits, an openly gay man, is appointed as a consultant to Defense Secretary Donald Rumsfeld. **May**: A panel of legal and military experts assembled by the National Institute of Military Justice calls on Congress to repeal a clause in the Uniform Code of Military Justice that outlaws acts of sodomy between consenting adults.

2002 March: The Service Members Legal Defense Network (SMLDN) report on the Pentagon's "Don't Ask, Don't Tell" policy uncovers disturbing trends in how service members suspected of being gay, lesbian, or bisexual continue to be discriminated against in the military.

Topic 9
DOES THE CONSTITUTION PROTECT RELIGIOUS FREEDOM?

YES

FROM *CHURCH OF THE LUKUMI BABALU AYE V. CITY OF HIALEAH*
508 U.S. 520 (1993)
JUSTICE ANTHONY M. KENNEDY

NO

FROM *MINERSVILLE SCHOOL DISTRICT V. BOARD OF EDUCATION*
310 U.S. 586 (1940)
JUSTICE FELIX FRANKFURTER

INTRODUCTION

When the Framers of the United States enshrined the civil rights of all American citizens in the 1791 Bill of Rights (the first 10 amendments to the Constitution), the first principles they set out concerned religious freedom. They believed it was vital to protect this freedom because many of the early settlers were escaping religious persecution in Europe. A democratic government, the Framers felt, should respect its citizens' beliefs, and the best way to ensure this was to exclude it from religious matters.

The First Amendment has two parts commonly called the Establishment clause and the Free Exercise clause. The Establishment clause effectively prevents Congress from "establishing" any religion, whether by endorsement, financial support, or by passing laws that favor one religion over another. Thus Congress cannot promote an official religion in the same way that the United Kingdom recognizes

Christianity as the official Church of England, for example. The Free Exercise clause prevents Congress from passing any laws that penalize or interfere with religious activities and specifies that citizens be allowed the freedom to follow any religion or none at all.

Since 1791 the Supreme Court has upheld people's religious rights in many circumstances. In *McCollum v. Board of Education* (1948), for instance, it ruled that religious teaching in public schools (which are state funded) violated the Establishment clause. Similarly, in the case of *Santa Fe Independent School District v. Doe* (2000) it found that student prayers at public school football games violated the same clause. And in *Torcaso v. Watkins* (1961) the court held that by requiring applicants for public office to swear that they believed in God, the state of Maryland was violating the Establishment clause.

The Supreme Court has also vacated laws that violate the Free Exercise clause. In the case of *United States v. Ballard, 322 U.S. 78* (1944) it ruled that religious teachings could not be prosecuted for fraud even if they seemed preposterous to others. And in *Martin v. Struthers* (1943) it ruled that the town of Struthers in Ohio could not legitimately outlaw the door-to-door selling of religious literature.

"Congress shall make no law respecting an establishment of religion, or prohibiting the free exercise thereof...."

—FIRST AMENDMENT TO THE CONSTITUTION

But have the courts ever interfered with people's pursuit of their religious beliefs? The Supreme Court has usually interpreted the Free Exercise clause as prohibiting laws leveled against any specific religion or religion in general. However, it has sometimes limited certain religious actions and rituals for compelling government reasons, or the so-called common-good argument, which it has invoked when religious practices break general laws. In the case of *Reynolds v. United States* (1878), for example, it upheld the federal law prohibiting polygamy after a Mormon defendant claimed it was his religious duty to take more than one wife. Similarly, when two members of the Native American Church defended their right to take the hallucinogenic drug peyote, used in traditional religious rituals (*Employment Division v. Smith*,

1990), the Supreme Court ruled that the Free Exercise clause did not allow them to violate laws prohibiting drug use. Opponents of this approach contend that the common-good argument has far-reaching implications. They argue that it allows the state to involve itself in religion at will, since "compelling reasons" are vague enough to enable action without any real justification.

The following two articles both summarize court cases challenging legal aspects of the right to religious freedom. In the first case, *Church of the Lukumi Babalu Aye v. City of Hialeah* (1993), Justice Anthony M. Kennedy rules unconstitutional ordinances (municipal laws) passed by the city of Hialeah, Florida, to prevent members of the Santeria religion from sacrificing animals in their ceremonies. Santeria, or "way of the saints," is a mix of Roman Catholicism and the traditional worship and beliefs of the Yoruba and Bantu peoples, who were brought from Africa to the Caribbean as slaves. While the judge recognized that religious actions should not violate general laws, he concluded that laws aimed at a specific religious practice were unconstitutional.

In the second case, *Minersville School District v. Board of Education* (1940), Justice Felix Frankfurter describes the case of Lillian and William Gobitis, two students who were expelled from school for refusing to salute the national flag on religious grounds. The Supreme Court decided that a public school may require students to show respect for the flag even if it violates their religious scruples, Justice Frankfurter basing his decision on the question of national cohesion. He pointed out that religious convictions do not excuse citizens from carrying out responsibilities regarded as being for the general good of the nation.

CHURCH OF THE LUKUMI BABALU AYE V. CITY OF HIALEAH
Justice Anthony M. Kennedy

YES

☑ … According to Santeria teaching, the orishas [spirits, or guardian angels] are powerful but not immortal. They depend for survival on the sacrifice. Sacrifices are performed at birth, marriage, and death rites, for the cure of the sick, for the initiation of new members and priests, and during an annual celebration. Animals sacrificed in Santeria rituals include chickens, pigeons, doves, ducks, guinea pigs, goats, sheep, and turtles. The animals are killed by the cutting of the carotid arteries in the neck. The sacrificed animal is cooked and eaten, except after healing and death rituals.

Santeria adherents faced widespread persecution in Cuba, so the religion and its rituals were practiced in secret. The open practice of Santeria and its rites remains infrequent. The religion was brought to this Nation most often by exiles from the Cuban revolution. The District Court estimated that there are at least 50,000 practitioners in South Florida today.

The Cuban revolution of 1959 resulted in the overthrow of the dictatorship of Fulgencio Batista (1901–1973) and brought to power Fidel Castro (1927–).

A distressing prospect

Petitioner Church of the Lukumi Babalu Aye, Inc. (Church), is a not for profit corporation organized under Florida law in 1973. The Church and its congregants practice the Santeria religion…. In April 1987, the Church leased land in the city of Hialeah, Florida, and announced plans to establish a house of worship as well as a school, cultural center, and museum. Pichardo indicated that the Church's goal was to bring the practice of the Santeria faith, including its ritual of animal sacrifice, into the open…. The prospect of a Santeria church in their midst was distressing to many members of the Hialeah community, and the announcement of the plans to open a Santeria church in Hialeah prompted the city council to hold an emergency public session on June 9, 1987….

Ernesto Pichardo was the president and priest of the Church of the Lukumi Babalu Aye and a petitioner in the case.

The Free Exercise Clause of the First Amendment, which has been applied to the States through the Fourteenth Amendment, provides that "Congress shall make no law respecting an establishment of religion, or prohibiting the free exercise thereof…." The city does not argue that Santeria is not a "religion" within the meaning of the First

Amendment. Nor could it. Although the practice of animal sacrifice may seem abhorrent to some, "religious beliefs need not be acceptable, logical, consistent, or comprehensible to others in order to merit First Amendment protection." Given the historical association between animal sacrifice and religious worship, petitioners' assertion that animal sacrifice is an integral part of their religion "cannot be deemed bizarre or incredible." Neither the city nor the courts below, moreover, have questioned the sincerity of petitioners' professed desire to conduct animal sacrifices for religious reasons. We must consider petitioners' First Amendment claim....

> Whether it is done sincerely or not, is animal sacrifice in religion acceptable?

Santeria sacrifice targeted

The record in this case compels the conclusion that suppression of the central element of the Santeria worship service was the object of the ordinances. First, though use of the words "sacrifice" and "ritual" does not compel a finding of improper targeting of the Santeria religion, the choice of these words is support for our conclusion. There are further respects in which the text of the city council's enactments discloses the improper attempt to target Santeria. Resolution 87–66, adopted June 9, 1987, recited that "residents and citizens of the City of Hialeah have expressed their concern that certain religions may propose to engage in practices which are inconsistent with public morals, peace or safety," and "reiterate[d]" the city's commitment to prohibit "any and all [such] acts of any and all religious groups." No one suggests, and on this record it cannot be maintained, that city officials had in mind a religion other than Santeria.

A "religious gerrymander"

It becomes evident that these ordinances target Santeria sacrifice when the ordinances' operation is considered. Apart from the text, the effect of a law in its real operation is strong evidence of its object. To be sure, adverse impact will not always lead to a finding of impermissible targeting. For example, a social harm may have been a legitimate concern of government for reasons quite apart from discrimination. The subject at hand does implicate, of course, multiple concerns unrelated to religious animosity, for example, the suffering or mistreatment visited upon the sacrificed animals, and health hazards from improper disposal. But the ordinances when considered together disclose an object remote from these legitimate concerns. The design of these laws accomplishes instead a "religious gerrymander," an impermissible attempt to target petitioners and their religious practices.

> Although used figuratively here, according to Webster's New Collegiate Dictionary to "gerrymander" is "to divide (a territorial unit) into election districts to give one political party an electoral majority in a large number of districts while concentrating the voting strength of the opposition in as few districts as possible." The term was coined after a use of this practice in Massachusetts during the governorship of Elbridge Gerry (1744–1814). The shape of the reformed electoral districts resembled a salamander— hence "gerry" plus "mander."

It is a necessary conclusion that almost the only conduct subject to Ordinances 87–40, 87–52, and 87–71 is the religious exercise of Santeria church members. The texts show that they were drafted in tandem to achieve this result. We begin with Ordinance 87–71. It prohibits the sacrifice of animals but defines sacrifice as "to unnecessarily kill ... an animal in a public or private ritual or ceremony not for the primary purpose of food consumption." The definition excludes almost all killings of animals except for religious sacrifice, and the primary purpose requirement narrows the proscribed category even further, in particular by exempting Kosher slaughter.... We need not discuss whether this differential treatment of two religions is itself an independent constitutional violation. It suffices to recite this feature of the law as support for our conclusion that Santeria alone was the exclusive legislative concern....

> *"Kosher" means satisfying Jewish law and applies in particular to food. For more information on kosher practice go to www.ou.org/kosher/primer.html.*

Operating in similar fashion is Ordinance 87–52, which prohibits the "possess[ion], sacrifice, or slaughter" of an animal with the "inten[t] to use such animal for food purposes." This prohibition, extending to the keeping of an animal as well as the killing itself, applies if the animal is killed in "any type of ritual" and there is an intent to use the animal for food.... The ordinance exempts, however, "any licensed [food] establishment" with regard to "any animals which are specifically raised for food purposes," if the activity is permitted by zoning and other laws. This exception, too, seems intended to cover Kosher slaughter. Again, the burden of the ordinance, in practical terms, falls on Santeria adherents, but almost no others....

Unnecessary killings?

Ordinance 87–40 incorporates the Florida animal cruelty statute. Its prohibition is broad on its face, punishing "[w]hoever ... unnecessarily ... kills any animal." The city claims that this ordinance is the epitome of a neutral prohibition.... The problem, however, is the interpretation given to the ordinance by respondent and the Florida attorney general. Killings for religious reasons are deemed unnecessary, whereas most other killings fall outside the prohibition. The city, on what seems to be a per se basis, deems hunting, slaughter of animals for food, eradication of insects and pests, and euthanasia as necessary. There is no indication in the record that respondent has concluded that hunting or fishing for sport is unnecessary. Indeed, one of the few reported Florida cases decided under § 828.12 concludes that the use of live rabbits to train greyhounds is not unnecessary....

> *On what grounds might hunting be necessary? What difference does it make what purpose an animal is killed for?*

Ordinance 87-72—unlike the three other ordinances—does appear to apply to substantial nonreligious conduct and not to be overbroad. For our purposes here, however, the four substantive ordinances may be treated as a group for neutrality purposes. Ordinance 87-72 was passed the same day as Ordinance 87-71 and was enacted, as were the three others, in direct response to the opening of the Church. It would be implausible to suggest that the three other ordinances, but not Ordinance 87-72, had as their object the suppression of religion. We need not decide whether the Ordinance 87-72 could survive constitutional scrutiny if it existed separately; it must be invalidated because it functions, with the rest of the enactments in question, to suppress Santeria religious worship....

Hostility toward the Santeria religion

That the ordinances were enacted "'because of,' not merely 'in spite of,'" their suppression of Santeria religious practice ... is revealed by the events preceding enactment of the ordinances. Although respondent claimed at oral argument that it had experienced significant problems resulting from the sacrifice of animals within the city before the announced opening of the Church ... the city council made no attempt to address the supposed problem before its meeting in June 1987, just weeks after the Church announced plans to open. The minutes and taped excerpts of the June 9 session, both of which are in the record, evidence significant hostility exhibited by residents, members of the city council, and other city officials toward the Santeria religion and its practice of animal sacrifice. The public crowd that attended the June 9 meetings interrupted statements by council members critical of Santeria with cheers and the brief comments of Pichardo with taunts. When Councilman Martinez, a supporter of the ordinances, stated that in prerevolution Cuba "people were put in jail for practicing this religion," the audience applauded....

In sum, the neutrality inquiry leads to one conclusion: The ordinances had as their object the suppression of religion....

We conclude, in sum, that each of Hialeah's ordinances pursues the city's governmental interests only against conduct motivated by religious belief. The ordinances "ha[ve] every appearance of a prohibition that society is prepared to impose upon [Santeria worshippers] but not upon itself." This precise evil is what the requirement of general applicability is designed to prevent....

"Oral argument" is a stage in a court case. In the Supreme Court attorneys for the petitioner and the respondent each have 30 minutes in which to present their point of view to the justices and answer questions from them. For more on the Supreme Court go to www.supremecourtus.gov/about/about.html.

Do you think that resistance to animal sacrifice may have had anything to do with prejudice toward a different community?

MINERSVILLE SCHOOL DISTRICT V. BOARD OF EDUCATION
Justice Felix Frankfurter

NO

The pledge detailed here is the original written in 1892. In 1924 it was altered to read "I pledge allegiance to the flag of the United States of America...." In 1954 the words "under God" were added after "one nation." The constitutionality of the pledge was challenged by a federal court in 2002. For more on the pledge go to www.cnn.com/2002/LAW/06/26/pledge.allegiance.

X … Lillian Gobitis, aged 12, and her brother William, aged 10, were expelled from the public schools of Minersville, Pennsylvania, for refusing to salute the national flag as part of a daily school exercise. The local Board of Education required both teachers and pupils to participate in this ceremony. The ceremony is a familiar one. The right hand is placed on the breast and the following pledge recited in unison: "I pledge allegiance to my flag, and to the Republic for which it stands; one nation indivisible, with liberty and justice for all." While the words are spoken, teachers and pupils extend their right hands in salute to the flag. The Gobitis family are affiliated with "Jehovah's Witnesses," for whom the Bible as the Word of God is the supreme authority. The children had been brought up conscientiously to believe that such a gesture of respect for the flag was forbidden by command of Scripture....

The Jehovah's Witness sect originated in the United States in 1872. It views flags as "graven images," or symbols of power forbidden in the Bible.

Religious freedom guaranteed

We must decide whether the requirement of participation in such a ceremony, exacted from a child who refuses upon sincere religious grounds, infringes without due process of law the liberty guaranteed by the Fourteenth Amendment.

Centuries of strife over the erection of particular dogmas as exclusive or all-comprehending faiths led to the inclusion of a guarantee for religious freedom in the Bill of Rights. The First Amendment, and the Fourteenth through its absorption of the First, sought to guard against repetition of those bitter religious struggles by prohibiting the establishment of a state religion and by securing to every sect the free exercise of its faith. So pervasive is the acceptance of this precious right that its scope is brought into question, as here, only when the conscience of individuals collides with the felt necessities of society.

Certainly the affirmative pursuit of one's convictions about the ultimate mystery of the universe and man's relation to it is placed beyond the reach of law. Government may not interfere with organized or individual expression of belief or disbelief. Propagation of belief—or even of disbelief—in the supernatural is protected, whether in church or chapel, mosque or synagogue, tabernacle or meetinghouse. Likewise, the Constitution assures generous immunity to the individual from imposition of penalties for offending, in the course of his own religious activities, the religious views of others, be they a minority or those who are dominant in government.

But the manifold character of man's relations may bring his conception of religious duty into conflict with the secular interests of his fellow men. When does the constitutional guarantee compel exemption from doing what society thinks necessary for the promotion of some great common end, or from a penalty for conduct which appears dangerous to the general good? To state the … problem is to recall the truth that no single principle can answer all of life's complexities. The right to freedom of religious belief, however dissident and however obnoxious to the cherished beliefs of others— even of a majority—is itself the denial of an absolute. But to affirm that the freedom to follow conscience has itself no limits in the life of a society would deny that very plurality of principles which, as a matter of history, underlies protection of religious toleration.…

Citizens have responsibilities

In the judicial enforcement of religious freedom, we are concerned with a historic concept. The religious liberty which the Constitution protects has never excluded legislation of general scope not directed against doctrinal loyalties of particular sects. Judicial nullification of legislation cannot be justified by attributing to the framers of the Bill of Rights views for which there is no historic warrant. Conscientious scruples have not, in the course of the long struggle for religious toleration, relieved the individual from obedience to a general law not aimed at the promotion or restriction of religious beliefs. The mere possession of religious convictions which contradict the relevant concerns of a political society does not relieve the citizen from the discharge of political responsibilities. The necessity for this adjustment has again and again been recognized. In a number of situations, the exertion of political authority has been sustained, while basic considerations of religious freedom have been left inviolate. In all these cases, the general laws in question, upheld in their application to those who refused obedience from religious conviction, were manifestations of specific powers of government deemed by the legislature essential to secure and maintain that orderly, tranquil, and free society without which religious toleration itself is

Compare this with the findings expressed by Justice Kennedy in Church of the Lukumi Babalu Aye v. City of Hialeah at the foot of page 119.

Should political concerns be more important than religious ones?

unattainable. Nor does the freedom of speech assured by Due Process move in a more absolute circle of immunity than that enjoyed by religious freedom. Even if it were assumed that freedom of speech goes beyond the historic concept of full opportunity to utter and to disseminate views, however heretical or offensive to dominant opinion, and includes freedom from conveying what may be deemed an implied but rejected affirmation, the question remains whether school children, like the Gobitis children, must be excused from conduct required of all the other children in the promotion of national cohesion. We are dealing with an interest inferior to none in the hierarchy of legal values. National unity is the basis of national security. To deny the legislature the right to select appropriate means for its attainment presents a totally different order of problem from that of the propriety of subordinating the possible ugliness of littered streets to the free expression of opinion through distribution of handbills....

"We live by symbols"

The ultimate foundation of a free society is the binding tie of cohesive sentiment. Such a sentiment is fostered by all those agencies of the mind and spirit which may serve to gather up the traditions of a people, transmit them from generation to generation, and thereby create that continuity of a treasured common life which constitutes a civilization. "We live by symbols." The flag is the symbol of our national unity, transcending all internal differences, however large, within the framework of the Constitution....

The wisdom of training children in patriotic impulses by those compulsions which necessarily pervade so much of the educational process is not for our independent judgment. Even were we convinced of the folly of such a measure, such belief would be no proof of its unconstitutionality. For ourselves, we might be tempted to say that the deepest patriotism is best engendered by giving unfettered scope to the most crochety beliefs.... But the courtroom is not the arena for debating issues of educational policy. It is not our province to choose among competing considerations in the subtle process of securing effective loyalty to the traditional ideals of democracy, while respecting at the same time individual idiosyncracies among a people so diversified in racial origins and religious allegiances. So to hold would, in effect, make us the school board for the country. That authority has not been given to this Court, nor should we assume it.

Minersville School District v. Board of Education was decided in 1940, ruling that students must take part in the daily flag salute. Three years later, however, this decision was reversed under West Virginia State Board of Education v. Barnette 319 U.S. 624 (1943), which ruled that the Jehovah's Witnesses did not have to salute the flag. For more on the latter case and the historical context go to http:// usinfo.state.gov/usa/i nfousa/facts/ democrac/46.htm, and also see http://atheism. about.com/library/ FAQs/blfaq_cs_jw_ flag1.htm and flag2.htm.

We are dealing here with the formative period in the development of citizenship. Great diversity of psychological and ethical opinion exists among us concerning the best way to train children for their place in society.... What the school authorities are really asserting is the right to awaken in the child's mind considerations as to the significance of the flag contrary to those implanted by the parent. In such an attempt, the state is normally at a disadvantage in competing with the parent's authority, so long—and this is the vital aspect of religious toleration—as parents are unmolested in their right to counteract by their own persuasiveness the wisdom and rightness of those loyalties which the state's educational system is seeking to promote. Except where the transgression of constitutional liberty is too plain for argument, personal freedom is best maintained—so long as the remedial channels of the democratic process remain open and unobstructed—when it is ingrained in a people's habits, and not enforced against popular policy by the coercion of adjudicated law. That the flag salute is an allowable portion of a school program for those who do not invoke conscientious scruples is surely not debatable. But for us to insist that, though the ceremony may be required, exceptional immunity must be given to dissidents, is to maintain that there is no basis for a legislative judgment that such an exemption might introduce elements of difficulty into the school discipline, might cast doubts in the minds of the other children which would themselves weaken the effect of the exercise.

Should parents who are Jehovah's Witnesses have the right to "implant" their own values in their children's minds? Is it really any concern of the government?

An ordered society

The preciousness of the family relation, the authority and independence which give dignity to parenthood, indeed the enjoyment of all freedom, presuppose the kind of ordered society which is summarized by our flag. A society which is dedicated to the preservation of these ultimate values of civilization may, in self-protection, utilize the educational process for inculcating those almost unconscious feelings which bind men together in a comprehending loyalty, whatever may be their lesser differences and difficulties.... Judicial review, itself a limitation on popular government, is a fundamental part of our constitutional scheme. But to the legislature no less than to courts is committed the guardianship of deeply cherished liberties. Where all the effective means of inducing political changes are left free from interference, education in the abandonment of foolish legislation is itself a training in liberty....

The right of judicial review gives the courts the power to consider the constitutionality of acts of Congress and the president. For further detail visit www.constitutioncenter.org/sections/basics/basic_1d.asp.

Summary

Although it may appear that the First Amendment to the Constitution provides cast-iron protection for religious freedom, there have been a number of court cases centered on this fundamental right. The Supreme Court opinions delivered by Justices Kennedy and Frankfurter are from two such cases. In *Church of the Lukumi Babalu Aye v. City of Hialeah* (1993) Justice Kennedy ruled that ordinances (municipal laws) enacted by the city of Hialeah, Florida, violated the Free Exercise clause of the First Amendment. The aim of the ordinances was to stop members of the Church of the Lukumi Babalu Aye from sacrificing animals, a central element of the church's religious practice. Since the ordinances "had as their object the suppression of religion," Justice Kennedy ruled that they were unconstitutional.

The second case, *Minersville School District v. Board of Education* (1940), involved two students who refused on religious grounds to salute the national flag. Justice Frankfurter ruled that students should be required to salute the flag even if the practice violated their religious beliefs, since "the mere possession of religious convictions which contradict the relevant concerns of a political society does not relieve the citizen from the discharge of political responsibilities." The judge based his ruling on the common good argument. Since the flag symbolized the unity of the United States, allowing some people to refuse to acknowledge the flag risked damaging that unity. It is perhaps interesting to note, as mentioned on page 122, that Justice Frankfurter's ruling was reversed three years later in *West Virginia State Board of Education v. Barnette* (1943).

FURTHER INFORMATION:

Books:

Canizares, Raul, *Cuban Santeria: Walking with the Night*. Rochester, VT: Destiny Books, 1999.
Noonan, John T. Jr., *The Lustre of Our Country: The American Experience of Religious Freedom*. Berkeley, CA: University of California Press, 2000.
Peters, Shawn Francis, *Judging Jehovah's Witnesses: Religious Persecution and the Dawn of the Rights Revolution*. Lawrence, KS: University Press of Kansas, 2002.

Useful websites:

www.aclu.org/students/slrelig.html
American Civil Liberties Union Freedom Network. Ask Sybil Liberty about your right to religious freedom.
www.firstthings.com
The journal of the Institute on Religion and Public Life.
http://religiousfreedom.lib.virginia.edu

The Religious Freedom page, a collection of articles and other resources examining the broad philosophical and theoretical issues concerning religious freedom.

The following debates in the Pro/Con series may also be of interest:

In *Individual and Society*:
Topic 9 Should there be a right to violate laws for religious reasons?

In *Science*:
Topic 11 Should religion affect parents' medical decisions?

DOES THE CONSTITUTION PROTECT RELIGIOUS FREEDOM?

YES: The judiciary has used it to stop the state from promoting one religious belief over another by ruling religious education in public schools unconstitutional, for example

YES: Laws targeting specific religious groups are held to be unconstitutional

FREE EXERCISE
Does the First Amendment protect Free Exercise of religion?

ESTABLISHMENT
Has the First Amendment prevented establishment of religion?

NO: General laws can be used to restrict religious practices

NO: By disallowing religious education in public schools, has not this part of the First Amendment infringed the Free Exercise clause?

DOES THE CONSTITUTION PROTECT RELIGIOUS FREEDOM?

KEY POINTS

YES: In a conflict of interests religious convictions come second to a citizen's political responsibilities

YES: Limits should be placed on religious activities if it is in the national interest

COMMON GOOD
Should there be limits on religious activities?

NO: The First Amendment provides for freedom in matters of religion

NO: "Compelling reasons" is too vague a term with which to sanction government interference in religion

PART 3
THE PROTECTION OF CIVIL LIBERTIES

INTRODUCTION

The Constitution—especially the Bill of Rights, the first 10 amendments added to the original document in 1791—guarantees Americans certain individual rights known collectively as "civil liberties." These rights are inherent or "natural" in that they are seen as belonging to all human beings and are beyond interference from government.

Key civil liberties include the freedom of speech, freedom of the press, freedom of assembly, and freedom of worship.

The Constitution protects civil liberties largely by limiting the power of the government to act against individuals. It does this by specifying a list of what Supreme Court Justice Hugo L. Black referred to as "thou shalt nots." In other words, the Bill of Rights lists a number of areas in which the government is prohibited from interfering, thereby protecting individuals against the state (see pages 10-11 and 24-25). State and federal laws further guarantee these rights.

Rights vs. what is right

As in other areas discussed in this volume, however, the Constitution is open to various interpretations. The question of precisely what civil liberties are and where their limits lie has long been the subject of debate. Many people, for example, argue that the Bill of Rights guarantees the right to bear arms. Others contend that the Second Amendment that grants that right does so specifically for the purpose of supporting a militia. In a nation without a militia, they argue, and with a high number of gun-related deaths, the Constitution no longer supports the individual's right to carry a firearm.

Over time, too, civil liberties have been the subject of considerable disagreement in relation to issues such as the rights of African Americans, the treatment of homosexuals, or the nation's obligations to immigrants.

Another cause of controversy about rights lies in contradictions within the nature of the rights themselves. The First Amendment, for example, guarantees freedom of speech. In theory, however, this right allows anybody to say anything they like: A white American can make racist slurs against a black neighbor, or a publisher can print pornographic material, for example.

Many critics believe that it is wrong to protect speech that offends or that incites violence or civil unrest. Advocates, however, counter that the application of the Bill of Rights cannot be selective: The liberties it enshrines are either rights, or they are not.

In 2001 freedom of expression came under intense scrutiny in the aftermath of the September 11 attacks on New

York and Washington, D.C. Young Muslims thought to sympathize with the terrorists' cause were jailed, while racially motivated hate crimes and hate speech—mainly against American Muslims—rose. Following the attacks, people called for greater restrictions on hate speech. Some of the strongest criticism of such measures, however, has come from civil rights groups, who argue that freedom of speech is precious and must be preserved.

The ACLU and feminist Andrea Dworkin discuss the argument in Topic 12.

Further questions about civil liberties concern the scope of government interference in other areas of Americans' lives. Can the government, for example, compel someone to fight for their country? The draft was used a number of times in the 20th century, but how does it fit in with people's freedom of religious and moral beliefs, which might be against violent conflict?

"When the architects of our republic wrote the magnificent words of the Constitution ... they were signing a promissory note ... that all men would be guaranteed the inalienable rights of life, liberty, and the pursuit of happiness."
—DR. MARTIN LUTHER KING, JR., FROM "I HAVE A DREAM," 1963

Charles R. Lawrence II and Jonathan Rausch argue for and against the prohibition of hate speech in Topic 10.

Topic 11 looks at another aspect of freedom of expression, the right to violent protest. If people have sincere objections to certain practices, such as abortion, does the Constitution give them the right to make themselves heard through violent acts? Articles by Duncan Campbell and the ACLU are used to examine this issue.

Freedom of speech is also a key consideration in pornography, which is legal in certain forms in the United States but banned in many other countries. Many people argue that pornography is protected by the First Amendment; others, particularly religious and feminist groups, argue that it is exploitative and unconstitutional.

In Topic 13 Justice White and Congressman Ron Paul look at the constitutionality of the draft.

Topics 14 and 15 consider the limits of interference in an individual's private life. In Topic 14 Justices Scalia and O'Connor argue about whether school boards have the right to impose random drug tests on teenage athletes. In Topic 15 Bryan Knowles and the ACLU consider the right of the government, employers, or others to monitor private e-mail correspondence. Some people believe such monitoring to be a gross invasion of privacy; others view it as a key element in preventing terrorism and other crime.

The final topic looks at the constitutionality of the death penalty. Justices Stewart and Marshall argue whether it is "cruel and unusual."

Topic 10

SHOULD THE GOVERNMENT BE ABLE TO PROHIBIT HATE SPEECH?

YES

FROM CHAPTER 2, "HATE CRIMES VIOLATE THE FREE SPEECH RIGHTS OF VICTIMS"
HATE CRIMES
CHARLES R. LAWRENCE, III

NO

FROM "IN DEFENSE OF PREJUDICE: WHY INCENDIARY SPEECH MUST BE PROTECTED"
HARPERS MAGAZINE, MAY 1995
JONATHAN RAUCH

INTRODUCTION

The Framers of the Constitution believed that freedom of expression was the foundation of a democratic society. So it is perhaps no surprise that the First Amendment to the Constitution provides that "Congress shall make no law … abridging the freedom of speech, or of the press…." While freedom of expression is seen as a fundamental right for all American citizens, its protection under the Constitution has provoked great controversy over the years. Much has centered around cases in which the First Amendment has been used to justify "hate speech"—words and symbols that discriminate against or ridicule a person, group, or institution on the basis of race, religion, national origin, or sexual preference.

At first glance it may look as if the state has no power to ban hate speech. But the First Amendment is a statement of intent, not a detailed article of law. Many people agree that there may be

circumstances in which free speech must be limited in the interest of a greater good. A precedent for this was established by Supreme Court Justice Oliver Wendell Holmes, Jr., during a landmark case in 1919. The case involved a socialist named Charles T. Schenck. During World War I (1914–1918) Schenck had mailed leaflets to potential recruits urging them to oppose conscription and the war itself. Schenck was later convicted of obstructing recruitment under the 1917 Espionage Act. Schenck's attorneys appealed the decision, claiming it had violated his First-Amendment right to free speech. In his summary Justice Holmes stated that "in ordinary times" Schenck may have had a right to free speech but added: "The question in every case is whether words used are of such a nature as to create a clear and present danger that they will bring about the substantive evils that Congress has a right to prevent."

Since that famous judgment other laws have been invoked to prevent speech and writings that might be inflammatory. If a court decides that speakers or writers are likely to inspire hatred or violence, their words can be banned without necessarily threatening general freedom of speech. Yet this is an area in which it is difficult to be completely objective. One person's utterances may be offensive to another person, or even to most other people, but does that give the state the right to gag the speaker? We may all agree that we do not want to have to listen to the views of bigots, but who has the right to define bigotry?

"Free speech is the whole thing, the whole ball game. Free speech is life itself."
—SALMAN RUSHDIE (1947–),

BRITISH AUTHOR

In 2001 Brown University became embroiled in a heated civil liberties debate after a campus newspaper ran an advertisement opposing reparations to compensate black descendants of American slaves. Some people argued that the paper had a right to publish its views regardless of any offense the ad might have caused. Others said: "This is not a free speech issue. It is a hate speech issue."

Can such distinctions be made fairly either at a university, which is supposed to be a melting pot for ideas, or anywhere else? In the first of the following articles Charles R. Lawrence, III, argues that the state must ban hate

speech because it subjugates its victims. Not only does hate speech undermine the principle of social equality; it may also intimidate victims into silence, therefore violating their constitutional right to free speech.

Others think that the only fair way of making up your mind about an issue is to listen to all sides of the argument. Anyone can say anything—we live in a pluralist world where every opinion has a place in society. Only by listening to views of others—no matter how intolerable they may seem—will we be able to move an argument on. The 1977 Skokie trial is a case in point. When the neo-Nazi group the National Socialist Party of America (NSPA) announced its intention of marching through Skokie, Illinois, the villagers won a court injunction against the march. Many of the villagers were survivors, or were related to survivors, of the Holocaust (the mass killing of Jews during World War II [1939-1945]). The villagers argued that the NSPA march would offend Jewish residents of Skokie. In the face of heavy criticism the American Civil Liberties Union (ACLU) appealed against the decision on behalf of the NSPA, claiming a violation of the First Amendment. The Supreme Court ruled in their favor, reaffirming the right to free speech for all citizens. However, the court added a provision that the First Amendment did protect people from offensive speech.

Jonathan Rauch, the author of the second article, opens the case of the American Civil Liberties Union (ACLU). Rauch agrees that the best way to counter hate speech is to address head-on all homophobic, racist, sexist, and xenophobic views with more speech. Persuasion is the key says Rauch; prohibition is counterproductive.

HATE CRIMES VIOLATE THE FREE SPEECH RIGHTS OF VICTIMS
Charles R. Lawrence, III

YES

In the first two paragraphs the author identifies the main reasons why hate speech undermines the principles of the Constitution. This makes his argument clear from the start.

Hate speech harms the rights of victims

… I have tried to articulate the ways in which hate speech harms its victims and the ways in which it harms us all by undermining core values in our Constitution.

The first of these values is full and equal citizenship expressed in the Fourteenth Amendment's Equal Protection clause. When hate speech is employed with the purpose and effect of maintaining established systems of caste and subordination, it violates that core value. Hate speech often prevents its victims from exercising legal rights guaranteed by the Constitution and civil rights statutes. The second constitutional value threatened by hate speech is the value of free expression itself. Hate speech frequently silences its victims, who, more often than not, are those who are already heard from least. An understanding of both of these injuries is aided by the methodologies of feminism and critical race theory that give special attention to the structures of subordination and the voices of the subordinated….

The author refers to Brown v. Board of Education of Topeka, Kansas (1954), a landmark decision of the Supreme Court that banned the "separate but equal" doctrine in public education and set the precedent for desegregation. To find out more information about this and related cases, visit http://library. thinkquest.org/ 10718.

Discrimination conveys a message

The "Whites Only" signs on the lunch counter, swimming pool and drinking fountain convey the same message. The antidiscrimination principle articulated in *Brown* presumptively entitles every individual to be treated by the organized society as a respected, responsible and participating member. This is the principle upon which all our civil rights laws rest. It is the guiding principle of the Equal Protection clause's requirement of nondiscriminatory government action. In addition, it has been applied in regulating private discrimination. The words "women need not apply" in a job announcement, the racially exclusionary clause in a restrictive covenant and the racial epithet scrawled on the locker of the new black employee at a previously all-white job site all convey a political message. But we treat these messages as "discriminatory practices" and outlaw them under federal and state civil rights legislation because they are more than speech. In the context of social inequality, these verbal and symbolic acts form integral links in historically ingrained systems of social discrimination. They work to keep traditionally victimized groups in socially isolated, stigmatized and disadvantaged positions through the promotion of fear, intolerance, degradation and violence. The Equal Protection clause of the Fourteenth Amendment requires the disestablishment of these practices and systems. Likewise, the First Amendment does *not* prohibit our accomplishment of this compelling constitutional interest simply because those discriminatory practices are achieved through the use of words and symbols....

> The author raises an important question. While the Fourteenth Amendment bans racial discrimination on the basis of equal opportunity, the guarantee of free speech provided by the First Amendment appears to condone hate speech. Do you think discriminatory practices do more harm than speech alone?

Verbal assaults are discrimination

Robinson v. Jacksonville Shipyards, Inc. (1991) ... presents a clear example of the tension between the law's commitment to free speech and its commitment to equality. Lois Robinson, a welder, was one of a very small number of female skilled craftworkers employed by Jacksonville Shipyards. She brought suit ... alleging that her employer had created and encouraged a sexually hostile, intimidating work environment. A U.S. District Court ruled in her favor, finding that the presence in the workplace of pictures of women in various stages of undress and in sexually suggestive or submissive poses, as well as remarks made by male employees and supervisors which demeaned women, constituted a violation of Title VII "through the maintenance of a sexually hostile work environment." Much of District Court Judge Howell Melton's opinion is a recounting of the indignities that Ms. Robinson and five other women experienced almost daily while working with 850 men over the course of ten years.... Male employees admitted that the shipyard was "a boys' club" and "more or less a man's world."

> By interfering with the woman's right to work at a job where she is free from sexual harassment, the speech violates the Equal Protection clause. This decision highlights the author's concerns that certain types of speech do more than just voice an idea.

The local chapter of the American Civil Liberties Union (ACLU) appealed the District Court's decision, arguing that "even sexists have a right to free speech." However, anyone who has read the trial record cannot help but wonder about these civil libertarians' lack of concern for Lois Johnson's right to do her work without being subjected to assault....

> Historically, the ACLU has always defended free speech no matter how offensive. The group argues that the same laws used to silence bigots could also be used to silence civil rights or gay rights activists.

Hate speech limits free speech for others

But it is not sufficient to describe the injury occasioned by hate speech only in terms of the countervailing value of equality. There is also an injury to the First Amendment. When Russ Jones looked out his window and saw that burning cross, he heard a message that said, "*Shut up, black man, or risk harm to you and your family.*" It may be that Russ

Professor Laurence H. Tribe is the Ralph S. Tyler, Jr., Professor of Constitutional Law at Harvard Law School. Tribe believes that speech is the cornerstone of democratic society since it is a vital form of self-expression that encourages public debate.

If Congress prevents people expressing hateful ideas and opinions, do you think this will "disempower" those people in the same way as homosexuals or African Americans are disempowered? Does the state become the oppressor?

The Constitutional Rights Foundation website at http://www.crf-usa.org/ has more information about the case of Russell and Laura Jones. Look for the links "School Violence" and "Should Hate Be Outlawed?"

Jones is especially brave, or especially foolhardy, and that he may speak even more loudly in the face of this threat. But it is more likely that he will be silenced, and that *we* will lose the benefit of his voice.

Professor Laurence H. Tribe has identified two values protected by the First Amendment. The first is the intrinsic value of speech, which is the value of individual self-expression. Speech is intrinsically valuable as a manifestation of our humanity and our individuality. The second is the instrumental value of speech. The First Amendment protects dissent to maximize public discourse, and to achieve the great flowering of debate and ideas that we need to make our democracy work. Both of these values are implicated in the silencing of Russ Jones by his nocturnal attacker.

For African Americans, the intrinsic value of speech as self-expression and self-definition has been particularly important. The absence of a "black voice" was central to the ideology of European–American racism, an ideology that denied Africans their humanity and thereby justified their enslavement. African American slaves were prevented from learning to read and write, and they were prohibited from engaging in forms of self-expression that might instill in them a sense of self-worth and pride. Their silence and submission was then interpreted as evidence of their subhuman status. The use of the burning cross as a method of disempowerment originates, in part, in the perpetrators' understanding of how, in the context of this ideology, their victims are rendered subhuman when they are silenced. When, in the face of threat and intimidation, the oppressors' victims are afraid to give full expression to their individuality, the oppressors achieve their purpose of denying the victims the liberty guaranteed to them by the Constitution.

When the Joneses moved to Earl Street in St. Paul, they were expressing their individuality. When they chose their house and their neighbors, they were saying, "This is who we are. We are a proud black family and we want to live here." This self-expression and self-definition is the intrinsic value of speech. The instrumental value of speech is likewise threatened by this terrorist attack on the Joneses. Russ and Laura Jones also brought new voices to the political discourse in this St. Paul community. Ideally, they will vote and talk politics with their neighbors. They will bring new experiences and new perspectives to their neighborhood. A burning cross not only silences people like the Joneses, it impoverishes the democratic process and renders our collective conversation less informed.

Regulating private behavior to guarantee equality

First Amendment doctrine and theory have no words for the injuries of silence imposed by private actors. There is no language for the damage that is done to the First Amendment when the hateful speech of the cross burner or the sexual harasser silences its victims. In antidiscrimination law, we recognize the necessity of regulating private behavior that threatens the values of equal citizenship. Fair housing laws, public accommodations provisions and employment discrimination laws all regulate the behavior of private actors. We recognize that much of the discrimination in our society occurs without the active participation of the state. We know that we could not hope to realize the constitutional ideal of equal citizenship if we pretended that the government was the only discriminator.

The author reinforces his argument by repeating the reason why he thinks hate speech undermines the principles of the Constitution.

But there is no recognition in First Amendment law of the systematic private suppression of speech. Courts and scholars have worried about the heckler's veto, and, where there is limited access to speech fora, we have given attention to questions of equal time and the right to reply. But for the most part, we act as if the government is the only regulator of speech, the only censor. We treat the marketplace of ideas as if all voices are equal, as if there are no silencing voices or voices that are silenced. In the discourse of the First Amendment, there is no way to talk about how those who are silenced are always less powerful than those who do the silencing. First Amendment law ignores the ways in which patriarchy silences women, and racism silences people of color. When a woman's husband threatens to beat her the next time she contradicts him, a First Amendment injury has occurred. "Gay-bashing" keeps gays and lesbians "in the closet." It silences them. They are denied the humanizing experience of self-expression. We *all* are denied the insight and beauty of their voices....

In the rush to protect the "speech" of cross burners, would-be champions of the First Amendment must not forget the voices of their victims. If First Amendment doctrine and theory is to truly serve First Amendment ideals, it must recognize the injury done by the private suppression of speech; it must take into account the historical reality that some members of our community are less powerful than others and that those persons continue to be systematically silenced by those who are more powerful. If we are truly committed to free speech, First Amendment doctrine and theory must be guided by the principle of antisubordination. There can be no free speech where there are still masters and slaves.

The author argues for changes to the First Amendment in order to protect the victims of hate speech. What measures do you think society can take to combat hate speech?

IN DEFENSE OF PREJUDICE: WHY INCENDIARY SPEECH MUST BE PROTECTED
Jonathan Rauch

NO

Jonathan Rauch's article was written and published in 1995, when the Lawrence case and Rogers' lawsuit were "hot topics" in the national press. By citing the two cases, Rauch used up-to-date examples and contemporized his article.

X The war on prejudice is now, in all likelihood, the most uncontroversial social movement in America. Opposition to "hate speech," formerly identified with the liberal left, has become a bipartisan piety. In the past year, groups and factions that agree on nothing else have agreed that the public expression of any and all prejudices must be forbidden. On the left, protesters and editorialists have insisted that Francis L. Lawrence resign as president of Rutgers University for describing blacks as "a disadvantaged population that doesn't have that genetic, hereditary background to have a higher average." On the other side of the ideological divide, Ralph Reed, the executive director of the Christian Coalition, responded to criticism of the religious right by calling a press conference to denounce a supposed outbreak of "name-calling, scapegoating, and religious bigotry." Craig Rogers, an evangelical Christian student at California State University, recently filed a $2.5 million sexual-harassment suit against a lesbian professor of psychology, claiming that anti-male bias in one of her lectures violated campus rules and left him feeling "raped and trapped."

In universities and on Capitol Hill, in workplaces and newsrooms, authorities are declaring that there is no place for racism, sexism, homophobia, Christian-bashing, and other forms of prejudice in public debate or even in private thought. "Only when racism and other forms of prejudice are expunged," say the crusaders for sweetness and light, "can minorities be safe and society be fair." So sweet, this dream of a world without prejudice. But the very last thing society should do is seek to utterly eradicate racism and other forms of prejudice.

Intellectual pluralism

Intellectual pluralists believe that all ideas and opinions—even homophobic or racist ones—have a place in democratic society.

I suppose I should say, in the customary I-hope-I-don't-sound-too-defensive tone, that I am not a racist and that this is not an article favoring racism or any other particular prejudice. It is an article favoring intellectual pluralism, which permits the expression of various forms of bigotry and always will. Although we like to hope that a time will come when no one will believe that people come in types and that each type belongs with its own kind, I doubt such a day will ever arrive. By all indications, *Homo sapiens* is a tribal species for whom "us versus them" comes naturally and must be continually pushed back. Where there is genuine freedom of expression, there will be racist expression. There will also be people who believe that homosexuals are sick or threaten children or—especially among teenagers—are rightful targets of manly savagery. Homosexuality will always be incomprehensible to most people, and what is incomprehensible is feared. As for anti-Semitism, it appears to be a hardier virus than influenza. If you want pluralism, then you get racism and sexism and homophobia, and communism and fascism and xenophobia and tribalism, and that is just for a start. If you want to believe in intellectual freedom and the progress of knowledge and the advancement of science and all those other good things, then you must swallow hard and accept this: for as thickheaded and wayward an animal as us, the realistic question is how to make the best of prejudice, not how to eradicate it....

The term antiSemitism encompasses all forms of hostility—economic, racial, or social—toward Jewish people. The term was coined in 1879 by the German agitator Wilhelm Marr, but antiSemitism dates back to at least 175 B.C., when tension arose between Jews and non-Jews in the eastern Mediterranean region of Europe.

All voices are equal

An enlightened and efficient intellectual regime lets a million prejudices bloom, including many that you or I may regard as hateful or grotesque. It avoids any attempt to stamp out prejudice, because stamping out prejudice really means forcing everyone to share the same prejudice, namely that of whoever is in authority. The great American philosopher Charles Sanders Peirce wrote in 1877: "When complete agreement could not otherwise be reached, a general massacre of all who have not thought in a certain way has proved a very effective means of settling opinion in a country." In speaking of "settling opinion," Peirce was writing about one of the two or three most fundamental problems that any human society must confront and solve. For most societies down through the centuries, this problem was dealt with in the manner he described: errors were identified by the authorities—priests, politburos, dictators—or by mass opinion, and then the error-makers were eliminated along with their putative mistakes. "Let all men who reject the established belief be terrified into silence," wrote Peirce, describing this system. "This method has, from the earliest times, been one of the chief means of upholding correct theological and political doctrines."

The author quotes the respected academic Charles Sanders Peirce to substantiate his argument. You can find out more about the life and work of Peirce at www.digitalpeirce. org.

Intellectual pluralism substitutes a radically different doctrine: we kill our mistakes rather than each other. Here I

Around 1508 the Polish astronomer Nicolaus Copernicus proposed that Earth and other planets in the Solar System orbit the Sun. Copernicanism challenged the widely held belief that Earth was the center of the universe. The Italian scientist Galileo Galilei agreed with Copernicus but was condemned to life imprisonment by the Inquisition, which viewed Copernicanism as heresy. We now know that Copernicus and Galileo were correct.

The author personalizes his argument by presenting some of his own opinions on homosexuality and religion.

The McCarthyites were an influential group of politicians under the leadership of Senator Joseph McCarthy. The McCarthyites tried to oust suspected communists from positions of influence in society during the 1940s and 1950s.

draw on another great philosopher, the late Karl Popper, who pointed out that the critical method of science "consists in letting our hypotheses die in our stead." Those who are in error are not (or are not supposed to be) banished or excommunicated or forced to sign a renunciation or required to submit to "rehabilitation" or sent for psychological counseling. It is the error we punish, not the errant. By letting people make errors—even mischievous, spiteful errors (as, for instance, Galileo's insistence on Copernicanism was taken to be in 1633)—pluralism creates room to challenge orthodoxy, think imaginatively, experiment boldly. Brilliance and bigotry are empowered in the same stroke.

Progress depends on dissidence

Pluralism is the principle that protects and makes a place in human company for that loneliest and most vulnerable of all minorities, the minority who is hounded and despised among blacks and whites, gays and straights, who is suspect or criminal among every tribe and in every nation of the world, and yet on whom progress depends: the dissident. I am not saying that dissent is always or even usually enlightened. Most of the time it is foolish and self-serving. No dissident has the right to be taken seriously, and the fact that Aryan Nation racists or Nation of Islam anti-Semites are unorthodox does not entitle them to respect. But what goes around comes around. As a supporter of gay marriage, for example, I reject the majority's view of family, and as a Jew I reject its view of God. I try to be civil, but the fact is that most Americans regard my views on marriage as a reckless assault on the most fundamental of all institutions, and many people are more than a little discomfited by the statement "Jesus Christ was no more divine than anybody else" (which is why so few people ever say it). Trap the racists and anti-Semites, and you lay a trap for me too. Hunt for them with eradication in your mind, and you have brought dissent itself within your sights.

The new crusade against prejudice waves aside such warnings. Like earlier crusades against antisocial ideas, the mission is fueled by good (if cocksure) intentions and a genuine sense of urgency. Some kinds of error are held to be intolerable, like pollutants that even in small traces poison the water for a whole town. Some errors are so pernicious as to damage real people's lives, so wrongheaded that no person of right mind or goodwill could support them. Like their forebears of other stripe—the Church in its campaigns against heretics, the McCarthyites in their campaigns against Communists—the modern anti-racist and anti-sexist and anti-homophobic campaigners are totalists, demanding not that misguided ideas and ugly expressions be corrected or criticized but that they be eradicated. They make war not on errors but on error, and like other totalists they act in the name of public safety—the safety, especially, of minorities....

The new purism sets out, to begin with, on a campaign against words, for words are the currency of prejudice, and if prejudice is hurtful then so must be prejudiced words. "We are not safe when these violent words are among us," wrote Mari Matsuda, then a UCLA law professor. Here one imagines gangs of racist words swinging chains and smashing heads in back alleys....

"The experience of being called 'nigger,' 'spic,' 'Jap,' or 'kike' is like receiving a slap in the face," Charles Lawrence wrote in 1990. "Psychic injury is no less an injury than being struck in the face, and it often is far more severe...."

The fear engendered by these words is real. The remedy is as clear and as imperfect as ever: protect citizens against violence. This, I grant, is something that American society has never done very well and now does quite poorly. It is no solution to define words as violence or prejudice as oppression, and then by cracking down on words or thoughts pretend that we are doing something about violence and oppression. No doubt it is easier to pass a speech code or hate-crimes law and proclaim the streets safer than actually to make the streets safer, but the one must never be confused with the other. Every cop or prosecutor chasing words is one fewer chasing criminals....

Indeed, equating "verbal violence" with physical violence is a treacherous, mischievous business. Not long ago a writer was charged with viciously and gratuitously wounding the feelings and dignity of millions of people. He was charged, in effect, with exhibiting flagrant prejudice against Muslims and outrageously slandering their beliefs. "What is freedom ayatollahs sentenced him to death and put a price on his head. "Without the freedom to offend, it ceases to exist." I can think of nothing sadder than that minority activists, in their haste to make the world better, should be the ones to forget the lesson of Rushdie's plight: for minorities, pluralism, not purism, is the answer. The campaigns to eradicate prejudice —all of them, the speech codes and workplace restrictions and mandatory therapy for accused bigots and all the rest— should stop, now. The whole objective of eradicating prejudice, as opposed to correcting and criticizing it, should be repudiated as a fool's errand. Salman Rushdie is right ... and minorities belong at his side....

Mari J. Matsuda is a professor of law at the Georgetown University Law Center and has written numerous books and articles on constitutional law, feminist theory, affirmative action, and hate speech.

The Indian-born British novelist Salman Rushdie (1947–) was sentenced to death by the former Iranian spiritual leader Ayatollah Ruhollah Khomeini on February 14, 1989. Khomeini's fatwa (death sentence) came in response to Rushdie's book The Satanic Verses (1988), which was seen as an attack on the Muslim faith. See Volume 12 Arts and Culture, page 193 for further information.

Summary

Hate speech is a difficult topic to reconcile for most liberal-minded people because it exposes a conflict between the values of liberty—the freedom to express one's opinions—and equality in cases in which those opinions bolster social discrimination through victimization. In the first article Charles R. Lawrence, III identifies the tension between the constitutional protection of free speech and the commitment to equality. He believes that hate speech breeds discrimination and therefore undermines the Fourteenth Amendment, which aims to provide full and equal citizenship for all Americans. Furthermore, Lawrence maintains that hate speech silences its victims and therefore violates those people's First Amendment right to free speech. In conclusion, he argues for changes to the Constitution to prohibit hate speech and to protect the persecuted minority. Only then, says the author, will victims be able to express themselves and establish independent identities.

The author of the second article, Jonathan Rauch, does not think that a democratic government can abolish extremist ideas simply by banning discussion of them. Rauch believes that a liberal democracy must protect the right of its citizens to hold such views no matter how repellent they may be to the majority. The author asserts that a liberal democracy should favor intellectual pluralism, in which "a million prejudices bloom." Intellectual pluralists believe that people should listen to all sides of the argument and correct and criticize prejudice rather than try to stamp it out.

FURTHER INFORMATION:

Books:

Lamarch, Gara (ed.), *Speech and Equality: Do We Really Have to Choose?* New York: New York University Press, 1996.

MacKinnon, Catharine A., *Only Words.* Cambridge, MA: Harvard University Press, 1993.

Matas, David, *Bloody Words: Hate and Free Speech.* Winnipeg, Manitoba: Blizzard Publishing Ltd., 2001.

Walker, Samuel, *Hate Speech: The History of an American Controversy.* Lincoln, NE: University of Nebraska Press, 1994.

Wolfson, Nicholas, *Hate Speech, Sex Speech, Free Speech.* Westport, CT: Praeger Publishers, 1997.

Articles:

Sunstein, Cass, "Is Violent Speech a Right?" 1992. *The American Prospect* 6:22.

Owen, Ursula, "Hate Speech: The Speech That Kills." *Index on Censorship*, Issue 1/98.

 Useful websites:

www.aclu.org

The American Civil Liberties Union site. Contains links to sites on cyber liberties, free speech, and racial equality.

www.freedomforum.org

The Freedom Forum site contains an extensive list of links to articles and publications dedicated to free speech.

www.article19.org

The ARTICLE 19 site—an organization whose aim is to combat censorship by promoting freedom of expression.

The following debates in the Pro/Con series may also be of interest:

In this volume:

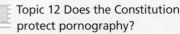 Topic 12 Does the Constitution protect pornography?

SHOULD THE GOVERNMENT BE ABLE TO PROHIBIT HATE SPEECH?

YES: Such a right is unconditional no matter how extreme the viewpoint

YES: Hate speech hurts the vulnerable. A society should protect the weak.

CONSTITUTIONAL FREEDOM
Should all the citizens in a democracy be able to say what they want?

EXCESSIVE INTERVENTION
Should governments try to control what people think?

NO: Just as no one is allowed to incite violence, people should not be allowed to express ideas that are hurtful to others

NO: You may be able to control what people say, but you cannot control what they think. Legislation will never make prejudice go away.

SHOULD THE GOVERNMENT BE ABLE TO PROHIBIT HATE SPEECH?
KEY POINTS

YES: The government creates the moral climate of a nation. If we want equality, we must pass laws that produce and preserve it.

YES: If hate speech is permitted, a culture of hate develops in which intolerance is accepted on a wider scale

WAR ON PREJUDICE
Should hate be a subject for legislation?

NO: Every society contains a wide range of opinions on every conceivable subject. If we censor undesirable speech, we place restrictions on everyone regardless of their opinions.

NO: A government should not attempt to control what people say. It must permit dissent and hope that people learn the truth for themselves.

Topic 11
IS THE RIGHT TO VIOLENT PROTEST PROTECTED BY THE CONSTITUTION?

YES

"SEVEN DOCTORS HAVE BEEN MURDERED, NOW JUDGES RULE IN FAVOUR
OF ABORTION HIT LIST"
THE GUARDIAN, MARCH 30, 2001
DUNCAN CAMPBELL

NO

"ABORTION CLINIC ACCESS LAW"
HTTP://WWW.ACLU.ORG/LIBRARY/AAABORT.HTML
AMERICAN CIVIL LIBERTIES UNION, 1997

INTRODUCTION

People throughout history have staged protests in an attempt to bring about change. Some of these protests have been peaceful; some have been violent. Protesters have often argued that the ends justified the means—especially when peaceful protests failed to have the desired effect.

During the 1960s, for example, the black civil rights movement in the United States drew support from, and in turn supported, Irish Nationalists who sought a united Ireland. Both groups were reacting to government discrimination in jobs, housing, and voting. When nonviolent protest failed in Ireland, some leading black activists supported the IRA's (Irish Republican Army) adoption of force. Similarly, during the era of apartheid in South Africa Nelson Mandela's African National Congress (ANC) often resorted to violence—the UK Prime Minister Margaret Thatcher even referring to

Mandela as a "terrorist." Animal rights organizations, environmentalists, the labor movement, suffragists, antinuclear weapons groups, and antiwar protesters have also resorted to violence.

But is the right to violent protest protected by the Constitution? The First Amendment states that "Congress shall make no law ... abridging the freedom of speech, or of the press; or the right of the people peaceably to assemble, and to petition the government for a redress of grievances." So while some issues might never have been highlighted nor changes brought about without what some have seen as justifiable violence, does this equate with a Constitution that mentions only peaceful forms of protest?

Some people have argued that violence becomes justified if they are prevented from exercising their legal rights. Toward the end of 1999, for example, various anticapitalist, trade union, and environmental organizations gathered in Seattle to protest against that year's round of talks by the World Trade Organization (WTO). On the second day of the meeting the mayor issued an emergency order establishing a 25-block zone in which all expressions of protest against the WTO were banned, which he justified on the basis of what he saw as a "threat to public safety" after some of the demonstrators committed acts of violence. Most of the protesters had been peaceful, however. Were the riots that followed justified on the basis that the government and the police acted unconstitutionally in infringing people's First Amendment rights? The Constitution might specify only peaceful assembly, but what recourse remains when people's rights to peaceful protest and freedom of speech are barred?

"… the way to reform has always led through prison."
—EMMELINE PANKHURST
(1858–1928), BRITISH SUFFRAGIST
AND POLITICIAN

Another issue that needs to be considered is that people's basic constitutional rights are continually being redefined by rulings of the Supreme Court. The right to free speech, for example, now has many legal exceptions, such as incitement to criminal behavior, fighting words, defamation, and obscenity. So what is and is not protected by the Constitution can become a complex matter of legal debate. In such cases the issue of due

process often comes into play: the Fourteenth Amendment provision that people cannot be subject to laws that are either arbitrary, unfair, or that permit unreasonable treatment of certain groups or individuals.

Even if a law is passed, due process can subsequently make it unconstitutional. Consequently, some protesters have contested legal attempts to restrict their behavior on the grounds that the laws were unconstitutional according to the limits of due process. Antiabortion protesters, for example, have claimed that laws restricting their behavior have discriminated against them on the basis of their religion.

The following articles look at the violent tactics used by some antiabortion campaigners in the United States and consider whether they are in any way protected by the Constitution. In the first article British journalist Duncan Campbell discusses the 2001 decision by the Court of Appeals that vacated an earlier ruling awarding substantial damages against a protest group that published "wanted posters" of doctors who provided abortions. Since one possible result of these actions was to encourage violent attacks on the doctors, Campbell argues that by implication the ruling has also deemed the right to violent protest constitutional.

The American Civil Liberties Union, on the other hand, agrees that the First Amendment protects people's right to protest, but argues that the Constitution at no point protects "the right to threaten abortion providers with harm." It also highlights the view that protesters cannot realistically claim that legal restrictions on their behavior infringe their constitutional rights when they themselves are infringing women's right to choose an abortion.

SEVEN DOCTORS HAVE BEEN MURDERED, NOW JUDGES RULE IN FAVOUR OF ABORTION HIT LIST
Duncan Campbell

YES

James Kopp has always protested his innocence, and after his arrest in May 2002 he decided to return to the United States to face the case against him. For further information about Kopp go to www.armyofgod.com/JamesKopp.html or to bcnews.go.com/sections/us/DailyNews/kopp_bio_990506.html.

Anti-abortionists in the United States have won the right to publish on the Internet what amounts to a hit list of doctors who provide terminations for pregnant women. The site, known as the Nuremberg Files, describes abortions as "Satan's food source." It prints "wanted" posters of the "baby butchers" and in some cases lists their addresses, car licence plate numbers and relatives' names. Seven doctors providing abortions in the US have been murdered in the past ten years.

The danger posed to doctors was underlined yesterday when one of the FBI's most wanted fugitives was arrested in France on suspicion of having murdered a gynaecologist in 1998. James Kopp, dubbed "Atomic Dog" by fellow anti-abortionists, was the subject of an international manhunt after Dr Barnett Slepian was shot dead at home near Buffalo, New York state. Within hours, Slepian's name was posted on the Nuremberg Files with a cross through it.

Cause for concern

The ruling was upheld because the site did not actually threaten violence. Web service providers have resisted putting the Nuremberg files back online, however, because they violate contract stipulations prohibiting hate speech. The files remain available as a CD-ROM.

The ruling upholding the right of the site to publish its content was upheld by a federal appeals court sitting in San Francisco. The decision aroused despair last night among pro-choice doctors and campaigners.

Warren Hern of Boulder, Colorado—one of the doctors who lodged the original lawsuit in Oregon that went on to the appeal court—said he was "shocked, disappointed and alarmed" by the decision. Dr Hern, who has been the target of an attack, said the ruling would be a "green light" for the most violent anti-abortionists.

Gloria Feldt, president of the Planned Parenthood Federation of America, condemned the decision: "Reasonable people understand the difference between free speech and harassment that creates a violent social climate."

In making its ruling the bench pointed to the First Amendment to the Constitution, which guarantees free

Prochoice campaigners protest against the tactics used by prolife campaigners.

One of the three judges said that "extreme rhetoric and violent action" had always played a part in American political life.

The ruling arose out of a 1999 case in Portland, Oregon, where a jury awarded $107m (then worth £66.5m) in mainly punitive damages against the American Coalition of Life Activists, the Advocates for Life Ministries and 13 individuals who had put wanted posters of doctors on the web and described them as baby butchers. The case had been brought by four doctors, a clinic and the Planned Parenthood organisation under the Freedom of Access to Clinics Act.

The identities of three of the seven doctors murdered in the past 10 years were listed on websites; there have been a further 17 attempted murders. Many such doctors now wear disguises and bullet-proof vests, live in fortified houses and vary their journeys to work.

"Political speech may not be punished just because it makes it more likely that someone will be harmed at some

The Portland judge awarded damages after deciding that the website constituted a "true threat." He based his ruling on the 1969 case Watts v. United States, in which a student was tried for threatening to kill President L.B. Johnson. The court ruled that since the student was not in Washington and no definite time was set, the threat was not sufficiently direct to constitute a "true threat."

COMMENTARY: Prolife violence

Attacks on abortion clinics began after the *Roe v. Wade* decision of 1973. The first arson was reported in 1977, and in 1982 several men identifying themselves as members of the Army of God kidnapped Dr. Hector Zevallos and torched his premises. One of them was later convicted of three bombings. Further bouts of violence occurred in 1983 and 1984, and members of the white-supremacist movement were also implicated.

In 1984 Randall Terry began organizing clinic actions in Binghamton, New York, using tactics such as obstruction, trespass, and vandalism. A book published by Joseph Scheidler of Chicago in 1985 advocated similar actions, including sit-ins, withholding taxes, and asking friends working in government offices to obtain opponents' addresses. Together, the two men launched a nationwide campaign called Operation Rescue, provoking clinic blockades throughout the country. Meanwhile, the number of bombings, arsons, and assaults was also rising.

Early in the 1990s the American Coalition of Life Advocates (ACLA) began publishing "wanted posters" of abortion providers. In 1991 the first reported shooting occurred at a clinic in Springfield, Missouri, where a masked gunman paralyzed one manager and wounded another. The first murder occurred in 1993, when Michael Griffin shot a doctor in Pensacola, Florida, prompting antiabortion leaders to sign a statement condoning his actions. Shortly afterward Shelley Shannon, who had already been on a year-long arson and butyric-acid bombing spree, shot Dr. George Tiller outside his clinic in Wichita, Kansas. In 1994 Paul Hill, a former Presbyterian minister, gunned down Dr. John Britton and his escort. Another shooting rampage in Brookline, Massachusetts, in 1995, left two clinic receptionists dead and wounded five others.

In 1997 Neal Horsley created the "Nuremberg Files" website for the ACLA. Named after the German city in which World War II criminals were tried, it listed the details of more than 200 abortion providers, including information such as addresses, photos, and family members. Horsley said his intention was to disseminate information, not to cause harm, but three doctors listed on the site have since been killed—their names appearing crossed-out to indicate fatalities. Bombings also increased that year, beginning with two explosions in an Atlanta clinic that injured seven people. In 1998 another bomb killed a clinic security guard and blinded a nurse. Meanwhile, antiabortionists began holding "White Rose Banquets" to honor the killers, arsonists, and bombers. One of the banquet leaders, Dennis Malvasi, was arrested as an accomplice to the murder of Dr. Barnett Slepian in 1998.

Between 1974 and 2000 the National Abortion Federation reported 2,584 violent crimes against abortion providers, while there were 224 reported arsons and bombings between 1982 and March 2000. Since 1993 seven clinic staff have been killed and many others dealt life-threatening injuries.

makes it more likely that someone will be harmed at some unknown time in the future by an unrelated third party," said Judge Alex Kozinski in the judgment.

"Extreme rhetoric and violent action have marked many political movements in American history. Patriots intimidated loyalists in both word and deed as they gathered support for American independence. John Brown and other abolitionists, convinced that God was on their side, committed murder in pursuit of their cause.

"In more modern times, the labour, anti-war, animal rights and environmental movements all have had their violent fringes," said Judge Kozinski, who was appointed under Ronald Reagan's presidency.

"As a result, much of what was said by non-violent participants acquired a tinge of menace.... If their (the websites') statements merely encouraged unrelated terrorists then their words are protected by the First Amendment."

Mixed reactions

The American Civil Liberties Union [ACLU] agreed that the First Amendment protected the right to protest against abortion, but argued that "it doesn't protect the right to threaten abortion providers with harm."

The ruling delighted anti-abortion groups. "Hallelujah!" said Neal Horsley of Carrollton, Georgia who runs the Nuremberg Files site.

Yesterday the site was posting new names of doctors, calling for fresh volunteers to carry out surveillance on doctors to protect "God's little babies." It also guided site visitors to the names of doctors killed.

"This is a reaffirmation of First Amendment liberty," said Christopher Ferrara of the American Catholic Lawyers Association [ACLA], an attorney in the case. "The posters do not contain any threats and in comparison to what we see in other protest movements, they are rather tame."

Do you think Judge Kozinski is supporting violent protest here, or is he merely upholding people's right to use extreme rhetoric in support of a cause—on the assumption that one person's words cannot be directly responsible for causing the actions of another unrelated party?

Christopher Ferrara is president of ACLA, a nonprofit body established in 1990 that provides free legal assistance to Roman Catholics in First Amendment and religious liberty cases. He was lead defense lawyer during the 1999 trial, arguing before the Ninth Circuit Court of Appeals on behalf of three of the defendants.

ABORTION CLINIC ACCESS LAW
American Civil Liberties Union

FACE was President Clinton's national response to earlier attempts to curb the tide of antiabortion violence. In 1993, for example, the governor of California signed the Assembly Bill, making it illegal to obstruct a person trying to enter or exit health-care facilities. Another bill in 1994 permitted private lawsuits to be filed against people who obstructed or disrupted the functioning of a health-care facility.

A friend-of-the-court brief is submitted by a party who is not directly involved in a case. The brief may provide information about legal arguments or how a case might affect other people. Briefs may be filed only if all parties give their written consent, or if the court grants a motion. Some organizations file these briefs in an attempt to lobby the Supreme Court, to obtain media attention, or to impress members.

NO

The Freedom of Access to Clinic Entrances Act, or FACE, was signed into law by President Clinton on May 26, 1994. It was intended to stem the well-documented and increasing violence against those who obtain and provide abortions. The law provides criminal and civil penalties against the use of force, threats of force, physical obstruction or property damage aimed at interfering with those obtaining or providing reproductive health services.

On the same day the law was signed, various anti-choice groups filed suit in federal courts in Virginia, Arizona and the District of Columbia to block enforcement of the law on the grounds that, as written, it infringed First Amendment and statutory rights to freedom of speech and religion. Following the first three lawsuits, cases were filed in federal courts in California, Florida, Virginia (a second case in the state) and Louisiana. A lawsuit already pending in federal court in North Carolina to challenge a state clinic access bill was amended to challenge FACE as well.

To date, the United States Department of Justice has filed two criminal prosecutions under FACE. In Milwaukee, Wisconsin, six demonstrators are charged with attaching themselves by handcuffs, cement, and other means to an automobile or a 55-gallon drum employed to block a clinic's entrances. And in Pensacola, Florida, Paul Holl is accused of murdering a doctor and his volunteer escort and wounding another escort. In each case, anti-abortion protesters clearly engaged in criminal conduct chargeable under FACE, not in constitutionally protected expression. In both of these cases, defendants' motions to dismiss the charges on constitutional grounds have been denied, making way for the prosecutions to proceed.

Federal courts in Arizona, California, Florida, Louisiana, and Virginia (two cases) have also rendered decisions upholding FACE's constitutionality. The courts concluded that Congress has the constitutional authority to enact FACE and that the law as drafted infringes no First Amendment freedoms. The Florida and both Virginia cases are now on appeal. The ACLU filed friend-of-the-court briefs supporting FACE in two of the district court cases and is filing as well in the pending appeals.

Having worked during the legislative process to assure that First Amendment rights were not infringed by the Act, the ACLU believes the new law, as it is written, does not violate the First Amendment. Wherever feasible, we will file friend-of-the-court briefs supporting the constitutionality of the law.

In brief

* As the nation's preeminent defender of the Constitution and the Bill of Rights, the ACLU ardently defends the right of all—including anti-abortion activists—to communicate their message by speaking, praying, chanting, singing and demonstrating. The ACLU has worked to make sure FACE protects the First Amendment rights of protesters. We have also defended anti-abortion activists from police abuse.

* What the First Amendment does not protect is criminal acts of violence—shooting doctors, kidnapping clinic staff, spraying butyric acid on clinic property, destroying medical equipment or making death threats. The Constitution does not—and never has—provided immunity to vigilantes.

* Blockades—physical obstruction that interferes with another person's rights—are not protected by the First Amendment, even when used as a tactic of political protest. A protester is protected when she sets up a table on a sidewalk and offers literature or distributes leaflets from the middle of a sidewalk. But the First Amendment does not protect a group of people when they link arms and prevent others from passing on the sidewalk or from entering or exiting a building.

* The claim that FACE discriminates on the basis of content or viewpoint is groundless. This charge simply does not apply when violence and physical obstruction, as opposed to expression, are the targets of the restriction.

* It does not matter whether those who violate the Act are motivated by religious belief or secular objection to abortion; intentional violent or obstructive interference is simply forbidden. FACE does not single out any religion or religious belief for discrimination.

ACLU policy

Protection of the First Amendment is part of the ACLU's "common law." Likewise, the ACLU has supported a woman's right to choose abortion since before *Roe v. Wade*, and in

To find out more about the ACLU, go to its website at www.aclu.org/.

Butyric acid is a vile-smelling chemical that is difficult to remove and that can make a building uninhabitable. It burns the skin and eyes and can cause vomiting and inflammation of the respiratory system. It can also damage the liver and cause death in extreme cases.

Until the mid-19th century abortion before fetal movement occurred at about 20 weeks was not considered wrong. But after a campaign by the American Medical Association (AMA) "unnecessary" abortions were criminalized in the early 1900s. Things changed again in the Roe v. Wade case of 1973, when the Supreme Court ruled that state abortion laws violated due process, and that women had a fundamental right to obtain abortions until the third trimester of pregnancy unless the state had a "compelling interest" in preventing them. For more information go to bostonreview.mit. edu/BR21.3/Paul. html.

This is a key point in the argument. Antiabortion activists often complain that their constitutional rights are being violated when they themselves are trying to restrict the constitutional rights of others.

recent years has argued the key cases opposing restrictions that deny women access to reproductive health care. Policy 263 states: "The ACLU holds that every woman, as a matter of her right to the enjoyment of life, liberty, and privacy, should be free to determine whether and when to bear children."

The ACLU has long distinguished between violence and non-violent protest. Policy 41 (section b) on picketing is illustrative: "Picketing is an expression of the rights of free speech and assembly protected by the First Amendment. The ACLU supports the right to picket in any circumstances, by any method, in any numbers. Neither the merits of the controversy nor the views expressed limit the right to picket. The right to picket does not, however, protect acts of violence, or the physical obstruction of persons and places."

Arguments, facts, and quotes

Congress has a dual obligation to protect women exercising their constitutional right to choose abortion and the medical providers who assist them, as well as to protect the First Amendment rights of anti-abortion activists. The new federal law, patterned after existing civil rights legislation, fulfills that dual obligation. It provides urgently needed protection for the constitutional rights of abortion clinic patients and providers, while still permitting protesters to express their views peacefully as guaranteed by the First Amendment.

FACE is aimed at punishing illegal conduct. From 1977 through April of 1993, reproductive health clinics and providers were the targets of an escalating epidemic of violence, with 36 bombings, 81 arsons, 84 assaults, two kidnappings, 327 clinic invasions and one murder. These are not activities protected by the First Amendment.

The law punishes: [whoever] by force or threat of force or by physical obstruction, intentionally injures, intimidates or interferes with or attempts to injure, intimidate or interfere with any person .... obtaining or providing reproductive health services ....

From the outset, the ACLU vigorously scrutinized the bill and worked with members of Congress to avoid infringement of expression protected by the First Amendment. The Act explicitly states:

Nothing in this section shall be construed to prohibit any expressive conduct (including peaceful picketing or other peaceful demonstration) protected from legal prohibition by the First Amendment to the Constitution.

Long-standing First Amendment law distinguishes between aggressive expression, on the one hand, and behavior that prevents others from exercising their rights, on the other. Anti-abortion activists, like all citizens espousing any cause, are properly protected by the First Amendment when they speak, march, demonstrate, pray or associate with others in these activities. Their expression may be harsh, vigorous, unsettling, and unpleasant and still be protected by the First Amendment. But protesters may not physically obstruct others from exercising their rights, nor break the bounds of peaceful expression and assembly.

Because FACE does not penalize expressive activities, claims of content or viewpoint discrimination fail. Just as Congress was free during the civil rights struggles of the 1960s to provide special protection for polling places, voters, and those assisting others to exercise their right to vote, Congress is free now to respond to violence at reproductive health facilities by protecting these facilities, their staffs and their patients.

Finally, guarantees of religious freedom are not shields for violence against or physical obstruction of those exercising protected rights. FACE does not target any religious practice or belief for discrimination; it punishes violations of its terms regardless of whether the perpetrators are motivated by religious belief or secular dogma.

Because all laws are susceptible to overreach by police or prosecutors, however, the ACLU plans to carefully monitor enforcement of the law. Should local authorities misinterpret the statute and apply it improperly, the ACLU will act to protect the constitutional rights of anti-abortion protesters.

Not all speech is protected by the First Amendment, which has many legal exceptions, such as incitement to illegal conduct, fighting words, and libel. Fighting words "...which by their very utterance inflict injury or tend to incite an immediate breach of the peace" were prohibited after the 1942 case of Chaplinsky v. New Hampshire.

The Framers created the First Amendment in an attempt to avoid religious conflicts by prohibiting government from either encouraging or promoting religion and giving people the right to worship or not as they chose.

Summary

In his article Duncan Campbell argues that during a federal appeals court session in San Francisco in March 2001 a panel of judges implicitly deemed the right to violent protest constitutional. The court was responding to a case in Portland, Oregon, in 1999 during which a jury awarded $107 million in damages against a group of antiabortionists who had posted "wanted posters" on the web of doctors who carried out abortions. In throwing out the earlier award, Judge Alex Kozinski said: "Political speech may not be punished just because it makes it more likely that someone will be harmed at some unknown time in the future by an unrelated third party." Kozinski thus upheld the antiabortionists' right to free speech as enshrined in the First Amendment, even though he acknowledged that their speech might provoke extreme followers of the movement into violent forms of protest.

In the second article the American Civil Liberties Union (ACLU) discusses the Freedom of Access to Clinic Entrances Act, which penalizes "the use of force, threats of force, physical obstruction, or property damage" aimed at women seeking abortions or doctors providing them. The ACLU maintains that the act in no way violates the First Amendment, since the Constitution has never provided protection or immunity for those carrying out criminal acts of violence as a form of protest. For the ACLU the difference between violent and nonviolent protest is key. It also contends that a woman's right to determine whether and when she has a child, and to seek out an abortion if she so chooses, is common law—a part of her constitutional right to the "enjoyment of life, liberty, and privacy." As such, it is unconstitutional for protesters to seek to prevent her exercising this right.

FURTHER INFORMATION:

Books:

Bader, Eleanor J. and Patricia Baird-Windle, *Targets of Hatred: Anti-Abortion Terrorism*. Basingstoke, Hampshire: Palgrave Macmillan, 2001.

Reiter, Jerry, *Live From the Gates of Hell: An Insider's Look at the Anti-Abortion Movement*. Amherst, New York: Prometheus Books, 2000.

Useful websites:

members.aol.com/abtrbng/
Abortion law homepage.
www-cse.stanford.edu/classes/cs201/projects/
nuremberg-files/
Stanford project discussing the Nuremberg files.
my.execpc.com/~awallace/choice1.htm
Prochoice links

The following debates in the Pro/Con series may also be of interest:

In this volume:

Topic 10 Should the government be able to prohibit hate speech?

Topic 15 Is Internet surveillance constitutional?

In *Arts and Culture*:

Topic 15 Should artists be held responsible for the effects of their work?

IS THE RIGHT TO VIOLENT PROTEST PROTECTED BY THE CONSTITUTION?

YES: Doctors have a right to carry out their work without fear or intimidation; women have a right to choose when and whether to have a child

RIGHTS OF OTHERS
Does violent protest undermine other people's constitutional rights?

NO: In some circumstances the rights of others should be overruled, for example, when attempting to protect an unborn child's right to life

YES: The constitutional right to freedom of political speech is paramount even if it later inspires some unrelated third party to act violently

FREE SPEECH
Is the right to freedom of speech paramount, even when it may lead to violence?

NO: Incitement of racial, religious, or political violence is not protected by the Constitution; free speech should not be protected when this is its intention

IS THE RIGHT TO VIOLENT PROTEST PROTECTED BY THE CONSTITUTION?
KEY POINTS

YES: Sometimes it is not possible to draw attention to a grievance or to bring about change without resorting to forceful means

YES: If the government or police are themselves acting unconstitutionally, protesters have little choice but to respond by using force

JUSTIFICATION
Can violent protest ever be justified?

NO: Resorting to violence only detracts from real issues, weakening public and media support for protesters

NO: The Constitution explicitly states its protection of "peaceable assembly," so violent protest cannot be justified under any circumstances

Topic 12
DOES THE CONSTITUTION PROTECT PORNOGRAPHY?

YES
FROM "A CONVERSATION WITH NADINE STROSSEN
AUTHOR OF *DEFENDING PORNOGRAPHY: FREE SPEECH, SEX AND THE
FIGHT FOR WOMEN'S RIGHTS"*
HTTP://WWW.SEXUALITY.ORG/L/ACTIVISM/PORNOGRA.HTML
AMERICAN CIVIL LIBERTIES UNION

NO
FROM THE "INTRODUCTION"
PORNOGRAPHY: MEN POSSESSING WOMEN
ANDREA DWORKIN

INTRODUCTION

Is the right to produce and supply pornography (defined in the quotation opposite) protected by the Constitution? Or should the government be able to censor—in other words, suppress—pornographic material in the interests of the public? This is an especially controversial issue now that the Internet has become such a powerful means of making pornography readily available to so many.

The First Amendment of the Constitution (see page 24) states that "Congress shall make no law … abridging the freedom of speech or of the press…." (The clause is generally agreed to apply to images as well as the spoken and written word.) Some people might argue that, according to the strict wording, absolutely all forms of expression, irrespective of whether society approves of them, are therefore constitutionally protected.

Many people believe, however, that not *everything* should be protected by the First Amendment. For example, few would disagree with the Supreme Court's view that child pornography should be excluded. In this instance the need to shield minors from sexual abuse is clearly much more important than the need to uphold absolute freedom of speech. Yet, the Supreme Court has also held that material deemed "obscene" is also not protected by the First Amendment. This has proved much more controversial because of the difficulty in determining what actually constitutes obscenity. Relatively little material has therefore been categorized as legally obscene.

One test often invoked is that of "literary, artistic, political, or scientific value." Opponents of pornography argue that depictions of sex that have none of these values are obscene and therefore not protected. But others point out that judgments of this kind are subjective and depend on cultural values that change with time and place. Several now celebrated works of art, literature, and film—including James Joyce's landmark 1922 novel *Ulysses*—were initially banned because of their alleged pornographic content.

Many people thus acknowledge that censoring obscenity on the basis of judgments about value will inevitably result in censoring art, which they believe would be regrettable.

"Pornography...
1. the depiction of erotic behavior (as in pictures or writing) intended to cause sexual excitement."
—MERRIAM-WEBSTER'S COLLEGIATE DICTIONARY

Another consideration, people often argue, is that access to important information about health issues, such as birth control and sexually transmitted diseases, might be blocked if the obscenity laws were thoroughly and vigorously enforced.

Despite these concerns, some opponents argue that pornography should be outlawed on the grounds that everybody—but especially women—ought to be protected from the harm caused by it. Others claim that adults, unlike children, do not need such protection and can make informed decisions of their own about what is or is not harmful.

Supporters of censorship include the religious right and some, but not all, feminists. Many claim that rising sex-crime rates, including child abuse, are linked to the increasing availability of pornographic material and ask why the Constitution should protect anything that incites sexual crime. Many people further claim that pornography necessarily involves the subordination, humiliation, and exploitation of women, and that it is they who need to be protected from its debasing effects.

Others, though—and feminists are also among them—insist that censorship violates civil liberties. They point out the difficulty of proving that pornography leads to violence and argue that it is not justifiable to encroach on civil liberties on that basis. They also argue that though pornography, like many jobs, can involve exploitation, many women also participate in it voluntarily. To prevent them from exercising their right to choose to produce pornography—which is a legitimate expression of human sexual behavior—would be to treat them as less than adults and to stifle their freedom of expression.

Pornography is an issue that has greatly divided feminists, and the following opposing articles are both by women's rights campaigners. In the first article Nadine Strossen of the American Civil Liberties Union (ACLU) defends pornography on the grounds of freedom of expression. She thinks censorship laws risk "punishing the very individuals and ideas they are supposed to protect." In the second article feminist Andrea Dworkin argues for a change in the law to protect women whose freedom, she believes, is in fact being jeopardized by the First Amendment.

A CONVERSATION WITH NADINE STROSSEN ...
American Civil Liberties Union

YES

Q: Why did you write this book now?

A: As a human rights advocate, I find myself increasingly concerned about the growing influence of the feminist pro-censorship movement, led by law professor Catharine Mackinnon and writer Andrea Dworkin. This movement has had a devastating impact on many human rights—not only free speech, but women's rights, reproductive freedom, and lesbian and gay rights. Its influence is especially apparent on college and law school campuses nationwide, leading to a series of unfortunate incidents in which feminist students and professors have been instrumental in censoring speech and works of art, including works by women, which they have labelled "pornographic."

I am also disturbed by the aftermath of the Canadian Supreme Court's 1992 decision to incorporate the "MacDworkinite" concept of pornography into that country's obscenity law. Since that ruling, more than half of all feminist bookstores in Canada have had materials confiscated or detained by Customs. Lesbian and gay writers and bookstores have also been hard hit. American women, as well as the broader public, need to know that these laws end up punishing the very individuals and ideas they are supposed to protect.

Q: What is the MacDworkinite definition of pornography?

A: Basically, the MacDworkinites argue that pornography is "the sexually explicit subordination of women through pictures and/or words." The problem, of course, is that this definition can sweep in everything from religious imagery to film footage about the mass rapes in the Balkans to self-help books about women's health and sexuality. In Canada, Customs officials concluded that two of Andrea Dworkin's own books were pornographic under her own definition, and therefore seized the books at the U.S.–Canadian border.

Q: Why did you choose the title, "Defending Pornography"? Isn't this really a book about free speech and women's rights?

MacKinnon (1946–) and Dworkin (1946–) have fought since the 1970s to outlaw pornography in the name of women's rights.

The Canadian Supreme Court ruled that obscenity should be defined as that which harms women, not that which offends against taste.

During the 1990s wars in Yugoslavia many rapes and other war crimes were reported.

See www.nostatusquo. com/ACLU/dworkin/ OrdinanceCanada. html for Dworkin and Mackinnon's response to these allegations.

A: The fact that the title is so provocative shows how influential both pro-censorship feminists and their right-wing allies have been in demonizing the word "pornography" and the sexual expression to which it refers according to its dictionary definition. I don't think a book title such as "Defending Sexually Explicit Expression" would be particularly provocative, but "Defending Pornography" has a different connotation precisely because pro-censorship forces have turned the term "pornography" into an epithet, much the way "communist" was during the McCarthy era.

Many people use the term "pornography" to stigmatize whatever sexually oriented expression they dislike. Similarly, legal powers to restrict sexual expression are always used to suppress speech on behalf of relatively unpopular ideas and groups. Thus, throughout history, laws against "obscenity" (the legal term for sexual expression that the Supreme Court now deems to lack constitutional protection) have always been used to stifle feminist speech, information about contraception and abortion, and lesbian and gay writing and art.

I defend pornography against all efforts to suppress it— including in the name of feminism—because those efforts are so damaging to women's rights....

In the late 1940s and early 1950s Cold War paranoia fueled fears of communism in the United States. Between 1952 and 1954 Senator Joseph McCarthy (1908–1957) chaired hearings that investigated those suspected— often on little evidence—of being communists.

Q: You argue in your book that the First Amendment has furthered the struggle for women's rights. Can you give examples?

A: The guiding principles of the First Amendment—freedom of speech, press, and association—have historically benefitted civil rights struggles, whether of women, African Americans or lesbians and gay men. From the sit-ins and picket lines of the Civil Rights Movement of the 1960's to the pro-choice and gay rights demonstrations of today, the First Amendment, as the Supreme Court now interprets it, guarantees freedom from government repression of unpopular images and ideas. This was not always so. During the first women's rights movement at the turn of the century, Margaret Sanger, Emma Goldman, and others were repeatedly arrested and charged with "obscenity" for giving birth control information to poor women.

Ironically, the current feminist anti-pornography movement depends on free speech rights including the right to display pornographic pictures on sidewalks and in other public places. These feminists have effectively used their First Amendment rights to raise public consciousness about the serious problems of violence and discrimination against

For more about the First Amendment see page 24.

Margaret Sanger (1883–1966) founded the American Birth Control League in 1921. Radical political activist Emma Goldman (1869–1940) campaigned for women's rights, including birth control.

women. Therefore, they themselves demonstrate the wisdom of our constitutional principle that the appropriate response to any speech you disagree with or that offends you is not to censor it but rather, to answer it. More speech, not less, is the solution.

See www.aclu.org/issues/women/nadine.html for more about the ACLU's fight for women's rights.

Q: You are the President of the ACLU. Where does the ACLU stand on these issues?
A: Ever since its founding 75 years ago, the ACLU has battled the forces of repression and upheld all fundamental rights for all members of American society. We neutrally defend all rights because experience shows that they are indivisible; if the government gets the power to suppress one right for one person, then no right is secure for any person. That's why the pro-censorship feminists are so wrong when they argue that we have to choose between free speech and gender equality. Nothing could be further from the truth! Women, along with everyone else in our society, are entitled to both free speech and equality, and it hardly advances the women's rights cause to say we can have only one, but not both. Moreover, history shows that we can't have one without the other— that without free speech, women will never enjoy political equality or reproductive freedom.

This mutually reinforcing relationship has been clear in many ACLU cases. In our earliest years we defended Margaret Sanger and other pioneering birth control advocates when they were prosecuted under anti-obscenity laws. More recently, we brought a lawsuit challenging the "gag rule" all the way to the Supreme Court, arguing that the bar on information about abortion at federally funded family planning clinics violated women's reproductive rights and free speech rights.

So-called "gag rules" restrict the activities, including counseling, of family-planning services funded by the government.

I'm especially proud of the ACLU's landmark work and achievements on behalf of women's rights. Under the leadership of Ruth Bader Ginsberg, the founding director of our Women's Rights Project, we won many important cases securing women's constitutional equality rights and that work continues today through such historic cases as *Faulkner v. Jones*, in which we are representing Shannon Faulkner in her challenge to the exclusion of women from The Citadel, a taxpayer-funded military school in South Carolina. I am also proud of the ACLU's leading work on behalf of lesbians and gay men. We handle more cases in this area than any other organization.

Ruth Bader Ginsberg (1933–) founded the project in 1972. She is now a Supreme Court justice.

See http://leon.law.harvard.edu/vaw00/Faulkner.html for more about this case.

And the ACLU has always been the preeminent defender of free speech rights for all unpopular expression, including sexual expression. ACLU lawyers have played a major role in defending the victims of today's pornophobia—writers, artists, filmmakers, and others whose work has been censored because it deals with sexual themes. Many of these censorship victims are women and gay people, who have explored issues of feminism and homoeroticism. Again, the interrelationship of all rights, and the importance of the ACLU's unique commitment to defending all of them, is reaffirmed.

> Do you think Strossen is justified in using the term "pornophobia" to describe concerns about obscenity?

Q: Some have said that your attacks on MacKinnon and Dworkin are personal. Why have you focused so much of your book on what they have said and written?
A: I make no personal attacks on MacKinnon and Dworkin. Rather than criticizing them as persons, I criticize their ideas. I do so because, as I previously noted, their ideas have been so influential. In fact, too many people seem to think that Dworkin and MacKinnon speak for all women, or all feminists, on pornography and censorship. This is absolutely wrong, but the feminist anti-censorship movement has not gotten nearly as much media attention. To correct this imbalance, and the resulting misperception, my book quotes extensively from the many women, in all walks of life, who have powerfully explained why censoring pornography would do more harm than good to the crucially important causes of women's safety and equality. My book focuses far more on what other women have said and written, in response to MacKinnon and Dworkin, than it does on what MacKinnon and Dworkin themselves have said and written....

> Is the feminist anticensorship movement under-represented in the media, as Strossen claims? If so, why might that be?

INTRODUCTION, *PORNOGRAPHY: MEN POSSESSING WOMEN*
Andrea Dworkin

I did not hesitate to let it be known of me, that the white man who expected to succeed in whipping, must also succeed in killing me.
—Frederick Douglass, *Narrative of the Life of Frederick Douglass, An American Slave: Written by Himself*

> Frederick Douglass (1817–1895) published his autobiography in 1845.

In 1838, at the age of 21, Frederick Douglass became a runaway slave, a hunted fugitive. Though later renowned as a powerful political orator, he spoke his first public words with trepidation at an abolitionist meeting-—a meeting of white people-—in Massachusetts in 1841. Abolitionist leader William Lloyd Garrison recalled the event:

> "Abolitionists" were those who campaigned to abolish slavery in the 19th century.

> *He came forward to the platform with a hesitancy and embarrassment, necessarily the attendants of a sensitive mind in such a novel position. After apologizing for his ignorance, and reminding the audience that slavery was a poor school for the human intellect and heart, he proceeded to narrate some of the facts in his own history as a slave. …*
> *As soon as he had taken his seat, filled with hope and admiration, I rose … [and] reminded the audience of the peril which surrounded this self-emancipated young man at the North—even in Massachusetts, on the soil of the Pilgrim Fathers, among the descendants of revolutionary sires; and I appealed to them, whether they would ever allow him to be carried back into slavery—law or no law, constitution or no constitution.*

> John Brown (1800–1859) was tried and hanged in 1859 after trying to free Southern slaves by means of armed intervention. Elizabeth Cady Stanton (1815–1902) campaigned for women's suffrage and called for the first U.S. women's rights convention at Seneca Falls in 1848.

Always in danger as a fugitive, Douglass became an organizer for the abolitionists; the editor of his own newspaper, which advocated both abolition and women's rights; a station chief for the underground railroad; a close comrade of John Brown's; and the only person willing, at the Seneca Falls Convention in 1848, to second Elizabeth Cady Stanton's resolution demanding the vote for women. To me, he has been a political hero: someone whose passion for human rights was both visionary and rooted in action; whose risk was real, not rhetorical; whose endurance in pursuing equality set a standard for political honor. In his writings, which were as eloquent as his orations, his repudiation of subjugation was uncompromising. His political intelligence, which was both analytical and strategic, was suffused with emotion: indignation at human pain, grief at degradation, anguish over suffering, fury at apathy and collusion. He hated oppression. He had an empathy for those hurt by inequality that crossed lines of race, gender, and class because it was an empathy animated by his own experience—his own experience of humiliation and his own experience of dignity.

> Why do you feel Dworkin focuses so much on Frederick Douglass?

Taking freedom seriously

To put it simply, Frederick Douglass was a serious man—a man serious in the pursuit of freedom. Well, you see the problem. Surely it is self-evident. What can any such thing have to do with us—with women in our time? Imagine—in present time—a woman saying, and meaning, that a man who expected to succeed in whipping, must also succeed in killing her. Suppose there were a politics of liberation premised on that assertion—an assertion not of ideology but of deep and stubborn outrage at being misused, a resolute assertion, a serious assertion by serious women. What are serious women; are there any; isn't seriousness about freedom by women for women grotesquely comic; we don't want to be laughed at, do we? What would this politics of liberation be like? Where would we find it? What would we have to do? Would we have to do something other than dress for success? Would we have to stop the people who are hurting us from hurting us? Not debate them; stop them. Would we have to stop slavery? Not discuss it; stop it. Would we have to stop pretending that our rights are protected in this society? Would we have to be so grandiose, so arrogant, so unfeminine, as to believe that the streets we walk on, the homes we live in, the beds we sleep in, are ours—belong to us—really belong to us: we decide what is right and what is wrong and if something hurts us, it stops. It is, of course, gauche to be too sincere about these things, and it is downright ridiculous to be serious. Intelligent people are well mannered and moderate, even in pursuing freedom. Smart women whisper and say please.

> What effect does Dworkin create by asking so many questions?

Now imagine Cherry Tart or Bunny or Pet or Beaver saying, and meaning, that a man who expected to succeed in whipping must also succeed in killing her. She says it; she means it. It is not a pornographic scenario in which she is the dummy forced by the pimp-ventriloquist to say the ubiquitous *No-That-Means-Yes*. It is not the usual sexual provocation created by pornographers using a woman's body, the subtext of which is: I refuse to be whipped so whip me harder, whip me more; I refuse to be whipped, what I really want is for you to kill me; whip me, then kill me; kill me, then whip me; whatever you want, however you want it—was it good for you? Instead, the piece on the page or in the film steps down and steps out: I'm real, she says. Like Frederick Douglass, she will be hesitant and embarrassed. She will feel ignorant. She will tell a first-person story about her own experience in prostitution, in pornography, as a victim of incest, as a victim of rape, as someone who has been beaten or tortured, as someone who has been bought and sold. She may not remind her audience that sexual servitude is a poor school for the human intellect and heart—sexually violated, often since childhood, she may not know the value of her human intellect or her human heart—and the audience cannot be counted on to know that she deserved better than she got. Will there be someone there to implore the audience to help her escape the pornography—law or no law, constitution or no constitution; will the audience understand that as long as the pornography of her exists she is a captive of it, a fugitive from it? Will the audience be willing to fight for her freedom by fighting against the pornography of her, because, as Linda Marchiano said of *Deep Throat*, "every time someone watches that film, they are watching me being raped"? Will the audience understand that she is standing in for those who didn't get away; will the audience understand that those who didn't get away were someone—each one was someone? Will the audience understand what stepping down from the page or out of the film cost her—what it took for her to survive, for her to escape, for her to dare to speak now about what happened to her then?

> *"I'm an incest survivor, ex-pornography model, and ex-prostitute," the woman says. "My incest story begins before preschool and ends many years later—this was with my father. I was also molested by an uncle and a minister ... my father forced me to perform sexual acts with men at a stag party when I was a teenager. ... My father was my pimp in pornography. There were three occasions from ages nine to sixteen when he forced me to be a pornography model ... in Nebraska, so, yes, it does happen here."*

Has Dworkin convinced you of the comparison between Douglass and women who work in pornography? Is her comparison effective?

Under the name Linda Lovelace Linda Marchiano (1949–2002) made the infamous porn movie Deep Throat in 1972. She later became an active campaigner against pornography.

I was thirteen when I was forced into prostitution and pornography, the woman says. I was drugged, raped, gang-raped, imprisoned, beaten, sold from one pimp to another, photographed by pimps, photographed by tricks; I was used in pornography and they used pornography on me; "[t]hey knew a child's face when they looked into it. It was clear that I was not acting of my own free will. I was always covered with welts and bruises. … It was even clearer that I was sexually inexperienced. I literally didn't know what to do. So they showed me pornography to teach me about sex and then they would ignore my tears as they positioned my body like the women in the pictures and used me."

"As I speak about pornography, here, today," the woman says, "I am talking about my life." I was raped by my uncle when I was ten, by my stepbrother and stepfather by the time I was twelve. My stepbrother was making pornography of me by the time I was fourteen. "I was not even sixteen years old and my life reality consisted of sucking cocks, posing nude, performing sexual acts and actively being repeatedly raped."

> *Dworkin never specifies that these are the words of a real woman. Do you think they are, or might they be Dworkin creating a character? Would that make a difference in how you treated her argument?*

Serious women

These are the women in the pictures; they have stepped out, though the pictures may still exist. They have become very serious women; serious in the pursuit of freedom. There are many thousands of them in the United States, not all first put in pornography as children though most were sexually molested as children, raped or otherwise abused again later, eventually becoming homeless and poor. They are feminists in the antipornography movement, and they don't want to debate "free speech." Like Frederick Douglass, they are fugitives from the men who made a profit off of them. They live in jeopardy, always more or less in hiding. They organize to help others escape. They write—in blood, their own. They publish sometimes, including their own newsletters. They demonstrate; they resist; they disappear when the danger gets too close. The Constitution has nothing for them —no help, no protection, no dignity, no solace, no justice. The law has nothing for them—no recognition of the injuries done them by pornography, no reparations for what has been taken from them. They are real, and even though this society will do nothing for them, they are women who have resolved that the man who expects to succeed in whipping must also succeed in killing them. This changes the nature of the women's movement. It must stop slavery. The runaway slave is now part of it.…

> *Dworkin implies that free speech is not the most important factor in this debate. Do you agree?*

> *Is Dworkin justified in saying that the Constitution has nothing to offer the women she describes?*

Summary

Nadine Strossen argues that because it is not always easy to decide what is or is not pornographic, censorship of pornography will likely mean censorship of sexually explicit materials that are beneficial to women's rights, including art and information about health issues. She argues that terms like "obscenity" and "pornography" are often used too widely, and—as in Margaret Sanger's campaign for access to birth control—sometimes work against women's interests. For women as for men, she argues, the freedom of speech protected by the First Amendment is the best weapon against oppression.

Andrea Dworkin, on the other hand, argues that the First Amendment merely allows pornographers to prey on the vulnerability of women. Explicitly comparing pornography with slavery, Dworkin holds up escaped slave Frederick Douglass as an example to women of successful resistance to oppression. She cites the personal testimonies of women determined to speak out against the abuse they have suffered through their involvement in pornography and urges others to do the same. She argues that the Constitution, in its present form, does not do enough to protect women.

FURTHER INFORMATION:

Books:

Assiter, Alison, *Bad Girls and Dirty Pictures: The Challenge to Reclaim Feminism.* London: Pluto Press, 1993.

Cornell, Drucilla (ed.), *Feminism and Pornography.* New York: Oxford University Press, 2000.

Gibson, Pamela Church, and Rosa Gibson (eds.), *Dirty Looks: Women, Pornography, Power.* London: British Film Institute, 1993.

Itzin, Catherine (ed.), *Pornography: Women, Violence, and Civil Liberties: A Radical New View.* New York: Oxford University Press, 1993.

Kappeler, Susanne, *The Pornography of Representation.* Cambridge, UK: Polity Press, 1986.

MacKinnon, Catharine A., and Andrea Dworkin (eds.), *In Harm's Way: The Pornography Civil Rights Hearings.* Cambridge, MA: Harvard University Press, 1998.

MacKinnon, Catharine A., and Andrea Dworkin, *Pornography and Civil Rights: A New Day for Women's Equality.* Minneapolis, MN: Organizing Against Pornography, 1988.

Strossen, Nadine, *Defending Pornography: Free Speech, Sex, and the Fight for Women's Rights.* New York: New York University Press, 2000.

Useful websites:

www.aclu.org
American Civil Liberties Union site.

www.ifeminists.com
Individualist Feminists site, including search tool and links to useful essays and articles on women's rights issues.

www.nostatusquo.com/ACLU/dworkin/OnlineLibrary.html
Andrea Dworkin's online archive of articles.

www.obscenitycrimes.org
Educational site about fighting obscenity on the Internet, with section on pornography and the First Amendment.

www.zetetics.com/mac/topics.html
Propornography article by feminist writer Wendy McElroy.

The following debates in the Pro/Con series may also be of interest:

In *Individual and Society:*

Topic 3: Are women still the second sex?

Topic 15: Is abortion a right?

DOES THE CONSTITUTION PROTECT PORNOGRAPHY?

YES: First Amendment protections should not be applied selectively but should protect free speech of every kind, however distasteful

YES: There is no proof that the consumption of pornography makes anybody more likely to commit sexual crimes

FIRST AMENDMENT
Is the constitutional protection of free speech of paramount concern?

CRIME
If pornography is protected, can sexual crimes be kept in check?

NO: The First Amendment was not intended to protect the production of material that is obviously harmful—such as child pornography

NO: Pornography corrupts those who use it and makes them more likely to commit rape or child abuse

DOES THE CONSTITUTION PROTECT PORNOGRAPHY? KEY POINTS

YES: If pornography is censored, information that is beneficial to women—about birth control and sexually transmitted diseases, for example—may be censored as well

YES: Women are not forced to work in pornography, which is often a legitimate expression of human sexual behavior, and they can make their own decisions about how they use their bodies

WOMEN'S RIGHTS
Are women's rights best served by protecting pornography against censorship?

NO: Making pornography illegal is the best way to protect women from the abuses of pornographers and the harmful effects pornography has on society

NO: Women may be left with little or no choice but to work in pornography, where they are exploited and dehumanized. It's they who need protecting, not the pornographers.

NERVES AND PUBLIC SPEAKING

Anxiety is a natural human emotion with which most people are familiar. The physical effects of nervousness, such as blushing, trembling, and sweating, can be distressing. But nerves can also have a positive effect on performance because they produce adrenaline, which sharpens reflexes and heightens energy. The guidelines below will help you overcome any fear you may have of speaking in public and enable you to channel the adrenaline for your own benefit. You may also find these guidelines useful in everyday situations. Preparation, relaxation, and delivery are all key to overcoming anxiety.

PREPARATION   How to make a confident, informative presentation.
RELAXATION   How to reduce the physical effects of nervousness.
DELIVERY   How to turn nervous energy into positive energy.

Preparation
a. Know your material: You will feel more confident speaking about a topic you have thoroughly researched.
b. Anticipate questions: Make a list of possible questions or points that might be discussed. Write your responses on cue cards.
c. Organize notes: Decide whether you will be reading from a manuscript or from cue cards. Check that your material is in order.
d. Practice: It is invaluable to practice your presentation. Ask peers, family, and colleagues for positive criticism and suggestions.

Relaxation
a. Get a good nights sleep: You should feel refreshed and energetic before your presentation.
b. Warm up excercises: Shrug your shoulders up to your ears, then drop them down; turn your head slowly from left to right, and repeat; drop your chin to touch your chest, and then look up to relieve tension in the neck area.
c. Breathing: Make sure you breathe deeply before you begin your speech to help fill your lungs and steady your voice.

Delivery
a. Eye contact: Find a friendly face in the audience to help reassure you.
b. Adrenaline: You will experience a natural energy from the adrenaline; it will help you sound enthusiastic and lively when speaking.
c. Speech: Speak clearly; do not talk too quickly; change your pitch and tone by putting feeling into your speech. If your mouth becomes dry, sip tepid water to ease the discomfort.
d. Body language: Avoid crossing your arms, fiddling with pieces of paper or clothing, pacing the stage, or large, unnecessary gestures. Move naturally, use controlled gestures to make specific points, and stand confidently with your shoulders back.

PRACTICAL CHECKLIST

Arrive early   Give yourself plenty of time to prepare your
                          presentation. You will be anxious if you arrive late.

Prepare the room   Familiarize yourself with the room. Are the seating,
                          lighting, and audio facilities suitable?

Check equipment   All equipment should be checked before you begin your
                          speech. Be prepared for technical problems. If you are
                          using visual aids such as overhead projectors or
                          PowerPoint, consider preparing handouts in case
                          technical difficulties arise.

Quick rehearsal   A run-through of your presentation may help build
                          your confidence. Check the pace of your speech, and
                          remember to make eye contact.

Know your audience   You will benefit from meeting your audience
                          beforehand. It is easier to talk to people you have met
                          than strangers.

POINTS TO REMEMBER

The key to dealing with nerves is good preparation. Being well prepared will make you more confident with your material. It will not, however, dispel all your anxiety. Here are some points to remember.

Do
- Smile. Look relaxed, and your audience will believe you. Only you know how you are feeling.
- Remember that people want you to do well.
- Visualize yourself making the speech successfully.
- Concentrate on the message you want to communicate. That is all you should be focusing on.

Don't
- Apologize for your nerves. There is no need to highlight what may not be noticeable to your audience.
- Worry about mistakes. Continue your presentation regardless.
- Be negative. It is a valuable experience, whatever the outcome.
- Rush through your presentation. You will be more likely to make mistakes.

Topic 13

IS THE MILITARY DRAFT CONSTITUTIONAL?

YES

FROM *ARVER V. U.S.*, 245 U.S. 366 (1918)
HTTP://CASELAW.LP.FINDLAW.COM/SCRIPTS/GETCASE.PL?NAVBY=CASE&COURT=
US&VOL=245&INVOL=366, THE OPINION OF THE COURT
JUSTICE EDWARD DOUGLASS WHITE

NO

"THE MILITARY DRAFT AND SLAVERY"
COUNTERPUNCH, MARCH 24–30, 2002
REP. RON PAUL

INTRODUCTION

The military draft, also known as conscription, is the compulsory enrollment by the national government of people, usually young men, into military service. It is used to meet the occasional need for extra personnel, in addition to full-time professionals (regulars), especially in wartime. It also has the advantage of providing additional manpower at low cost: Conscripts are paid less than regulars.

The United States has adopted the draft at various times in its history. The draft's supporters claim it is an essential mechanism for use in times of war. Yet its critics argue that it is unconstitutional and a threat to civil rights.

Early American colonial laws required all adult males to do military service, but the practice had waned by the time of the American Revolution (1775–1783). For this war the revolutionary army introduced a short-term draft. Later, during the American Civil War

(1861–1865) both sides employed limited conscription, but it was more effective in the Confederacy than in the Union, where the Draft Act of 1863 met widespread resistance from northerners who wanted no part in the conflict.

The first successful conscription policy, the World War I Selective Service Act of 1917, chose some youths to meet the national military draft quota, but exempted others (reserved manpower) who were working in essential services and production. (The unfit have always been exempt.) There was also selective conscription after 1940 in World War II (1939–1945) and again during the Vietnam War (1964–1975).

Since the draft was first introduced, the United States has undergone major changes, which some people think have rendered any form of conscription redundant. First, the population is now much larger than before, and there are more people who voluntarily take up a military career. Second, modern weaponry is now highly sophisticated and needs skilled operators rather than manual laborers. Critics also object that the draft weakens the armed forces by causing rivalries between conscripts and volunteers that undermine cohesiveness—a vital element of an effective military organization. They argue that it is of no benefit to the military to draft people who do not want to serve and who spend their whole time in uniform looking for the first available way out of it.

> *"In this country, [a draft to the militia] ever was the most unpopular and impractical thing that could be attempted. Our people ... had learnt to consider it as the last of all oppressions."*
>
> —THOMAS JEFFERSON (1743–1826),
>
> THIRD PRESIDENT

However, the military draft is still an option available to the government. Although it was suspended in 1973, when the United States began to withdraw from Vietnam, it was revived in 1980, when young men were again registered for possible future conscription. (At the same time, Congress ruled against conscription for women.) Since the terrorist attacks of September 11, 2001, there have been fresh calls to reactivate the draft.

Yet despite the draft's long history in the United States, the Constitution is unclear about its desirability. No court has ruled the draft to be illegal, yet many people have questioned whether the government has the proper authority to enforce it. Those who think that it has see the possibility of conscription as a necessary condition of citizenship: Fighting for the nation is the price we may have to pay for living in a free country. Others think that compulsory military service contradicts the guarantees of individual liberty enshrined by the Constitution. They cite the Thirteenth Amendment, which states that "neither slavery nor involuntary servitude" shall exist in the United States, and believe that the government should not force a citizen to work for it. They believe that federal authority may only be allowed to call up an army when its citizens support its aims and are willing to do their duty. The author of the second article claims that conscription is more suited to a totalitarian country, such as Afghanistan under the Taliban, than to a democracy.

Opponents of the draft further maintain that the Constitution regards every American as primarily a citizen of his or her state, and that citizenship of the United States as a whole is a secondary consideration. Yet advocates of the draft insist that Congress is rightly empowered to have supremacy over every component state of the Union and all the inhabitants thereof. To maintain that position, it must be entitled to raise armies. That is one of the main points highlighted in the first of the following articles.

Given the Constitution's lack of clarity on this point, it is no surprise that the issue should have divided American opinion since the Declaration of Independence. The following articles argue both the pro and con viewpoints.

ARVER V. U.S.
Justice Edward Douglass White

YES

The possession of authority to enact the statute must be found in the clauses of the Constitution giving Congress power "to declare war; ... to raise and support armies, but no appropriation of money to that use shall be for a longer term than two years; ... to make rules for the government and regulation of the land and naval forces." And of course the powers conferred by these provisions, like all other powers given, carry with them as provided by the Constitution the authority "to make all laws which shall be necessary and proper for carrying into execution the foregoing powers."

> *The two quotes in this paragraph are both from Article I, Section 8 of the Constitution.*

An army without men

As the mind cannot conceive an army without the men to compose it, on the face of the Constitution the objection that it does not give power to provide for such men would seem to be too frivolous for further notice. It is said, however, that since under the Constitution as originally framed state citizenship was primary and United States citizenship but derivative and dependent thereon, therefore the power conferred upon Congress to raise armies was only coterminous with United States citizenship, and could not be exerted so as to cause that citizenship to lose its dependent character and dominate state citizenship. But the proposition simply denies to Congress the power to raise armies which the Constitution gives. That power by the very terms of the Constitution, being delegated, is supreme. In truth the contention simply assails the wisdom of the Framers of the Constitution in conferring authority on Congress and in not retaining it as it was under the Confederation in the several states.

> *Article VI of the Constitution says that it is the duty of all federal and state officers to support the Constitution, the supreme law of the land.*

Further it is said, the right to provide is not denied by calling for volunteer enlistments, but it does not and cannot include the power to exact enforced military duty by the citizen. This however ... challenges the existence of all power, for a governmental power which has no sanction to it and which therefore can only be exercised provided the citizen consents to its exertion is in no substantial sense a power. It is argued, however, that although this is abstractly true, it is not concretely so because as compelled military service is repugnant to a free government and in conflict with all the great guarantees of the Constitution as to individual liberty, it must be assumed that the authority to raise armies was intended to be limited to the right to call an army into existence, counting alone upon the willingness of the citizen to do his duty in time of public need, that is, in time of war. But the premise of this proposition is so devoid of foundation that it leaves not even a shadow of ground upon which to base the conclusion.

Conflict and the draft

In that year [1861] when the mutterings of the dread conflict which was to come began to be heard, and the proclamation of the President calling a force into existence was issued, it was addressed to the body organized out of the militia and trained by the states in accordance with the previous acts of Congress.... That force being inadequate to meet the situation, an act was passed authorizing the acceptance of 500,000 volunteers by the President to be by him organized into a national army (Act of July 22, 1861).

For the full transcript of the proclamation of President Abraham Lincoln, made on April 15, 1861, go to http://pub76. ezboard.com/ ftheanglecivilwar frm57.showMessage ?topicID=17.topic.

This was soon followed by another act increasing the force of the militia to be organized by the states for the purpose of being drawn upon when trained under the direction of Congress (Act of July 29, 1861), the two acts when considered together presenting in the clearest possible form the distinction between the power of Congress to raise armies and its authority under the militia clause. But it soon became manifest that more men were required. As a result the Act of March 3, 1863, was adopted entitled "An act for enrolling and calling out the national forces and for other purposes."

This act, also known as the Conscription Act, marked the first time that the draft was enacted.

By that act, which was clearly intended to directly exert upon all the citizens of the United States the national power which it had been proposed to exert in 1814, on the recommendation of the then Secretary of War, Mr. Monroe, every male citizen of the United States between the ages of 20 and 45 was made subject by the direct action of Congress to be called by compulsory draft to service in a national army at such time and in such numbers as the President in his discretion might find necessary. In that act, as in the one of 1814, and in this one, the means by which the act was to be enforced were directly federal and the force to be raised as a result of the draft was therefore typically national as distinct from the call into active service of the militia as such. And under the power thus exerted, four separate calls for draft were made by the President and enforced, that of July, 1863, of February and March, 1864, of July and December, 1864,

COMMENTARY: The draft

The military draft has operated on and off in the United States since 1863, when it was first used in the Civil War to enlarge military ranks. Since then it has developed into a system with specific rules, methods, and practices.

Most of the time the nation has enough troops to fulfill its military responsibilities using its body of volunteer soldiers, who receive certain benefits in exchange for their active service. If more soldiers are needed, a trained volunteer National Guard and volunteer reserve troops can also be called on to provide further assistance. There are times, however, when all these forces are still not considered adequate to meet the country's military needs. At such times the Selective Service System (SSS), created by the Selective Training and Service Act signed by President Franklin Roosevelt in 1940, is used to call up extra manpower. The role of the SSS is to oversee the provision of military backup by using the draft to fill vacancies that the nation has been unable to fill using voluntary personnel.

During peacetime the main task of the SSS is to keep a list of potential draftees. Generally this list includes all male residents between 18 and 25 years of age, except for those already involved in the military or excused for medical or psychiatric reasons, foreign citizens on valid student, visitor, or diplomatic visas, and prisoners. Those eligible for the draft must register within 30 days of reaching eligibility, either by mail, Internet, at a post office, or at a high-school Selective Service register. The SSS keeps all registered names and addresses on file so that they can be easily accessed if the draft is mobilized. Men eligible for the draft who do not register could be jailed for up to five years and fined up to $250,000.

To reactivate the draft, Congress must pass the necessary legislation, and the president must approve it. The SSS is informed of how many extra men are required and institutes a national draft lottery to determine an order in which eligible draftees would be enlisted, starting with all males who turned 20 in the year of the draft. Devised by the National Institute of Standards and Technology (NIST), the draft lottery is a random, impartial system based on numbers and birthdates. The SSS oversees the lottery draw and notifies by mail those draftees in the order of their birthdates. Those who receive induction notices must report to a regional military entrance processing station for physical, mental, psychological, and moral tests. They then have 10 days to file a claim for exemption, postponement, or deferment from the draft. Those eligible to make this claim must belong to one of the following groups: high-school or college students, religious ministers or students, men with dependents, government officials, aliens and dual nationals, and conscientious objectors. Each claim is judged on its own merits. Finally, if all eligible 20-year-olds have been drafted, and extra manpower is still needed, the SSS starts the same process with 21-year-olds to 25-year-olds, in succession, then with 19-year-olds, then 18-year-olds.

producing a force of about a quarter of a million men. It is undoubted that the men thus raised by draft were treated as subject to direct national authority and were used either in filling the gaps occasioned by the vicissitudes of war in the ranks of the existing national forces, or for the purpose of organizing such new units as were deemed to be required. It would be childish to deny the value of the added strength which was thus afforded.

Indeed in the official report of the Provost Marshal General ... it was stated that it was the efficient aid resulting from the forces created by the draft at a very critical moment of the civil strife which obviated a disaster which seemed impending and carried that struggle to a complete and successful conclusion. Thus sanctioned as is the act before us by the text of the Constitution, and by its significance as read in the light of the fundamental principles with which the subject is concerned, by the power recognized and carried into effect in many civilized countries, by the authority and practice of the colonies before the Revolution, of the states under the Confederation and of the government since the formation of the Constitution, the want of merit in the contentions that the act in the particulars which we have been previously called upon to consider was beyond the constitutional power of Congress, is manifest ... as we are unable to conceive upon what theory the exaction by government from the citizen of the performance of his supreme and noble duty of contributing to the defense of the rights and honor of the nation as the result of a war declared by the great representative body of the people can be said to be the imposition of involuntary servitude in violation of the prohibitions of the Thirteenth Amendment, we are constrained to the conclusion that the contention to that effect is refuted by its mere statement. Affirmed.

The position of provost marshal general in the Army was introduced during the Civil War and combined the role of a chief of police with that of a magistrate. It entailed such duties as preserving good order among the troops and disciplining stragglers and marauders. It gave the authority to make searches, seizures, and arrests of suspected offenders.

In the case of Arver v. U.S. Justice White affirms that the military draft is indeed supported by the Constitution.

THE MILITARY DRAFT AND SLAVERY
Rep. Ron Paul

This refers to September 11, 2001, when four passenger planes were hijacked by members of the Al Qaeda terrorist group, supported by Afghanistan's government, known as the Taliban. They were used to attack locations in the United States, including the World Trade Center in New York and the Pentagon in Washington, D.C.

NO

I rise to introduce legislation expressing the sense of Congress that the United States government should not revive military conscription. Supporters of conscription have taken advantage of the events of September 11 to renew efforts to reinstate the military draft. However, reviving the draft may actually weaken America's military. Furthermore, a military draft violates the very principles of individual liberty this country was founded upon. It is no exaggeration to state that military conscription is better suited for a totalitarian government, such as the recently dethroned Taliban regime, than a free society.

Since military conscription ended over 30 years ago, voluntary armed services have successfully fulfilled the military needs of the United States. The recent success of the military campaign in Afghanistan once again demonstrates the ability of the volunteer military to respond to threats to the lives, liberty, and property of the people of the United States.

Military weakened by the draft

A draft weakens the military by introducing tensions and rivalries between those who volunteer for military service and those who have been conscripted. This undermines the cohesiveness of military units, which is a vital element of military effectiveness. Conscripts also are unlikely to choose the military as a career; thus, a draft will do little to address problems with retention. With today's high-tech military, retention is the most important personnel issue and it seems counter-productive to adopt any policy that will not address this important issue.

Why do you think that the high-tech nature of current military procedures makes the retention of military personnel an important issue?

If conscription helps promote an effective military, then why did General Vladisova Putilin, Chief of the Russian General Staff, react to plans to end the military draft in Russia, by saying "This is the great dream of all servicemen, when our army will become completely professional...?"

Instead of reinstating a military draft, Congress should make military service attractive by finally living up to its responsibility to provide good benefits and pay to members of the armed forces and our nation's veterans. It is an outrage that American military personnel and veterans are given a

COMMENTARY: Daniel Webster

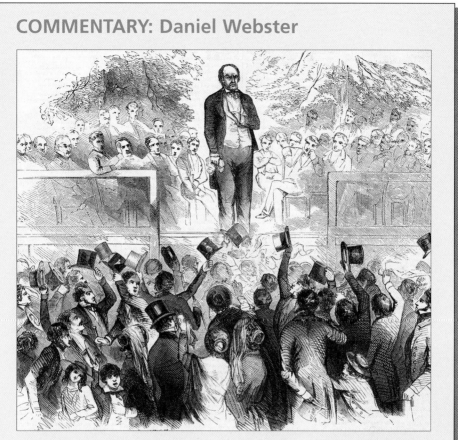

Daniel Webster gives one of his political speeches to a crowd on Boston Common.

Daniel Webster (1782–1852) was a great American lawyer, orator, and statesman. Born the son of a farmer in Salisbury, New Hampshire, he graduated in law from Dartmouth College in 1801 and set up a legal practice in Portsmouth, New Hampshire. His strong opposition to the War of 1812 led him into politics, and he was elected to the House of Representatives that same year as a member of the Federal Party. He served two terms before leaving Congress in 1816 to pursue his law practice in Boston, Massachusetts.

Webster took on a number of constitutional cases in his legal career and established himself as an expert in legal aspects of the Constitution. One of the quotes he is famous for is "One country, one constitution, one destiny." He was elected to Congress again in 1823 as a member of the National Republican Party and to the Senate in 1827. As leader of the Whig Party he ran for president in 1841, but lost the election. He was appointed secretary of state by President William Henry Harrison in 1841 and again by President Millard Fillmore in 1850.

lower priority in the federal budget than spending to benefit politically powerful special interests. Until this is changed, we will never have a military which reflects our nation's highest ideals.

A violation of principles

Mr. Speaker, the most important reason to oppose reinstatement of a military draft is that conscription violates the very principles upon which this country was founded. The basic premise underlying conscription is that the individual belongs to the state, individual rights are granted by the state, and therefore politicians can abridge individual rights at will. In contrast, the philosophy which inspired America's founders, expressed in the Declaration of Independence, is that individuals possess natural, God-given rights which cannot be abridged by the government. Forcing people into military service against their will thus directly contradicts the philosophy of the Founding Fathers. A military draft also appears to contradict the constitutional prohibition of involuntary servitude.

During the War of 1812, Daniel Webster eloquently made the case that a military draft was unconstitutional:

> *Where is it written in the Constitution, in what article or section is it contained, that you may take children from their parents, and parents from their children, and compel them to fight the battles of any war, in which the folly or the wickedness of Government may engage it? Under what concealment has this power lain hidden, which now for the first time comes forth, with a tremendous and baleful aspect, to trample down and destroy the dearest rights of personal liberty? Sir, I almost disdain to go to quotations and references to prove that such an abominable doctrine had no foundation in the Constitution of the country. It is enough to know that the instrument was intended as the basis of a free government, and that the power contended for is incompatible with any notion of personal liberty. An attempt to maintain this doctrine upon the provisions of the Constitution is an exercise of perverse ingenuity to extract slavery from the substance of a free government. It is an attempt to show, by proof and argument, that we ourselves are subjects of despotism, and that we have a right to chains and bondage, firmly secured to us and our children, by the provisions of our government.*

The War of 1812 between the United States and Great Britain is given less importance in history books than many other American wars, although it confirmed U.S. independence from Great Britain once and for all. It lasted two years, during which time the British seized U.S. ships, invaded the United States, and burned buildings in Washington, D.C. The Americans fought a number of battles against the British and tried to invade Canada three times but failed. The war was won by the Americans at the Battle of New Orleans in January 1815.

Daniel Webster (see box on page 173) equates the military draft with slavery. Do you think this is a fair comparison?

Opponents of the draft

Another eloquent opponent of the draft was former President Ronald Reagan who in a 1979 column on conscription said:

> ... [I]t rests on the assumption that your kids belong to the state. If we buy that assumption then it is for the state—not for parents, the community, the religious institutions or teachers—to decide who shall have what values and who shall do what work, when, where and how in our society. That assumption isn't a new one. The Nazis thought it was a great idea.

President Reagan and Daniel Webster are not the only prominent Americans to oppose conscription. In fact, throughout American history the draft has been opposed by Americans from across the political spectrum, from Henry David Thoreau to Barry Goldwater to Bill Bradley to Jesse Ventura. Organizations opposed to conscription range from the American Civil Liberties Union to the United Methodist Church General Board of Church and Society, and from the National Taxpayers Union to the Conservative Caucus. Other major figures opposing conscription include current Federal Reserve Chairman Alan Greenspan and Nobel Laureate Milton Friedman.

In conclusion, I ask my colleagues to stand up for the long-term military interests of the United States, individual liberty, and values of the Declaration of Independence by co-sponsoring my sense of Congress resolution opposing reinstatement of the military draft.

Ron Paul, M.D., represents the 14th Congressional District of Texas in the United States House of Representatives.

The author uses President Reagan's quote, in which he criticizes military conscription as an idea held by the Nazis, to good effect, since he assumes that many Americans are appalled by the concept of sharing Nazi ideas.

Henry David Thoreau (1817–1862) was an author, naturalist, and practical philosopher; Barry Goldwater (1909–) was a right-wing Republican senator (1952–1987) who ran for president in 1964 but lost to Lyndon B. Johnson; Bill Bradley (1943–) is a basketball star turned Democrat senator (1978–) who announced his candidacy for president in 2000 but was defeated in the primaries by Al Gore; and Jesse Ventura (1951–) is the governor of Minnesota (1998–) and member of the Reform Party, known for his libertarian views.

Summary

According to Justice White, the notion that the draft is unconstitutional is so flimsy that it is scarcely worth demolishing. No one disputes that the government has the power to assemble an army. Consequently, it must also have the right to compel citizens to join it. The judge regards it as self-evident that if the state is not able to do both these things, it has no power at all. Later in the article he raises the important question: What if the United States enters a war with an army composed entirely of regulars and volunteers, then discovers that it has insufficient manpower to pursue its objectives? Finally, he asserts that a democratically elected government is, by definition, exercising the will of the people; and if it decides it needs more soldiers, that is what the people want. Thus the contention that the draft is a violation of the Thirteenth Amendment "is refuted by its mere statement."

The second article is a transcript of a speech by Congressman Ron Paul to the House of Representatives in which he opposes the reinstatement of the draft. Paul argues that military conscription is contrary to the tenets of individual liberty enshrined by the Constitution. The state belongs to its citizens; they are not at the disposal of the government. He further claims that since the nation's armed forces have been fully and effectively staffed by volunteers for over 30 years, the draft is clearly unnecessary. If recruitment of soldiers were to fall, reinstating the draft would not be the best response, since it would bring in conscripts who would weaken the armed forces because they do not want to fight. The most effective way to maintain the required level of manpower would be to improve soldiers' pay and conditions.

FURTHER INFORMATION:

Books:

Flynn, George Q., *The Draft, 1940–1973*. Lawrence, KS: University Press of Kansas, 1993.

Graham, John R. *Constitutional History of the Military Draft*. Minneapolis, MN: Ross and Haines, 1971.

Lasson, Kenneth, *Your Rights and the Draft*. New York: Pocket Books, 1980.

Useful websites:

http://reason.com/sullum/111301.shtml
"Feel a Draft? What's Wrong with Forcing People into 'National Service'"? by Jacob Sullum.

http://cabreta. com/mib/glwdisap.htm
"Who Does the Second Amendment Protect"? by Charles E. Perry.

http://usmilitary.about.com/library/weekly/aa091401b.htm
"What you need to know about … the draft" site.

The following debates in the Pro/Con series may also be of interest:

In this volume:
Topic 1 Does it matter what the original intentions of the Framers were?

Topic 4 Should the president be able to lead the country into war without congressional approval?

In *Individual and Society*:
Topic 8 Should people have to obey unjust laws?

IS THE MILITARY DRAFT CONSTITUTIONAL?

YES: It says the government can raise an army, and an army needs soldiers

YES: Citizens should be free to decide for themselves whether they fight or not

UNCLEAR WORDING
Does the Constitution approve conscription?

INDIVIDUAL LIBERTY
Does the draft violate the right to individual liberty?

NO: The draft is a type of involuntary servitude, which is banned by the Thirteenth Amendment

NO: The people must obey the decisions they have empowered the government to make on their behalf

IS THE MILITARY DRAFT CONSTITUTIONAL?
KEY POINTS

YES: In time of war there may not be enough manpower to achieve military objectives without calling up draftees

YES: If we are to live in a free country, we must be ready to fight to protect it if required

PRACTICAL CONSIDERATIONS
Is conscription necessary or desirable?

NO: The armed forces have been fully staffed for 30 years without conscription

NO: Conscripts are unskilled and unwilling, and are therefore a liability to the armed forces

Topic 14
ARE RANDOM DRUG TESTS OF ATHLETES CONSTITUTIONAL?

YES
FROM *VERNONIA SCHOOL DIST. 47J V. ACTON*
WWW.FINDLAW.COM
JUSTICE ANTONIN SCALIA

NO
FROM *VERNONIA SCHOOL DIST. 47J V. ACTON*
WWW.FINDLAW.COM
JUSTICE SANDRA DAY O'CONNOR

INTRODUCTION

In the wake of growing public concern about the spread of drug abuse many private firms and sports organizations now require drug testing of applicants and athletes. Although there is no clear constitutional reason why a private organization should not be allowed to test its members, the Constitution does restrict what the government may do.

In the absence of any reasonable suspicion of drug abuses, is government drug testing an unreasonable search that the Constitution prohibits? The Fourth Amendment states: "The right of the people to be secure in their persons, houses, papers, and effects, against unreasonable searches and seizures, shall not be violated, and no Warrants shall issue, but upon probable cause, supported by Oath or affirmation, and particularly describing the place to be searched, and the persons or things to be seized." Security against arbitrary searches and seizures is one of the most fundamental liberties of citizens in free societies; it is not surprising that this liberty was included among those protected by the first ten amendments to the Constitution, known as the Bill of Rights, ratified in 1791.

Unlike some of the provisions in the Bill of Rights, the Fourth Amendment's prohibition against searches and seizures is not absolute. Even in a free society searches and seizures will sometimes be necessary for law enforcement and other purposes. Only "unreasonable" searches and seizures are prohibited. One specific limit on government's power to search or seize is provided by the requirement that warrants should be issued only when there is "probable cause." This limit on the power of government seems most suited to cases involving suspicion of criminal behavior: Only when there are reasonable grounds to believe that someone is guilty of a crime should a warrant be issued; mere belief in a person's guilt, without any supporting evidence, should not be sufficient to justify a warrant authorizing a search for incriminating evidence, for example. Among other things, the Fourth Amendment prohibits so-called "general warrants," a hated memory dating from colonial times that could authorize searches of all houses in a geographic area or all persons in a specified group. Such warrants are clearly offensive to liberty because they subject innocent persons to intrusions on their privacy without individualized suspicion of wrongdoing, and also because they place extraordinary power in the hands of law-enforcement officials that might easily be exercised in an arbitrary way.

"Who could deny that privacy is a jewel?"
PHYLLIS McGINLEY, POET

In accordance with the provisions of the Fourth Amendment, when a law-enforcement officer undertakes a search to discover evidence of criminal wrongdoing, it is almost always accompanied by a warrant issued by a magistrate. But when the government interest justifying a search is not a law-enforcement interest, the warrant and probable cause requirements may sometimes be dispensed with. For example, the Supreme Court held that the government's interest in ensuring railroad safety justifies a policy of state-compelled drug and urine testing of railroad employees involved in accidents, even without individualized suspicion of wrongdoing. So, too, the Supreme Court has upheld checkpoints looking for drunk drivers, on the grounds that

the need to prevent drunk driving outweighs such a minimal intrusion.

Thousands of public-school students are now subject to random drug testing as a means of deterring drug use. Is such testing a proper or improper "search" of a person? What is a "reasonable" search anyway? When does a search require a warrant, which can only be issued with probable cause? These are the questions that gave rise in 1995 to the Supreme Court case of *Vernonia School District v. Acton*, from which the following sections are excerpted.

In this case the school district is defending a drug-testing program that requires all students wanting to take part in interscholastic athletics to consent to random drug testing. Those who refuse are barred from taking part. Students who fail the tests are required to take part in counseling and may be excluded from further participation. Access to drug test results, however, is restricted, and the program serves no law-enforcement purpose.

In 2002 the Supreme Court expanded its endorsement of random drug testing in schools. In the case of *Board v. Earls* the court upheld an Oklahoma district's random testing of students engaged in extracurricular activities, including the future homemakers' club, the choir, and the cheerleading squad. The court suggested that under schools' "custodial responsibility" for students' welfare, testing all students would be acceptable.

The following extracts are taken from the Supreme Court judgment on the Vernonia School District policy, which was challenged by student James Acton and his parents. The first opinion upholds the right of the schools to conduct random testing; the second is a dissenting view from one of the minority of justices.

VERNONIA SCHOOL DIST. 47J V. ACTON
Justice Antonin Scalia

YES

The Fourth Amendment to the United States Constitution provides that the Federal Government shall not violate "the right of the people to be secure in their persons, houses, papers, and effects, against unreasonable searches and seizures...." We have held that the Fourteenth Amendment extends this constitutional guarantee to searches and seizures by state officers, including public school officials. In *Skinner v. Railway Labor Executives' Assn.*, we held that state-compelled collection and testing of urine, such as that required by the Student Athlete Drug Policy, constitutes a "search" subject to the demands of the Fourth Amendment.

As the text of the Fourth Amendment indicates, the ultimate measure of the constitutionality of a governmental search is "reasonableness." At least in a case such as this, where there was no clear practice, either approving or disapproving the type of search at issue, at the time the constitutional provision was enacted, whether a particular search meets the reasonableness standard "'is judged by balancing its intrusion on the individual's Fourth Amendment interests against its promotion of legitimate governmental interests.'" ...

> In 1989 the Supreme Court ruled that railroad staff could be subjected to alcohol and drug testing following serious accidents or breaches of safety procedures.

What the Fourth Amendment protects

The first factor to be considered is the nature of the privacy interest upon which the search here at issue intrudes. The Fourth Amendment does not protect all subjective expectations of privacy, but only those that society recognizes as "legitimate." What expectations are legitimate varies, of course, with context, depending, for example, upon whether the individual asserting the privacy interest is at home, at work, in a car, or in a public park. In addition, the legitimacy of certain privacy expectations vis-a-vis the State may depend upon the individual's legal relationship with the State. For example, in Griffin, supra, we held that, although a "probationer's home, like anyone else's, is protected by the Fourth Amendment," the supervisory relationship between probationer and State justifies "a degree of impingement upon [a probationer's] privacy that would not be constitutional if applied to the public at large." Central, in

> A person on probation is in effect in a halfway house between freedom and prison—and therefore must accept some loss of privacy.

our view, to the present case is the fact that the subjects of the Policy are (1) children, who (2) have been committed to the temporary custody of the State as schoolmaster....

Schools and school athletes

Fourth Amendment rights, no less than First and Fourteenth Amendment rights, are different in public schools than elsewhere; the "reasonableness" inquiry cannot disregard the schools' custodial and tutelary responsibility for children. For their own good and that of their classmates, public school children are routinely required to submit to various physical examinations, and to be vaccinated against various diseases.

Legitimate privacy expectations are even less with regard to student athletes. School sports are not for the bashful. They require "suiting up" before each practice or event, and showering and changing afterwards. Public school locker rooms, the usual sites for these activities, are not notable for the privacy they afford. The locker rooms in Vernonia are typical: no individual dressing rooms are provided; shower heads are lined up along a wall, unseparated by any sort of partition or curtain; not even all the toilet stalls have doors.

There is an additional respect in which school athletes have a reduced expectation of privacy. By choosing to "go out for the team," they voluntarily subject themselves to a degree of regulation even higher than that imposed on students generally. In Vernonia's public schools, they must submit to a preseason physical exam, they must acquire adequate insurance coverage or sign an insurance waiver, maintain a minimum grade point average, and comply with any "rules of conduct, dress, training hours and related matters as may be established for each sport by the head coach and athletic director with the principal's approval." Somewhat like adults who choose to participate in a "closely regulated industry," students who voluntarily participate in school athletics have reason to expect intrusions upon normal rights and privileges, including privacy.

Having considered the scope of the legitimate expectation of privacy at issue here, we turn next to the character of the intrusion that is complained of. We recognized in Skinner that collecting the samples for urinalysis intrudes upon "an excretory function traditionally shielded by great privacy." We noted, however, that the degree of intrusion depends upon the manner in which production of the urine sample is monitored. Under the District's Policy, male students produce samples at a urinal along a wall. They remain fully clothed and are only observed from behind, if at all. Female students

Across a wide variety of areas children have fewer rights than adults, who accept responsibility for them. Is this fair, or should children have the same rights as adults?

The implication is that because school athletes accept a lack of physical privacy, they should not be too worried about the further intrusion of random drug testing. Do you agree?

produce samples in an enclosed stall, with a female monitor standing outside listening only for sounds of tampering. These conditions are nearly identical to those typically encountered in public restrooms, which men, women, and especially school children use daily. Under such conditions, the privacy interests compromised by the process of obtaining the urine sample are in our view negligible. The other privacy-invasive aspect of urinalysis is, of course, the information it discloses concerning the state of the subject's body, and the materials he has ingested. In this regard it is significant that the tests at issue here look only for drugs, and not for whether the student is, for example, epileptic, pregnant, or diabetic. Moreover, the drugs for which the samples are screened are standard, and do not vary according to the identity of the student. And finally, the results of the tests are disclosed only to a limited class of school personnel who have a need to know; and they are not turned over to law enforcement authorities or used for any internal disciplinary function.

Do the conditions in which urine tests are obtained affect the principle of whether or not those tests are constitutional?

Accordingly, we reach the conclusion that the invasion of privacy was not significant.

Finally, we turn to consider the nature and immediacy of the governmental concern at issue here, and the efficacy of this means for meeting it. Is there a compelling state interest here? The phrase describes an interest which appears important enough to justify the particular search at hand, in light of other factors which show the search to be relatively intrusive upon a genuine expectation of privacy. Whether that relatively high degree of government concern is necessary in this case or not, we think it is met.

"Reasonableness" is a key concept when it comes to justifying intrusion by the state. Do these safeguards make the policy appear reasonable?

The special case of drugs

That the nature of the concern is important—indeed, perhaps compelling can hardly be doubted. Deterring drug use by our Nation's schoolchildren is at least as important as enhancing efficient enforcement of the Nation's laws against the importation of drugs. School years are the time when the physical, psychological, and addictive effects of drugs are most severe. "Maturing nervous systems are more critically impaired by intoxicants than mature ones are; childhood losses in learning are lifelong and profound"; children grow chemically dependent more quickly than adults, and their record of recovery is depressingly poor." And of course the effects of a drug-infested school are visited not just upon the users, but upon the entire student body and faculty, as the educational process is disrupted. In the present case, moreover, the necessity for the State to act is magnified by the fact that this evil is being visited not just upon individuals at large, but upon children for whom it has undertaken a special responsibility of care and direction. Finally, it must not be lost sight of that this program is directed more narrowly to drug use by school athletes, where the risk of immediate physical harm to the drug user or those with whom he is playing his sport is particularly high. Apart from psychological effects, which include impairment of judgment, slow reaction time, and a lessening of the perception of pain, the particular drugs screened by the District's Policy have been demonstrated to pose substantial physical risks to athletes.

International and professional athletes are subject to random drug tests. Why should school athletes be any different?

It seems to us self-evident that a drug problem largely fueled by the "role model" effect of athletes' drug use, and of particular danger to athletes, is effectively addressed by making sure that athletes do not use drugs. Respondents argue that a "less intrusive means to the same end" was available, namely, "drug testing on suspicion of drug use." Respondents' alternative entails substantial difficulties—if it is indeed practicable at all. It may be impracticable, for one thing, simply because the parents who are willing to accept random drug testing for athletes are not willing to accept accusatory drug testing for all students, which transforms the process into a badge of shame. Respondents' proposal brings the risk that teachers will impose testing arbitrarily upon troublesome but not drug-likely students. It generates the expense of defending lawsuits that charge such arbitrary imposition, or that simply demand greater process before accusatory drug testing is imposed. And not least of all, it adds to the ever-expanding diversionary duties of schoolteachers the new function of spotting and bringing to account drug abuse, a task for which they are ill prepared, and which is not readily compatible with their vocation.

Whether from a parent's or a student's perspective, do you think random drug tests are less intrusive than drug testing based on suspicion?

Taking into account all the factors we have considered above—the decreased expectation of privacy, the relative unobtrusiveness of the search, and the severity of the need met by the search—we conclude Vernonia's Policy is reasonable and hence constitutional.

VERNONIA SCHOOL DIST. 47J V. ACTON
Justice Sandra Day O'Connor

NO

X | **JUSTICE O'CONNOR, with whom JUSTICE STEVENS and JUSTICE SOUTER join, dissenting.**

The population of our Nation's public schools, grades 7 through 12, numbers around 18 million. By the reasoning of today's decision, the millions of these students who participate in interscholastic sports, an overwhelming majority of whom have given school officials no reason whatsoever to suspect they use drugs at school, are open to an intrusive bodily search.

This is a powerful way of opening an argument—by painting a vivid picture of the dangerous consequences of accepting the opposing view.

In justifying this result, the Court dispenses with a requirement of individualized suspicion on considered policy grounds. First, it explains that precisely because every student athlete is being tested, there is no concern that school officials might act arbitrarily in choosing who to test. Second, a broad-based search regime, the Court reasons, dilutes the accusatory nature of the search. In making these policy arguments, of course, the Court sidesteps powerful, countervailing privacy concerns. Blanket searches, because they can involve "thousands or millions" of searches, "pose a greater threat to liberty" than do suspicion-based ones, which "affect one person at a time," *Illinois v. Krull*. Searches based on individualized suspicion also afford potential targets considerable control over whether they will, in fact, be searched because a person can avoid such a search by not acting in an objectively suspicious way. And given that the surest way to avoid acting suspiciously is to avoid the underlying wrongdoing, the costs of such a regime, one would think, are minimal.

The spirit of the Fourth Amendment

The crux of O'Connor's argument is that the Fourth Amendment fundamentally opposes random searches.

But whether a blanket search is "better," than a regime based on individualized suspicion is not a debate in which we should engage. In my view, it is not open to judges or government officials to decide on policy grounds which is better and which is worse. For most of our constitutional history, mass, suspicionless searches have been generally considered per se unreasonable within the meaning of the Fourth Amendment. And we have allowed exceptions in recent years only where it has been clear that a suspicion-based regime would be ineffectual. Because that is not the case here, I dissent....

For another thing, the District's concern for the adversarial nature of a suspicion-based regime (which appears to extend even to those who are rightly accused) seems to ignore the fact that such a regime would not exist in a vacuum. Schools already have adversarial, disciplinary schemes that require teachers and administrators in many areas besides drug use to investigate student wrongdoing (often by means of accusatory searches); to make determinations about whether the wrongdoing occurred; and to impose punishment. To such a scheme, suspicion-based drug testing would be only a minor addition. The District's own elaborate disciplinary scheme is reflected in its handbook, which, among other things, lists the following disciplinary "problem areas" carrying serious sanctions: "DEFIANCE OF AUTHORITY," "DISORDERLY OR DISRUPTIVE CONDUCT INCLUDING FOUL LANGUAGE," "AUTOMOBILE USE OR MISUSE," "FORGERY OR LYING," "GAMBLING," "THEFT," "TOBACCO," "MISCHIEF," "VANDALISM," "RECKLESSLY ENDANGERING," "MENACING OR HARASSMENT," "ASSAULT," "FIGHTING," "WEAPONS," "EXTORTION," "EXPLOSIVE DEVICES," and "ARSON."

> Do you agree that testing for drugs on suspicion is quite in keeping with normal school disciplinary procedures? What rules apply in your school? And what rules should apply?

In addition to overstating its concerns with a suspicion-based program, the District seems to have understated the extent to which such a program is less intrusive of students' privacy. By invading the privacy of a few students rather than many (nationwide, of thousands rather than millions), and by giving potential search targets substantial control over whether they will, in fact, be searched, a suspicion-based scheme is significantly less intrusive.

> If testing were based on suspicion, how do you feel people would react to news that a fellow student had been tested? Would people's reaction to a random test be the same?

In any event, whether the Court is right that the District reasonably weighed the lesser intrusion of a suspicion-based scheme against its policy concerns is beside the point. As stated, a suspicion-based search regime is not just any less intrusive alternative; the individualized suspicion requirement has a legal pedigree as old as the Fourth Amendment itself, and it may not be easily cast aside in the name of policy concerns. It may only be forsaken, our cases in the personal search context have established, if a suspicion-based regime would likely be ineffectual.

But having misconstrued the fundamental role of the individualized suspicion requirement in Fourth Amendment analysis, the Court never seriously engages the practicality of such a requirement in the instant case. And that failure is crucial because nowhere is it less clear that an individualized suspicion requirement would be ineffectual than in the school context. In most schools, the entire pool of potential search targets—students—is under constant supervision by teachers and administrators and coaches, be it in classrooms, hallways, or locker rooms.

The record here indicates that the Vernonia schools are no exception. The great irony of this case is that most (though not all) of the evidence the District introduced to justify its suspicionless drug-testing program consisted of first- or second-hand stories of particular, identifiable students acting in ways that plainly gave rise to reasonable suspicion of in-school drug use—and thus that would have justified a drug-related search. Small groups of students, for example, were observed by a teacher "passing joints back and forth" across the street at a restaurant before school and during school hours. Another group was caught skipping school and using drugs at one of the students' houses. Several students actually admitted their drug use to school officials (some of them being caught with marijuana pipes). One student presented himself to his teacher as "clearly obviously inebriated" and had to be sent home. Still another was observed dancing and singing at the top of his voice in the back of the classroom; when the teacher asked what was going on, he replied, "Well, I'm just high on life." To take a final example, on a certain road trip, the school wrestling coach smelled marijuana smoke in a hotel room occupied by four wrestlers, an observation that (after some questioning) would probably have given him reasonable suspicion to test one or all of them.

> *Do you agree that such behavior would be reasonable grounds for suspicion of drug abuse?*

The merits of suspicion-based testing

In light of all this evidence of drug use by particular students, there is a substantial basis for concluding that a vigorous regime of suspicion-based testing (for which the District appears already to have rules in place), would have gone a long way toward solving Vernonia's school drug problem while preserving the Fourth Amendment rights of James Acton and others like him. And were there any doubt about such a conclusion, it is removed by indications in the record that suspicion-based testing could have been supplemented by an equally vigorous campaign to have Vernonia's parents encourage their children to submit to the District's voluntary drug testing program. In these circumstances, the Fourth Amendment dictates that a mass, suspicionless search regime is categorically unreasonable.

> *When asked why he objected to being tested, James Acton said, "Because I feel that they have no reason to think I was taking drugs." Is this a strong enough reason?*

I recognize that a suspicion-based scheme, even where reasonably effective in controlling in-school drug use, may not be as effective as a mass, suspicionless testing regime. In one sense, that is obviously true just as it is obviously true that suspicion-based law enforcement is not as effective as mass, suspicionless enforcement might be. "But there is nothing new in the realization" that Fourth Amendment protections come with a price. Indeed, the price we pay is higher in the criminal context, given that police do not closely observe the entire class of potential search targets (all citizens in the area) and must ordinarily adhere to the rigid requirements of a warrant and probable cause.

> *In police states, as opposed to democracies, law enforcement is naturally easier because the police do not have to respect citizens' rights.*

The principal counterargument to all this, central to the Court's opinion, is that the Fourth Amendment is more lenient with respect to school searches. That is no doubt correct, for, as the Court explains, schools have traditionally had special guardian-like responsibilities for children that necessitate a degree of constitutional leeway.

Schoolchildren are not prisoners

[This] case, however, asks whether the Fourth Amendment is even more lenient than that, i.e., whether it is so lenient that students may be deprived of the Fourth Amendment's only remaining, and most basic, categorical protection: its strong preference for an individualized suspicion requirement, with its accompanying antipathy toward personally intrusive, blanket searches of mostly innocent people. It is not at all clear that people in prison lack this categorical protection, and we have said "we are not yet ready to hold that the schools and the prisons need be equated for purposes of the Fourth Amendment." Thus, if we are to mean what we often proclaim—that students do not "shed their constitutional rights ... at the schoolhouse gate," *Tinker v. Des Moines Independent Community School Dist.*,—the answer must plainly be no....

> *Even prisoners, O'Connor argues, are not necessarily outside the protection of the Fourth Amendment. So why should schoolchildren be?*

Having reviewed the record here, I cannot avoid the conclusion that the District's suspicionless policy of testing all student-athletes sweeps too broadly, and too imprecisely, to be reasonable under the Fourth Amendment.

Summary

Justice Scalia argues, on behalf of the majority of the Supreme Court, that the random drug tests introduced by the Vernonia School District are a reasonable response to the problem of drug use in the nation's schools. He suggests that in the public school context, the intrusions on privacy involved are in fact relatively limited. And he argues that the schools must in some respects act in place of parents, and that this "custodial" role of the schools requires a reduced expectation of privacy, especially for athletes who have elected to take part in visible activities. As a result, it is "reasonable and hence constitutional" for the school district to employ such tests, even though the searches involved are not based on probable cause or any individualized suspicion of wrongdoing.

Justice Sandra O'Connor, in dissent, argues that random tests are effectively a form of blanket search, as prohibited by the Fourth Amendment. As such, she argues that they pose a greater threat to liberty than searches based on individualized suspicion, since they will inevitably subject many innocent persons to invasions of privacy. Policy concerns about the severity of the problem of drug use in America's schools should not be permitted, she argues, to override fundamental individual rights, including the right to privacy. In the case of school athletes, or of school students in general, there is no reason to think that a plan based on individualized suspicion would not be effective, because teachers and other educational professionals are able to recognize signs of potential drug abuse. The Fourth Amendment requires that searches be based on such individualized suspicion, wherever possible, in order to be held reasonable. Nor, O'Connor concludes, does the fact that schools have "guardian-like responsibilities" for children justify greater constitutional leniency with respect to school searches than searches in other settings.

FURTHER INFORMATION:

Books:

Wetterer, Charles, E., *The Fourth Amendment: Search and Seizure*. Berkeley Heights, NJ: Enslow Publishers, 1998.

Useful websites:

http://www.aclu.org/community/newjers/c092498a.html
"Say No To Random Drug Testing" ACLU factsheet.
http://www.ed.gov/offices/OESE/SDFS/actguid/drugath.htm
Article on drug testing in schools.
http://www.foxnews.com/story/0,2933,56387,00.html
Article on Supreme Court ruling on random drug tests.
http://supct.law.cornell.edu/supct/html/01-332.ZS.html
Court case that involved school drugs policy.

http://www.drugs.indiana.edu/issues/suspicionless.html
Article on drug prevention.

The following debates in the Pro/Con series may also be of interest:

In this volume:
Part 3: The protection of civil liberties

In *Individual and Society*:
Part 2: Social responsibility in a civil society

ARE RANDOM DRUG TESTS OF ATHLETES CONSTITUTIONAL?

YES: Random drug tests are a great intrusion on privacy, and if we allow them to be conducted, it is just a matter of time before other rights are breached

YES: The amendment clearly states that people are protected from searches and seizures

CIVIL LIBERTIES
Do random drug tests violate civil liberties?

FOURTH AMENDMENT
Are random searches against the Fourth Amendment?

NO: Drugs are illegal and as such must be stopped—this is one effective way to prevent the spread of drugs

NO: The Fourth Amendment only protects against unwarranted seizures and searches; drug-related searches are not "unwarranted"

ARE RANDOM DRUG TESTS OF ATHLETES CONSTITUTIONAL?
KEY POINTS

YES: Such searches, especially in a school environment, should only take place under strict guidelines and under supervision

YES: People will only be searched if the authorities are sure there are clear grounds for suspicion

ABUSE
Does random drug testing have any guarantees against being abused by the authorities?

NO: Because the searches are unconstitutional, their subjects have no recourse or protection

NO: There is nothing to stop minority groups from being targeted, rather as in racial profiling

189

Topic 15

IS INTERNET SURVEILLANCE CONSTITUTIONAL?

YES

"ARE EMPLOYERS VIOLATING WORKERS' PRIVACY WITH ELECTRONIC MONITORING"?
SPEAKOUT.COM, JUNE 15, 2000
BRYAN KNOWLES

NO

FROM "STATEMENT OF GREGORY T. NOJEIM ON THE FOURTH AMENDMENT AND
THE INTERNET BEFORE THE HOUSE JUDICIARY COMMITTEE SUBCOMMITTEE
ON THE CONSTITUTION"
AMERICAN CIVIL LIBERTIES UNION, WASHINGTON OFFICE, APRIL 6, 2000
GREGORY T. NOJEIM

INTRODUCTION

There is currently widespread concern over the matter of Internet surveillance and its constitutional implications for Americans. This issue has been especially highlighted following the terrorist attacks on the World Trade Center and the Pentagon on September 11, 2001. The discussion about whether Internet and e-mail surveillance could help reduce terrorist activity globally has fueled an already heated debate. Do third parties, such as the government or employers, have the right to monitor e-mail communications and Internet use? Does this violate the constitutional rights of citizens?

Debate has mainly centered on alleged violations of both the Fourth Amendment and the 1986 Electronic Communications Privacy Act (ECPA). The Fourth Amendment (see quote on page 191) was designed primarily to stop the government from conducting unreasonable searches and seizures, while the ECPA established legal requirements limiting investigatory access to electronic communication.

But why is Internet surveillance necessary? Increasingly, employers are arguing that employee usage of the Internet is costing them money and efficiency. They also assert that Internet and e-mail surveillance is necessary to protect their own security. Secret information could be leaked easily to competitors, for example. They claim that any e-mails sent during company time are the property of the employer and are not protected by the Constitution. Many employees and civil liberties groups disagree, arguing that such surveillance is not only unconstitutional because it is in violation of the Fourth Amendment, but that it also undermines employer–employee trust.

Pre-September 11 one of the biggest threats to Internet privacy was the Federal Bureau of Investigation's (FBI's) Internet surveillance system Carnivore. The FBI developed the software to capture data about electronic communications of parties under investigation. Opponents of the system, however, argue that the data is gathered from sweeps of Internet traffic sent and received by both innocent and guilty individuals, and that this creates concerns about privacy. Civil liberties groups, such as the American Civil Liberties Union (ACLU), argue that the use of Carnivore and similar systems raises all kinds of privacy issues.

> *"The right of the people to be secure in their persons, houses, papers, and effects, against unreasonable searches and seizures, shall not be violated."*
>
> —FOURTH AMENDMENT,
>
> THE CONSTITUTION

Those who support the use of software like Carnivore, on the other hand, argue that criminals—and, more specifically, terrorists—are using everyday technology such as e-mail to plan, coordinate, and execute criminal acts. The terrorist action of September 11 and consequent debates about the importance of the Internet in terrorist communication and organization both contributed to the introduction of the USA PATRIOT Act by President George W. Bush in October 2001. The act states that it was established "… to deter and punish terrorist acts in the United States and around the world, to enhance law-enforcement investigatory tools, and for other purposes."

In practice, opponents argue, it has given the government and law-enforcement agencies too much power and has extended their power to monitor the movements and actions of citizens. The act was passed so easily, they claim, because of the shock surrounding the events of September 11, 2001.

Subsequent public reaction has, however, been strong—by July 2002 several cities, including Cambridge, Northampton, Amherst, and Leverett in Massachusetts and Carrboro in North Carolina, had all passed resolutions calling the USA PATRIOT Act a threat to their residents' civil rights.

Opponents, moreover, point to other countries, such as the United Kingdom, where government proposals to monitor the Internet and e-mail have been put on hold due to public outcry.

However, supporters of Internet monitoring argue that since September 11, surveillance measures have the support of a high percentage of the population. They assert that the government has the right to enact special measures to protect its people from similar attacks.

The following articles discuss some of these issues. Bryan Knowles argues that Internet surveillance is already a part of the modern workplace and is necessary to prevent misuse and safeguard company security.

Gregory T. Nojeim of the ACLU argues that such surveillance violates people's Fourth Amendment right of protection from unreasonable searches and is unconstitutional.

ARE EMPLOYERS VIOLATING WORKERS' PRIVACY WITH ELECTRONIC MONITORING?
Bryan Knowles

YES

With the development of affordable computer technology over the past two decades, coupled with the need for increased and faster communications, the American office place has experienced a significant metamorphosis. While it was once a luxury to have your own office phone extension, it is now common for workers to have voice mail, personal computers, e-mail and Internet connection. While these advances have aided productivity and business growth, they have also created new concerns over corporate security efforts and the privacy rights of employees.

As American workers generate billions of e-mails and phone calls every business day, employers are increasingly monitoring and cataloguing these and other employee communications. According to the American Management Association, 73.5 percent of major U.S. corporations record and monitor employee e-mails, computer files and phone conversations, as well as track Web sites workers visit on the Internet. These companies often perceive monitoring as the best means of limiting liability and increasing worker productivity. Companies vary on whether they inform employees of such tactics.

While the American Civil Liberties Union, numerous computer privacy groups and scores of employees condemn monitoring, arguing that it violates personal privacy, laws regarding workplace privacy indicate differently. Passed by Congress in 1986, the Electronic Communications Privacy Act (ECPA) gave employers the right to monitor electronic communications "in the ordinary course" of business. Public debate has grown over the ethics and legality of employer monitoring. In October 1999, California Governor Gray Davis vetoed a state bill that would have prohibited companies from secretly monitoring employee communications. Other states are addressing similar pieces of legislation.

COMMENTARY: Examples of Internet cases

Bourke v. Nissan Motor Corporation (1993)

During a training session for new employees of the Nissan Motor Corporation on how to use the company's e-mail system, a message from Internet systems specialist employee Bonita Bourke sent to a work colleague was selected at random and read out for demonstration purposes. The message contained information of a personal and sexual nature. The incident was reported to management, and Bourke's e-mails and those of others in her work group were reviewed. Nissan then issued written warnings to all employees they considered to have misused the e-mail system in a similar fashion and subsequently fired Bonita Bourke and Rhonda Hall in 1991. Bourke and Hall sued Nissan for wrongful discharge, common-law invasion of privacy, violation of constitutional privacy rights, and violation of criminal wiretapping and eavesdropping. The Los Angeles County Superior Court ruled in Nissan's favor because the company's employees were aware that e-mails could be accessed and read without the sender's knowledge; the plaintiffs' wrongful discharge claims were dismissed.

Smyth v. Pillsbury Company (1996)

In 1995 the Pillsbury Company fired employee Michael Smyth for sending e-mails that contained "inappropriate and unprofessional comments" from his home computer to his supervisor through the company's e-mail system. Smyth's e-mails were critical of and offensive to the management of the Pillsbury Company. Yet Pillsbury had clearly and repeatedly informed its employees that all e-mails were confidential, could not be intercepted by the management, and could not be used as grounds for employee reprimand or termination. Smyth therefore sued for wrongful discharge and violating privacy laws.

The Pennsylvania Eastern District court ruled that Pillsbury was not bound by its assurances of Internet privacy in its decision to fire an employee and that an employee's e-mail privacy was not protected if it interfered with the company's interests.

On one hand...

Monitoring the electronic communications of employees violates their Constitutional right to privacy established by the Fourth Amendment. Such practices alienate workers, increase their stress levels and destroy company loyalty, all of which are detrimental to overall company performance and customer service. Electronic communications, especially of a private nature, are the property of individuals. The ECPA and several current state laws regarding worker privacy hand too much authority to employers and are extremely antiquated.

According to a 2001 American Management Association (AMA) survey, almost 80 percent of employers admitted to engaging in the monitoring of employees' Internet and e-mail usage.

The Internet and e-mail were barely in existence when the ECPA became law. New laws must be enacted to prohibit electronic monitoring and protect worker privacy.

On the other hand...

The legal right of employers to intercept the electronic communications of employees is invaluable to the security and success of countless companies and must be protected. Considering several recent lawsuits in which plaintiffs sued employers over inappropriate office communications, many containing racial or sexually offensive material, employers must be able to review employee communications to limit their liability. Monitoring employee e-mails and computer hard drives combats the constant risk of internal hacking and sabotage by disgruntled workers. Employees should be focused on company goals and customer needs when on company time, not e-mail and Web surfing.

- It is estimated that U.S. workers generate 2.8 billion e-mails daily.
- A recent study by the American Management Association found that 55 percent of companies use electronic devices and programs to prevent their employees from dialing prohibited phone numbers.
- In 1996, the Morgan Stanley brokerage firm was sued for $70 million by employees offended by e-mails containing racial humor that were sent through the firm's e-mail system.
- An estimated 38 percent of major companies review employee e-mails.
- Despite deleting an e-mail from your work computer, many company e-mail systems produce copies of all messages that pass through the system.
- The New York Times Company recently fired 23 employees for sending e-mails containing pornographic images.
- An estimated quarter of all major corporations have released employees for inappropriately using electronic office equipment.

One such example was in 1995, when four female employees of the Chevron Corporation sued their employers for sexual harassment over the receipt of sexually offensive e-mails. Although Chevron denied the charges, it paid the employees $2.2 million plus all their legal fees and court costs.

The American Management Association (AMA) also reported that up to a quarter of companies that review employee e-mails do not tell their employees that they are doing so. Do you think that employees have the right to know if their e-mails are being monitored?

STATEMENT ON THE FOURTH AMENDMENT AND THE INTERNET …
Gregory T. Nojeim

NO

Gregory T. Nojeim was legislative counsel to the American Civil Liberties Union (ACLU) when this statement was given. In 2001 he was appointed Associate Director of the ACLU's Washington office.

X … As the 21st century begins, Americans have expressed overwhelming concern about their privacy. A *Wall Street Journal* poll conducted at the end of last year indicated that Americans were more concerned in the new millennium about loss of personal privacy than things like terrorism, crime or even the economy.

Today I will discuss the Fourth Amendment as it applies to certain Internet communications. I will explain that when it comes to protecting the privacy of communications on the Internet, the buck stops here, with Congress, and not in the courts through Fourth Amendment jurisprudence.…

Civil liberty threatened by electronic surveillance

Electronic surveillance of communications is conducted secretly and unlike most searches in the physical world, there is no simultaneous notice that a search is being conducted. Because electronic surveillance vacuums up both innocent and incriminating conversations, we believe it resembles the kind of general search warrant that the Fourth Amendment was adopted to preclude. Everyone would agree that law enforcement ought not search all of the houses on a street because it has probable cause that crime might be conducted in one of the houses on the street. This principle has not been carried forth into the world of electronic surveillance.…

"Probable cause" is a legal term defined in Merriam-Webster's Dictionary as "a reasonable ground for supposing a charge is well-founded." Read about it at www.lectlaw.com/def2/p089.htm and http://majoritywhip.house.gov/constitution/hints/amendment4.asp.

Electronic surveillance is increasingly a scattershot investigative tool. For the first five-year period for which statistics are available (1969–1973), more than half of the communications intercepted in law enforcement electronic surveillance were incriminating. However, over the most recent five-year period (1994–1998) only one-fifth of the communications intercepted in law enforcement electronic surveillance were incriminating conversations. Each time a federal or state electronic surveillance intercept is installed, on average, 1608 innocent conversations are intercepted. In 1998, the most recent year for which statistics are available in the Wiretap Report published annually by the Administrative Office of the U.S. Courts, a record number of

For the 2001 Wiretap Report see www.uscourts.gov/wiretap01/contents.html.

electronic intercept applications were installed by federal and state law enforcement officials. At the same time, less than 19% of the millions of communications intercepted in 1998 were incriminating, and 1.9 million innocent communications were intercepted.

This is a tremendous loss of personal privacy. It is one of the reasons Americans overwhelmingly oppose wiretapping. Each year the Department of Justice asks Americans whether all things considered, they oppose or support wiretapping. Nearly 3/4th's of the respondents consistently indicate opposition. Because it is conducted secretly, electronic surveillance undermines trust in the government and trust between individuals. For some, it inhibits communication by putting them in fear that their words might be recorded and one day be used against them....

Why do you think the Department of Justice consults the public every year if it then does nothing about wiretapping? Is it merely for show, or does it hope public opinion will eventually change?

The Fourth Amendment and electronic surveillance

The Fourth Amendment provides:

The right of the people to be secure in their persons, houses, papers, and effects, against unreasonable searches and seizures, shall not be violated, and no Warrants shall issue, but upon probable cause, supported by Oath or affirmation, and particularly describing the place to be searched, and the persons or things to be seized.

Our freedom against unreasonable searches depends on crafting Fourth Amendment principles that make sense in the digital age. It used to be the case that most of the information people wanted to be kept private was stored in their home. To the extent that third parties obtained a person's most private information, it was difficult to store and difficult to collate. Now, with the advent of the Internet, the World Wide Web and instantaneous electronic communication, an invasion of privacy is only a point and a click away.

Olmstead v. United States, 277 U.S. 438 (1928) is often cited as the Court's first foray into cyberspace. The Court held that a warrant is not required for a wiretap of a home or an office telephone because law enforcement officers had not physically entered the home or office, or any other place deemed constitutionally protected. The Court reasoned that since the language of the Fourth Amendment refers only to tangible things, such as houses, papers, effects and people, its reach extended only to physical intrusions.

See Topic 1 Does it matter what the original intentions of the Framers were?

The author gives a short account of the legal history of electronic surveillance. Does this add to or interrupt his argument?

The Court reversed itself in *Katz v. United States*, 389 U.S. 347 (1967). It declared, "the Fourth Amendment protects people, not places." It held that what a person seeks to preserve as private might be constitutionally protected even if it is in an area accessible to the public. In Katz, the Court held that a telephone conversation could not be intercepted without a warrant....

In response to the Court's decision in *Katz*, Congress enacted Title III of the Omnibus Crime Control and Safe Streets Act of 1968 (18 U.S.C.2510-20). It established procedures for court-ordered wire-taping and bugging. Because Congress recognized that electronic surveillance was so invasive of privacy, it included a number of safeguards....

Congress and Internet surveillance

The Electronic Communications Privacy Act of 1986 is the comprehensive legislation Congress enacted to protect the privacy of electronic communications such as e-mail. An individual's e-mail message stored by a third party was viewed as likely unprotected by the Fourth Amendment....

...ECPA has a number of shortcomings that should be addressed. It is not as protective of e-mail and other electronic communications as Title III is of voice communications:

Only a high-ranking DOJ official can authorize an application for wiretap order; "any attorney for the Government" may authorize an application for an order to intercept e-mail and other electronic communications.... Electronic communications ought to be afforded the same protections as voice communications because they are functionally similar.

A "provider of electronic communications service" might be a cellphone network or an Internet service provider (ISP).

Second, under the scheme adopted in ECPA, real-time interception of e-mail messages is given greater protection than is acquisition of the message from a "provider of electronic communications service" after it has been stored. Under ECPA, real-time interception of e-mail messages and other electronic communications requires a court order based on probable cause of crime, interception is an investigative technique of the last resort, and continuing judicial oversight is required. 18 U.S.C. 2510-22. However, since real-time interception of electronic communications is not necessary in most cases, these provisions do not afford the protection for electronic communications that Congress likely intended. Instead, law enforcement need only wait until the provider stores the e-mail message; it is stored immediately upon delivery.

Once in storage, law enforcement access is obtained more readily under 18 U.S.C. 2703. A search warrant based on probable cause issued by a federal magistrate (as opposed to a court order with the protections mentioned above) is all that is required to access e-mail in storage for less than 180 days. 18 U.S.C. 2703(a)....

What does this mean for a service like AOL's "Instant Messaging?" It resembles a phone conversation over the Internet. But if AOL stores the messages—even for an instant—the communication has lesser protection than would a phone conversation.

Importantly, once the e-mail has been stored with the provider for over 180 days, it can be made available to law enforcement acting with only an administrative subpoena and delayed notice to the customer, or with a warrant without notice. 18 U.S.C. 2703(b). Most importantly, such e-mail can be obtained by law enforcement acting with a court order issued based upon a showing of only "specific and articulable facts showing that there are reasonable grounds to believe" that the contents of the communication are "relevant" to an ongoing investigation. "Relevance" is a far lower threshold for a search than is "probable cause." In effect, the privacy of the contents of an e-mail message or other electronic communication diminishes just because a service provider retained the message an inordinately long time....

> Do you think e-mail and instant messaging communications should have privacy safeguards equal to those of telephone conversations?

Conclusion

There is an urgent need for active Congressional oversight in this area. To the extent that courts have failed to extend Fourth Amendment principles to protect the privacy of communications held by third parties, Congress must step in. Clear rules governing surveillance of communications on the Internet need to be established.... As Congress recognized when it enacted ECPA, "...the law must advance with the technology to ensure the continued vitality of the Fourth Amendment... [Privacy] will gradually erode as technology advances."...

> Do you think advances in technology will inevitably lead to the loss of privacy? Or can changes in the law keep pace with technology to safeguard privacy?

Summary

Bryan Knowles highlights the fact that employers are increasingly monitoring employees' e-mail and Internet usage and that the Electronic Communications Privacy Act (ECPA), passed by Congress in 1986, protects employers' rights to do so. Although he recognizes that the monitoring of electronic communication could be said to violate the individual's right to privacy established by the Constitution's Fourth Amendment, he defends employers' rights to Internet surveillance in order to protect company information and avoid liability for the circulation of sexually or racially offensive material by their employees.

Gregory T. Nojeim cites a poll showing Americans' concern about loss of privacy. He believes Internet surveillance occurs frequently and is often arbitrary. (In 1998 fewer than 19 percent of intercepted communications were criminal.) Surveillance, he believes, defies the Fourth Amendment—even though privacy is invaded electronically rather than physically—and undermines trust in the government and between individuals. He advocates that Internet communications be given the same legal protections as voice communications and warns that electronic communication is particularly vulnerable because it is stored, which means fewer legal safeguards limit access to it. He concludes by urging Congress to establish clear rules that secure privacy and that can then be updated in step with technology.

FURTHER INFORMATION:

Books:

Alderman, Ellen, and Caroline Kennedy, *The Right to Privacy*. New York: Alfred A. Knopf, 1995.
Banisar, David, and Bruce Schneier (eds.), *The Electronic Privacy Papers: Documents on the Battle for Privacy in the Age of Surveillance*. New York:John Wiley & Sons, 1997.
Dempsey, James X., and David Cole, *Terrorism and the Constitution: Sacrificing Civil Liberties in the Name of National Security*. (2nd edition) Washington, D.C.: First Amendment Foundation, 2002.

Useful websites:

www.fbi.gov
FBI site, including section on fight against terrorism.
www.fbi.gov/hq/lab/carnivore/carnivore.htm
FBI file on Carnivore, including congressional statements.
www.whitehouse.gov
White House site. Explains government response to September 11, 2001, including USA PATRIOT Act.
www.epic.org
Electronic Privacy Information Center site. Sections on workplace privacy and suing of FBI over Carnivore.
www.eff.org
Electronic Frontier Foundation site has critical analyses of Carnivore and USA PATRIOT Act and text of the act itself.
www.aclu.org
American Civil Liberties Union site. Includes a section on cyber-liberties.
www.privacy.org
Useful news site about surveillance/privacy issues.
www.howstuffworks.com/workplce-surveillance.htm
Detailed look at workplace monitoring.

The following debates in the Pro/Con series may also be of interest:

In this volume:

Topic 1 Does it matter what the original intentions of the Framers were?

IS INTERNET SURVEILLANCE CONSTITUTIONAL?

YES: Electronic surveillance is a vital tool for law-enforcement agencies

YES: Employers have a right to know how their equipment is being used by employees

YES: E-mail and other Internet communications are not the same as telephone communications, and no one expects them to be private

PRIVACY
Should we expect our electronic communications to be monitored?

NO: Employers should not monitor employees' communications without notifying them that monitoring is taking place

TECHNOLOGY
Should different rules apply to Internet surveillance from those that apply to wiretapping?

NO: Law-enforcement agencies should only monitor a person's communications when they have good reason to suspect them of a specific crime

NO: Electronic communications should have the same privacy safeguards as voice communications

IS INTERNET SURVEILLANCE CONSTITUTIONAL?
KEY POINTS

YES: The government's first duty is to protect its citizens from terrorists, and it must take all necessary steps to secure their safety

SECURITY
Do the heightened security concerns following September 11, 2001, justify increased Internet surveillance?

YES: Increased surveillance can enable the government to prevent terrorist acts, instead of merely prosecuting terrorists when the damage has been done

NO: If the government ignores civil liberties, then terrorism has already won a significant victory against the values enshrined in the Constitution

NO: Surveillance is not certain to prevent terrorist acts, but is certain to affect civil liberties

Topic 16

IS THE DEATH PENALTY CONSTITUTIONAL?

YES

FROM *GREGG V. GEORGIA* 428 U.S. 153 (1976)
ARGUED MARCH 31, 1976, AND JULY 2, 1976
OPINION OF JUSTICES STEWART, POWELL, AND STEVENS,
ANNOUNCED BY JUSTICE POTTER STEWART

NO

FROM *FURMAN V. GEORGIA* 408 U.S. 328 (1972)
DECIDED JUNE 29, 1972
OPINION OF JUSTICE THURGOOD MARSHALL

INTRODUCTION

The execution of George Kendall—a spy put to death in 1608 in the Colony of Virginia—is the first recorded use of the death penalty in colonial America. The death penalty has been an ever-present—although controversial—feature of the American criminal justice system ever since. Death-penalty statistics were first recorded by the Bureau of Justice Statistics in 1930. By 2001 a total of 4,608 people had been executed. Although attention usually focuses on the ethical and moral issues involved with capital punishment, there is the additional controversy of whether or not the death penalty fits into the framework of the Constitution.

Supporters of the death penalty believe that the punishment must fit the crime in cases of serious felonies such as murder and sexual or violent assaults. While the Constitution does not provide specifically for a death penalty, supporters believe that the

Fifth Amendment has always permitted it in reasonable circumstances. The Fifth Amendment states that no person shall be deprived of "life, liberty, or property, without due process of the law."

Opponents suggest that there are no reasonable circumstances in which people should be executed for their crimes. Although some critics accept that much of their objection to capital punishment centers on ethical issues, many others point to a constitutional conflict surrounding interpretation of the Eighth Amendment, in which the Constitution specifically forbids "cruel and unusual punishments."

The critics claim that the death penalty violates the Eighth Amendment since execution is excessively painful or brutal and, in addition, that the death penalty is not applied consistently to all serious crimes, such as first-degree murder. This argument became popular in the late 1950s and 1960s following

Trop v. Dulles (1958), in which the Supreme Court decided that the Eighth Amendment contained an "evolving standard of decency that marked the progress of maturing society." Although this case did not involve the death penalty, abolitionists claimed that the argument could equally be applied to capital punishment and that the United States had reached a point at which its "standard of decency" made the death penalty intolerable.

"The choice for the judge who believes the death penalty to be immoral is resignation rather than simply ignoring duly enacted constitutional laws and sabotaging the death penalty."

—JUSTICE ANTONIN SCALIA,

PEW FORUM CONFERENCE,

JANUARY 25, 2002

By the end of the 1960s 40 states had laws to authorize the use of the death penalty in certain cases. However, the precedent set by *Trop v. Dulles,* along with strong opposition from the NAACP Legal Defense Fund, meant that support for the death penalty reached an all-time low. Indeed, no one was executed for several years after 1967.

One of the most important legal cases concerning the death penalty came in 1972 with *Furman v. Georgia.* In this case the Supreme Court invalidated all federal and state death-penalty laws. A majority ruling upheld that many of these laws violated both the Eighth Amendment, by inflicting "cruel and unusual punishment," and also the due-process guarantees of the Fourteenth Amendment. Justice Brennan and Justice Marshall (whose opinion is summarized in the second article that follows) struck down the state and federal death-penalty laws because the arbitrary application of the death penalty and its racial bias made the laws "unusual." In his summary Justice Marshall argued that "the history of the Eighth Amendment supports only the conclusion that retribution for its own sake is improper." No executions took place in the United States for four years. By striking down specific federal and state legislature, however, the judgment did not mean that the death penalty was unconstitutional in itself. So, in response to this case 35 states rewrote their death-penalty statutes to respond to the court's decision.

Four years after *Furman v. Georgia,* Georgia's new statutes were challenged in *Gregg v. Georgia.* The first extract is taken from the opinion on this case by Justices Stewart, Powell, and Stevens as announced by Justice Stewart. The petitioner argued that the imposition of a death sentence violated the "cruel and unusual punishment" clause of the Eighth Amendment. The Supreme Court upheld the sentence, however, stating that "punishment of death does not invariably violate the Constitution."

Execution rates have soared since *Gregg*—683 people were executed between 1977 and 2000; 85 of them were executed in 2000 alone. By the end of 2000 a further 3,593 prisoners in 38 states were awaiting their execution on death row.

GREGG V. GEORGIA
Justice Potter Stewart

YES

The case involves Troy Gregg, who was charged with armed robbery and the murders of Fred Simmons and Bob Moore in Atlanta in 1973. The jury found Gregg guilty on two counts of murder and two counts of armed robbery, returning verdicts of death on each count. Gregg challenged the decision on the basis that the death sentence violated the Eighth and Fourteenth amendments to the Constitution. You can read more about Troy Gregg's life, his trial and conviction, and his life on death row in Reidsville, Georgia, in Waiting For It *by Kit Davis (New York: Harper & Row, 1980).*

✓ III

We address initially the basic contention that the punishment of death for the crime of murder is, under all circumstances, "cruel and unusual" in violation of the Eighth and Fourteenth Amendments of the Constitution. In Part IV of this opinion, we will consider the sentence of death imposed under the Georgia statutes at issue in this case. The Court on a number of occasions has both assumed and asserted the constitutionality of capital punishment. In several cases that assumption provided a necessary foundation for the decision, as the Court was asked to decide whether a particular method of carrying out a capital sentence would be allowed to stand under the Eighth Amendment. But until *Furman v. Georgia,* 408 U.S. 238 (1972), the Court never confronted squarely the fundamental claim that the punishment of death always, regardless of the enormity of the offense or the procedure followed in imposing the sentence, is cruel and unusual punishment in violation of the Constitution. Although this issue was presented and addressed in *Furman,* it was not resolved by the Court. Four Justices would have held that capital punishment is not unconstitutional *per se;* two Justices would have reached the opposite conclusion; and three Justices, while agreeing that the statutes then before the Court were invalid as applied, left open the question whether such punishment may ever be imposed. We now hold that the punishment of death does not invariably violate the Constitution....

In the discussion to this point we have sought to identify the principles and considerations that guide a court in addressing an Eighth Amendment claim. We now consider specifically whether the sentence of death for the crime of murder is a *per se* violation of the Eighth and Fourteenth Amendments to the Constitution. We note first that history and precedent strongly support a negative answer to this question....

It is apparent from the text of the Constitution itself that the existence of capital punishment was accepted by the Framers. At the time the Eighth Amendment was ratified, capital punishment was a common sanction in every State. Indeed, the First Congress of the United States enacted

The judge presents the court's opinion in a clear and concise manner. He repeats the main point of his first paragraph and then outlines the next part of his argument.

legislation providing death as the penalty for specified crimes. The Fifth Amendment, adopted at the same time as the Eighth, contemplated the continued existence of the capital sanction by imposing certain limits on the prosecution of capital cases:

> *No person shall be held to answer for a capital, or otherwise infamous crime, unless on a presentment or indictment of a Grand Jury…; nor shall any person be subject for the same offense to be twice put in jeopardy of life or limb;… nor be deprived of life, liberty, or property, without due process of law….*

And the Fourteenth Amendment, adopted over three-quarters of a century later, similarly contemplates the existence of the capital sanction in providing that no State shall deprive any person of "life, liberty, or property" without due process of law.

For nearly two centuries, this Court, repeatedly and often expressly, has recognized that capital punishment is not invalid *per se*. In *Wilkerson v. Utah*, 99 U.S., at 134-135, where the Court found no constitutional violation in inflicting death by public shooting, it said:

> *Cruel and unusual punishments are forbidden by the Constitution, but the authorities referred to are quite sufficient to show that the punishment of shooting as a mode of executing the death penalty for the crime of murder in the first degree is not included in that category, within the meaning of the eighth amendment….*

Four years ago, the petitioners in *Furman* and its companion cases predicated their argument primarily upon the asserted proposition that standards of decency had evolved to the point where capital punishment no longer could be tolerated. The petitioners in those cases said, in effect, that the evolutionary process had come to an end, and that standards of decency required that the Eighth Amendment be construed finally as prohibiting capital punishment for any crime regardless of its depravity and impact on society. This view was accepted by two Justices. Three other Justices were unwilling to go so far; focusing on the procedures by which convicted defendants were selected for the death penalty rather than on the actual punishment inflicted, they joined in the conclusion that the statutes

You can read more about the implications of the Fifth and Eighth amendments for the death penalty at the University of Missouri-Kansas City Law School's "Exploring Constitutional Conflicts" website at www.law.umkc.edu/faculty/projects/ftrials/conlaw/home. Click on "The Death Penalty" link.

The judge refers to Wilkerson v. Utah (1878), in which the Supreme Court first ruled on the death penalty. The court upheld the use of a firing squad as a form of execution because death by public shooting was quick and minimized cruelty.

See pages 208–211 of this topic for a full account of the opinion of Justice Marshall, one of five justices who filed opinions on the Furman v. Georgia (1972) case.

before the Court were constitutionally invalid. The petitioners in the capital cases before the Court today renew the "standards of decency" argument, but developments during the four years since *Furman* have undercut substantially the assumptions upon which their argument rested. Despite the continuing debate, dating back to the 19th century, over the morality and utility of capital punishment, it is now evident that a large proportion of American society continues to regard it as an appropriate and necessary criminal sanction.

The most marked indication of society's endorsement of the death penalty for murder is the legislative response to *Furman*. The legislatures of at least 35 States have enacted new statutes that provide for the death penalty for at least some crimes that result in the death of another person. And the Congress of the United States, in 1974, enacted a statute providing the death penalty for aircraft piracy that results in death. These recently adopted statutes have attempted to address the concerns expressed by the Court in *Furman* primarily (i) by specifying the factors to be weighed and the procedures to be followed in deciding when to impose a capital sentence, or (ii) by making the death penalty mandatory for specified crimes. But all of the post-*Furman* statutes make clear that capital punishment itself has not been rejected by the elected representatives of the people.

The jury also is a significant and reliable objective index of contemporary values because it is so directly involved. It may be true that evolving standards have influenced juries in recent decades to be more discriminating in imposing the sentence of death. But the relative infrequency of jury verdicts imposing the death sentence does not indicate rejection of capital punishment *per se.* Rather, the reluctance of juries in many cases to impose the sentence may well reflect the humane feeling that this most irrevocable of sanctions should be reserved for a small number of extreme cases. Indeed, the actions of juries in many States since *Furman* are fully compatible with the legislative judgments, reflected in the new statutes, as to the continued utility and necessity of capital punishment in appropriate cases. At the close of 1974 at least 254 persons had been sentenced to death since *Furman,* and by the end of March 1976, more than 460 persons were subject to death sentences.

As we have seen, however, the Eighth Amendment demands more than that a challenged punishment be acceptable to contemporary society. The Court also must ask whether it comports with the basic concept of human dignity at the core of the Amendment. Although we cannot "invalidate a

---

In a nationwide survey conducted by Gallup in May 2002 adults were asked: "Are you in favor of the death penalty for a person convicted of murder?" Of the 1,012 adults surveyed, 72 percent favored the death penalty, 25 percent opposed it, and 3 percent did not have an opinion.

Only a jury can decide whether the death sentence is a suitable penalty for a particular crime. This was highlighted by a Supreme Court ruling in June 2002, suggesting that in cases in which judges impose death sentences, this violates defendants' Sixth Amendment right to a jury trial.

Check out the Bureau of Justice Statistics website at www.ojp.usdoj.gov/ bjs/ for more statistics about the death penalty. Click on the "Capital Punishment" link under "Corrections."

category of penalties because we deem less severe penalties adequate to serve the ends of penology[.]"

The death penalty is said to serve two principal social purposes: retribution and deterrence of capital crimes by prospective offenders.

In part, capital punishment is an expression of society's moral outrage at particularly offensive conduct. This function may be unappealing to many, but it is essential in an ordered society that asks its citizens to rely on legal processes rather than self-help to vindicate their wrongs....

Statistical attempts to evaluate the worth of the death penalty as a deterrent to crimes by potential offenders have occasioned a great deal of debate. The results simply have been inconclusive. Although some of the studies suggest that the death penalty may not function as a significantly greater deterrent than lesser penalties, there is no convincing empirical evidence either supporting or refuting this view.

In sum, we cannot say that the judgment of the Georgia Legislature that capital punishment may be necessary in some cases is clearly wrong. Considerations of federalism, as well as respect for the ability of a legislature to evaluate, in terms of its particular State, the moral consensus concerning the death penalty and its social utility as a sanction, require us to conclude, in the absence of more convincing evidence, that the infliction of death as a punishment for murder is not without justification and thus is not unconstitutionally severe....

How does the court decide what kind of crimes merit the death penalty? Should people who kill in self-defense be sentenced to death? Why not confer death sentences on all violent criminals?

Many critics believe that electrocution causes an undue amount of suffering and therefore violates the Eighth Amendment prohibition of "cruel and unusual punishments." Do you think the court's opinion in this case implies that all forms of execution are constitutional?

FURMAN V. GEORGIA
Justice Thurgood Marshall

NO

X …Whether the English Bill of Rights prohibition against cruel and unusual punishments is properly read as a response to excessive or illegal punishments, as a reaction to barbaric and objectionable modes of punishment, or as both, there is no doubt whatever that in borrowing the language and in including it in the Eighth Amendment, our Founding Fathers intended to outlaw torture and other cruel punishments.

The precise language used in the Eighth Amendment first appeared in America on June 12, 1776, in Virginia's "Declaration of Rights," § 9 of which read: "That excessive bail ought not to be required, nor excessive fines imposed, nor cruel and unusual punishments inflicted." This language was drawn verbatim from the English Bill of Rights of 1689. Other States adopted similar clauses, and there is evidence in the debates of the various state conventions that were called upon to ratify the Constitution of great concern for the omission of any prohibition against torture or other cruel punishments.

The Virginia Convention offers some clues as to what the Founding Fathers had in mind in prohibiting cruel and unusual punishments. At one point George Mason advocated the adoption of a Bill of Rights, and Patrick Henry concurred, stating:

"By this Constitution, some of the best barriers of human rights are thrown away. Is there not an additional reason to have a bill of rights? …

Congress, from their general powers, may fully go into business of human legislation. They may legislate, in criminal cases, from treason to the lowest offence —petty larceny. They may define crimes and prescribe punishments. In the definition of crimes, I trust they will be directed by what wise representatives ought to be governed by. But when we come to punishments, no latitude ought to be left, nor dependence put on the virtue of representatives. What says our Bill of Rights?—'that excessive bail ought not to be required, nor excessive fines imposed, nor cruel and unusual punishments inflicted.' Are you not, therefore, now calling on those gentlemen who are to compose Congress, to prescribe trials and define punishments without this control? Will they find sentiments there similar to this bill of rights? You let them loose; you do more—you depart from the genius of your country. …

"In this business of legislation, your members of Congress will loose the restriction of not imposing excessive fines, demanding excessive bail, and inflicting cruel and unusual punishments. These are prohibited by your declaration of rights. What has distinguished our ancestors?—That they would not admit of tortures, or cruel and barbarous punishment. But Congress may introduce the practice of the civil law, in preference to that of the common law. They may introduce the practice of France, Spain, and Germany—of torturing, to extort a confession of the crime. They will say that they might as well draw examples from those countries as from Great Britain, and they will tell you that there is such a necessity of strengthening the arm of government, that they must have a criminal equity, and extort confession by torture, in order to punish with still more relentless severity. We are then lost and undone."

Henry's statement indicates that he wished to insure that "relentless severity" would be prohibited by the Constitution. Other expressions with respect to the proposed Eighth Amendment by Members of the First Congress indicate that they shared Henry's view of the need for and purpose of the Cruel and Unusual Punishments Clause.

Thus, the history of the clause clearly establishes that it was intended to prohibit cruel punishments. We must now turn to the case law to discover the manner in which courts have given meaning to the term "cruel." …

> *Look up the Death Penalty Information Center's website at www. deathpenaltyinfo. org/history1 for a detailed account of the history of the death penalty in the United States and its relationship to the Constitution.*

II

The Court used the same approach seven years later in the landmark case of *Weems v. United States*, 217 U.S. 349 (1910). Weems, an officer of the Bureau of Coast Guard and Transportation of the United States Government of the Philippine Islands, was convicted of falsifying a "public and official document." He was sentenced to 15 years' incarceration at hard labor with chains on his ankles, to an unusual loss of his civil rights, and to perpetual surveillance. Called upon to determine whether this was a cruel and unusual punishment, the Court found that it was....

In striking down the penalty imposed on Weems, the Court examined the punishment in relation to the offense, compared the punishment to those inflicted for other crimes and to those imposed in other jurisdictions, and concluded

Although the court agreed that Weems's sentence did not fit the crime, it also accepted that a clear definition of the term "cruel and unusual punishment" was difficult to make.

that the punishment was excessive. Justices White and Holmes dissented and argued that the cruel and unusual prohibition was meant to prohibit only those things that were objectionable at the time the Constitution was adopted.

Weems is a landmark case because it represents the first time that the Court invalidated a penalty prescribed by a legislature for a particular offense. The Court made it plain beyond any reasonable doubt that excessive punishments were as objectionable as those that were inherently cruel....

Trop v. Dulles, 356 U.S. 86 (1958), marked [another] major cruel and unusual punishment case in this Court. Trop, a native-born American, was declared to have lost his citizenship by reason of a conviction by court-martial for wartime desertion. Writing for himself and Justices Black, Douglas, and Whittaker, Chief Justice Warren concluded that loss of citizenship amounted to a cruel and unusual punishment that violated the Eighth Amendment.

Emphasizing the flexibility inherent in the words "cruel and unusual," the Chief Justice wrote that "the Amendment must draw its meaning from the evolving standards of decency that mark the progress of a maturing society...."

Justice Marshall reaches the central premise of the court's judgment. While the death penalty may have been acceptable in the past, Marshall implies that "standards of decency" have progressed to the point where the death penalty should no longer be tolerated. Do you agree that laws should evolve over time?

III

Perhaps the most important principle in analyzing "cruel and unusual" punishment questions is one that is reiterated in the prior opinions of the Court: *i. e.,* the cruel and unusual language "must draw its meaning from the evolving standards of decency that mark the progress of a maturing society." Thus, a penalty that was permissible at one time in our Nation's history is not necessarily permissible today.

The fact, therefore, that the Court, or individual Justices, may have in the past expressed an opinion that the death penalty is constitutional is not now binding on us....

To clarify the court's position, Justice Marshall lists examples in which punishments may violate the "cruel and unusual" provision of the Eighth Amendment.

Faced with an open question, we must establish our standards for decision. The decisions discussed in the previous section imply that a punishment may be deemed cruel and unusual for any one of four distinct reasons.

First, there are certain punishments that inherently involve so much physical pain and suffering that civilized people cannot tolerate them—*e. g.,* use of the rack, the thumbscrew, or other modes of torture. Regardless of public sentiment with respect to imposition of one of these punishments in a particular case or at any one moment in history, the Constitution prohibits it. These are punishments that have been barred since the adoption of the Bill of Rights.

Second, there are punishments that are unusual, signifying that they were previously unknown as penalties for a given offense[.] In light of the meager history that does exist, one would suppose that an innovative punishment would probably be constitutional if no more cruel than that punishment which it superseded. We need not decide this question here, however, for capital punishment is certainly not a recent phenomenon.

Third, a penalty may be cruel and unusual because it is excessive and serves no valid legislative purpose....

Fourth, where a punishment is not excessive and serves a valid legislative purpose, it still may be invalid if popular sentiment abhors it. For example, if the evidence clearly demonstrated that capital punishment served valid legislative purposes, such punishment would, nevertheless, be unconstitutional if citizens found it to be morally unacceptable. A general abhorrence on the part of the public would, in effect, equate a modern punishment with those barred since the adoption of the Eighth Amendment.

There are no prior cases in this Court striking down a penalty on this ground, but the very notion of changing values requires that we recognize its existence.

It is immediately obvious, then, that since capital punishment is not a recent phenomenon, if it violates the Constitution, it does so because it is excessive or unnecessary, or because it is abhorrent to currently existing moral values....

In addition to the legal interpretation of the "cruel and unusual" clause of the Eighth Amendment, Justice Marshall also notes moral issues involved with the death penalty.

V

In order to assess whether or not death is an excessive or unnecessary penalty, it is necessary to consider the reasons why a legislature might select it as punishment for one or more offenses, and examine whether less severe penalties would satisfy the legitimate legislative wants as well as capital punishment. If they would, then the death penalty is unnecessary cruelty, and, therefore, unconstitutional.

There are six purposes conceivably served by capital punishment: retribution, deterrence, prevention of repetitive criminal acts, encouragement of guilty pleas and confessions, eugenics, and economy....

[Among these] the concept of retribution is one of the most misunderstood in all of our criminal jurisprudence.... Punishment as retribution has been condemned by scholars for centuries, and the Eighth Amendment itself was adopted to prevent punishment from becoming synonymous with vengeance....

Many people believe that the death penalty is suitable retribution for murder. Does this also imply that rapists should be raped or that muggers who use violence should be beaten?

The history of the Eighth Amendment supports only the conclusion that retribution for its own sake is improper....

Summary

Although the Framers of the Constitution did not rule out the idea of a death penalty in their wording of the Fifth Amendment, much of the current controversy surrounding the constitutionality of the death penalty centers around the Eighth Amendment. It states that "cruel and unusual punishments are forbidden by the Constitution." The two preceding court cases explore this constitutional conflict. The first extract is the opinion of Justice Stewart in *Gregg v. Georgia* (1976), in which the petitioner, Troy Gregg, challenged his death sentence on the grounds that it violated the Eighth and Fourteenth amendments. Justice Stewart rules that "the infliction of death as a punishment for murder is not without justification and thus is not unconstitutionally severe...." Justice Stewart interprets the Fifth Amendment—that no one should be deprived of life "without due process of law"—as confirmation that the death penalty is constitutional.

The second extract is the opinion of Justice Marshall in *Furman v. Georgia* (1972). Citing several notable cases in legal history, Justice Marshall argues that the death penalty is unconstitutional because it violates the "cruel and unusual "punishment clause of the Eighth Amendment. Justice Marshall argues that "evolving standards of decency" now mark a point at which the death penalty should no longer be tolerated.

FURTHER INFORMATION:

Books:

Banner, Stuart, *The Death Penalty: An American History.* Cambridge, MA: Harvard University Press, 2002.

Bedau, Hugo Adam (ed.), *The Death Penalty in America: Current Controversies.* New York: Oxford University Press, 1998.

Costanzo, Mark, *Just Revenge: Costs and Consequences of the Death Penalty.* New York: Worth Publishers, 1997.

Jackson, Jesse L., Sr., et al., *Legal Lynching: The Death Penalty and America's Future.* New York: The New Press, 2001.

Prejean, Helen, *Dead Man Walking: An Eyewitness Account of the Death Penalty in the United States.* New York: Vintage Books, 1996.

Sarat, Austin (ed.), *The Killing State: Capital Punishment in Law, Politics, and Culture.* New York: Oxford University Press, 2001.

Sarat, Austin, *When the State Kills: Capital Punishment and the American Condition.* Princeton, NJ: Princeton University Press, 2001.

 Useful websites:

www.aclu.org
American Civil Liberties Union (ACLU) site.

www.web.amnesty.org
Amnesty International site. A human rights organization that lobbies against the death penalty.

The following debates in the Pro/Con series may also be of interest:

In this volume:
Topic 2 Is the Supreme Court too powerful?

Topic 5 Is the Constitution racist?

In *Criminal Justice and the Penal System*:
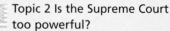 Topic 9 Should juveniles be sentenced to death?

IS THE DEATH PENALTY CONSTITUTIONAL?

YES: *The death penalty is barbaric and does not have a place in civilized society*

YES: *The Fifth Amendment suggests that the Framers made provision for a death penalty*

EIGHTH AMENDMENT
Is the death penalty "cruel and unusual"?

THE FRAMERS
Did the Framers intend for the Constitution to protect the death penalty?

NO: *Legal precedent suggests that the death penalty is a justified form of punishment as long as it fits the crime*

NO: *Nowhere in the Constitution does it state that the death penalty is a protected right*

IS THE DEATH PENALTY CONSTITUTIONAL? KEY POINTS

YES: *The death penalty is 100 percent effective. Once a criminal has been executed, he or she will never commit another crime.*

YES: *Many people suggest that the death penalty is racist. There must be some measure to protect minorities from discrimination.*

DETERRENT
Does the death penalty deter against violent crime?

EYE FOR AN EYE
As long as the criminal is punished, does it really matter if the death penalty is constitutional?

NO: *Most murders are committed in the "heat of the moment," under the influence of drink or drugs, when people do not necessarily think about the consequences of their actions*

NO: *The legality of the death penalty should not be the main issue. Criminals must pay for their crimes, especially if they have taken a life.*

GLOSSARY

abortion the premature delivery of a human fetus, either naturally through miscarriage or by artificial methods. Usually the term refers to the latter definition.

AIDS (acquired immune deficiency syndrome) a disease that destroys the ability of the immune system to combat infections and certain cancers, exposing the victim to repeated infections that may eventually be fatal. AIDS is caused by the human immunodeficiency virus (HIV).

Al Qaeda an international terrorist group thought to be behind several major acts of terrorism, including the events of September 11, 2001. It was formed initially to unite Arabs fighting in Afghanistan against the Soviet Union.

amendment an addition or change to a constitution or law. There have been 27 amendments to the U.S. Constitution, each one requiring the approval of two-thirds of both houses of Congress and ratification from three-quarters of the states. For a comprehensive overview of the amendments go to www.usconstitution. net/constquick.html. *See also* Bill of Rights; Equal Protection clause; Free Exercise clause.

American Civil Liberties Union (ACLU) an organization that aims to preserve constitutional liberties regardless of race, creed, or color. *See also* civil rights.

Articles of Confederation adopted in 1777, the articles established a league of friendship among the 13 states during the American Revolution (1775–1783).

Articles of War a law passed in 1916 that enshrined the punishment of homosexual soldiers, stating that assault with the intent to commit sodomy was a capital offense. A 1919 revision of the law made consensual sodomy a punishable offense.

Bill of Rights the first 10 amendments to the Constitution, which were ratified on December 15, 1791 (see pages 24–25).

capital punishment the legal ending of a person's life as punishment for a serious or violent offense.

censorship the altering or outlawing of writing, speech, or other forms of expression that those in authority believe threaten the social or political order.

civil rights entitlements that are guaranteed by law to all citizens, such as the right to vote and equality in law.

Civil Rights Act an act passed in 1964 to end discrimination based on race, color, or religion. The act guaranteed equal voting rights, banned segregation in public places, and outlawed discrimination by labor unions, schools, or businesses with government contracts. A new Civil Rights Act was passed in 1991 extending the 1964 law to cover such areas as the right to a jury trial. *See also* civil rights.

Cold War the social, political, and economic rivalry between the United States and the Soviet Union that lasted from the end of World War II until the breakup of the Soviet Union in 1991. *See also* communism.

communism a system of political and economic organization based on collective ownership. It was the official ideology of the Soviet Union from 1917 to 1991.

conscription the compulsory enrollment by a government of (usually male) citizens for military service. Also known as the draft.

constitution a written codification of the basic principles and laws under which a government operates.

Constitutional Convention the meeting in Philadelphia (May to September 1787) of delegates from every state except Rhode Island that drew up the Constitution.

Declaration of Independence a document drafted by Thomas Jefferson and issued on July 4, 1776, to proclaim the separation of the 13 North American British colonies from Great Britain.

Don't Ask, Don't Tell an interim policy set in 1993 by then President Bill Clinton. It effectively meant that gay men and lesbian women could serve in the military provided that they kept their sexual orientation to themselves.

Drug Enforcement Administration (DEA) a federal agency that implements drug and controlled substances laws and regulations.

Electronic Communications Privacy Act (ECPA) an act passed in 1986 to extend privacy protection laws to cover communication via computer transmission and electronic mail, mobile phones, and pagers.

Equal Protection clause a clause in the Fourteenth Amendment that prevents states from denying any person within their jurisdiction equal protection under the law. *See also* amendment.

Federalist Papers a series of political essays written by Alexander Hamilton, John Jay, and James Madison in the 1780s.

Framers the men who attended the Constitutional Convention in 1787. Also known as the Founding Fathers.

freedom of speech the right of individuals and the media to freely express views and opinions under the protection of the First Amendment.

Free Exercise clause part of the First Amendment, it effectively prevents Congress from establishing any state religion and from passing laws that interfere with religious activities.

Great Compromise a proposal presented at the Constitutional Convention in Philadelphia on July 13, 1787, to allocate federal representation to the states. It advocated proportional representation in the House of Representatives and equal representation in the Senate; also known as the Connecticut Compromise. *See also* Constitutional Convention, Framers.

hate speech words and symbols that discriminate against or ridicule a person, group, or institution on the basis of race, religion, national origin, or sexual preference. *See also* homophobia.

homophobia a fear of or discrimination against homosexuals or homosexuality.

inequality a disparity in distribution of a specific resource or item such as income, education, employment, or health care.

marijuana the dried leaves and flowering tops of the female hemp plant. Although illegal in many countries, it is commonly used as a recreational drug, and some people claim it is useful in relieving pain.

noncooperation the refusal to comply with laws and decisions that are believed to be unjust as a form of protest to bring about social change. Noncooperation was developed by the Indian leader Mahatma Gandhi (1869–1948) and later taken up by the African American civil rights campaigner Dr. Martin Luther King, Jr. (1929–1968). *See also* civil rights.

pornography a depiction of erotic behavior, for example, in pictures or words, intended to cause sexual excitement.

prejudice a preconceived judgment or an irrational attitude toward individuals or groups. *See also* hate speech.

racial profiling the use of ethnic characteristics to decide if someone is a likely suspect in a crime.

rule of law the principle that a country is governed by a set of laws rather than by a government or an individual such as a monarch.

separation of powers keeping different parts of the government separate through a system of checks and balances so that no one element can become too powerful.

Supreme Court the final court of appeal and final interpreter of the Constitution.

Treaty of Paris a treaty signed by Britain and America on September 3, 1783, that recognized the United States as a sovereign nation.

welfare assistance in the form of money or necessities for people in need.

Acknowledgments

Topic 1 Does it Matter What the Original Intentions of the Framers Were?

Yes: From "Are the Federalist Papers Still Relevant"? by Kathleen M. Sullivan, The Century Foundation, 1997.

No: From "Constitutional Intentions" by Wendy McElroy. Article first appeared in *Ideas on Liberty*, June 2000. Copyright © 2000 by Wendy McElroy. Used by permission.

Topic 2 Is the Supreme Court Too Powerful?

Yes: From *Planned Parenthood of Southeastern PA v. Casey*, 505 U.S. 833 (1992) by Justice Antonin Scalia. Courtesy of Findlaw (www.findlaw.com).

No: From *Planned Parenthood of Southeastern PA v. Casey*, 505 U.S. 833 (1992) by Justice Sandra Day O'Connor. Courtesy of Findlaw (www.findlaw.com).

Topic 3 Does the President Have Residual Emergency Powers?

Yes: From "Message to Congress" by Abraham Lincoln, July 4, 1861 (http://alpha.furman.edu/~benson/docs/lincoln.htm).

No: From *Youngstown Sheet & Tube Co. v. Sawyer* (1952) in *Basic Readings in U.S. Democracy*, U.S. Department of State, International Information Programs (http://usinfo.state.gov/usa/infousa/facts/democrac/59.htm).

Topic 4 Should the President Be Able to Lead the Country into War without Congressional Approval?

Yes: From "Dangerous Constraints on the President's War Powers" by Caspar W. Weinberger in *The Fettered Presidency: Legal Constraints on the Executive Branch*, edited by L. Gordon Crovitz and Jeremy A. Rabkin, 1989. Copyright © 1989 by the American Enterprise Institute. Reprinted with the permission of the American Enterprise Institute for Public Policy Research, Washington, D.C.

No: From "Restoring Checks and Balances" in *Presidential War Power* by Louis Fisher, published by the University Press of Kansas, Lawrence, KS. Copyright © 1995 by the University Press of Kansas.

Topic 5 Is the Constitution Racist?

Yes: "Constitution Furthers Institutional Racism" by Michael Schwartz, UCLA Daily Bruin Online, October 22, 1999. Copyright © 1999 by UCLA Daily Bruin (www.dailybruin.ucla.edu/db/issues/99/10.22/view.schwartz.html).

No: "Bush Celebrates the Life of Martin Luther King at White House," U.S. Department of State press release, January 21, 2002. Courtesy of the U.S. Department of State.

Topic 6 Is Welfare Constitutional?

Yes: From "The Next Century of our Constitution: Rethinking our Duty to the Poor" by Peter B. Edelman. Copyright © 1997 by University of California, Hastings College of the Law. Reprinted from *Hastings Law Journal*, Vol. 39, No. 1, 39, November 1987, by permission.

No: Reprinted by permission of the publisher from *Takings: Private Property and the Power of Eminent Domain* by Richard A. Epstein, Cambridge, Mass.: Harvard University Press. Copyright © 1985 by the President and Fellows of Harvard College.

Topic 7 Does the Constitution Adequately Protect the Rights of the Disabled?

Yes: From *City of Cleburne, Texas v. Cleburne Living Center*, 473 U.S. 432, July 1, 1985 by Justice Byron R. White (www.law.cornell.edu).

No: From "Disability Rights" by the American Civil Liberties Union, *ACLU Briefing Paper* No. 21, Winter 1999 (www.aclu.org/library/pbp21.html). Copyright © 1999 by the American Civil Liberties Union. Used by permission.

Topic 8 Should Homosexuals Be Allowed to Serve in the Military?

Yes: "Broken Promise: Lawsuits, Protests, Confusion, and Condemnation Follow the President's Compromise on Gays in the Military" by Chris Bull. Reprinted from *The Advocate*, August 24, 1993. Copyright © 1993 by Liberation Publications Inc. All rights reserved. Used by permission.

No: From "Gays and Lesbians in the Armed Forces" by Senator Sam Nunn, delivered to the U.S. Senate on July 16, 1993 (http://www.stark.kent.edu/library/reserves/speeches/nunn.htm).

Topic 9 Does the Constitution Protect Religious Freedom?

Yes: From *Church of the Lukumi Babalu Aye v. City of Hialeah*, 508 U.S. 520 (1993) by Justice Anthony M. Kennedy (www.law.cornell.edu).

No: From *Minersville School District v. Board of Education*, 310 U.S. 520 (1993) by Justice Felix Frankfurter (www.law.cornell.edu).

Topic 10 Should the Government Be Able to Prohibit Hate Speech?

Yes: From "Hate Crimes Violate the Free Speech Rights of Victims" by Charles R. Lawrence III in *Hate Crimes*, edited by Paul A. Winters, published by Greenhaven Press, San Diego, CA, 1996. Article first appeared as "Crossburning and the Sound of Silence: Antisubordination Theory and the First Amendment" in *Villanova Law Review*, Vol. 37 No. 787, 1992. Copyright © 1992 by *Villanova Law Review*. Used by permission.

No: From "In Defense of Prejudice: Why Incendiary Speech Must Be Protected" by Jonathan Rauch, *Harper's Magazine*, May 1995. Copyright © 1995 by *Harper's Magazine*. All rights reserved. Reproduced from the May issue by special permission.

Topic 11 Is the Right to Violent Protest Protected by the Constitution?

Yes: "Seven Doctors Have Been Murdered, Now Judges Rule in Favour of Abortion Hit List" by Duncan Campbell in *The Guardian*, March 30, 2001. Copyright © 2001 by Duncan Campbell. Used by permission.
No: "Abortion Clinic Access Law" by the American Civil Liberties Union, 1997 (www.aclu.org/library/aaabort.html). Copyright © 1997 by the American Civil Liberties Union. Used by permission.

Topic 12 Does the Constitution Protect Pornography?

Yes: From "A Conversation with Nadine Strossen, Author of *Defending Pornography: Free Speech, Sex and the Fight for Women's Rights*," by the American Civil Liberties Union (www.sexuality.org/l/activism/pornogra.html). Reprinted with permission of Nadine Strossen.
No: From the Introduction to *Pornography: Men Possessing Women* by Andrea Dworkin, published by The Women's Press, London, 1981. Copyright © 1981 by Andrea Dworkin. Used by permission.

Topic 13 Is the Military Draft Constitutional?

Yes: From *Arver v. U.S.*, 245 U.S. 366 (1918), Justice Edward Douglass White (http://caselaw.lp.findlaw.com/scripts/getcase.pl?navby=case&court=us&vol=245&invol=366).

No: "The Military Draft and Slavery" by Ron Paul, speech to the U.S. House of Representatives. Reproduced in *Counterpunch*, May 24–30, 2002 (www.counterpunch.org). Public domain.

Topic 14 Are Random Drug Tests of Athletes Constitutional?

Yes: From *Vernonia School Dist. 47J v. Acton*, 515 U.S. 646 (1995) Justice Antonin Scalia (www.findlaw.com).
No: From *Vernonia School Dist. 47J v. Acton*, 515 U.S. 646 (1995), Justice Sandra Day O'Connor (www.findlaw.com).

Topic 15 Is Internet Surveillance Constitutional?

Yes: "Are Employers Violating Workers' Privacy with Electronic Monitoring"? by Bryan Knowles, SpeakOut.com, June 15, 2000 (www.speakout.com/activism/issue_briefs/1300b-1.html). Copyright © 2000 by SpeakOut.com.
No: From "Statement of Gregory T. Nojeim on the Fourth Amendment and the Internet Before the House Judiciary Committee Subcommittee on the Constitution" by Gregory T. Nojeim, the American Civil Liberties Union, April 6, 2000 (www.aclu.org/library/aaabort.html). Copyright © 2000 by the American Civil Liberties Union. Used by permission.

Topic 16 Is the Death Penalty Constitutional?

Yes: From *Gregg v. Georgia*, 428 U.S. 153 (1976) by Justice Potter Stewart (www.law.umkc.edu/faculty/projects/ftrials/conlaw/gregg.html).
No: From *Furman v. Georgia*, 408 U.S. 238 (1972) by Justice Thurgood Marshall (www.law.umkc.edu/faculty/projects/ftrials/conlaw/furman.html).

The Brown Reference Group plc has made every effort to contact and acknowledge the creators and copyright holders of all extracts reproduced in this volume. We apologize for any omissions. Any person who wishes to be credited in further volumes should contact The Brown Reference Group in writing: The Brown Reference Group plc, 8 Chapel Place, Rivington Street, London EC2A 3DQ, UK.

Picture credits

Cover: Corbis: Lester Lefkowitz; **Corbis:** 173; David Buton, 79; Owen Franken 143; Jose Luis Palaez 194; Neil Rabinowitz 84; Michael S. Yamashita 68; **Library of Congress:** 10/11; Richard Jenkins, 164/165; **Robert Hunt Library:** 24/25; 72; **U.S. Department of Defense:** 112/113

SET INDEX